Nikon D5100:
From
Snapshots to
Great Shots

Rob Sylvan

Peachpit
Press

Nikon D5100: From Snapshots to Great Shots
Rob Sylvan

Peachpit Press
1249 Eighth Street
Berkeley, CA 94710
510/524-2178
510/524-2221 (fax)

Find us on the Web at www.peachpit.com
To report errors, please send a note to errata@peachpit.com
Peachpit Press is a division of Pearson Education

Senior Acquisitions Editor: Nikki McDonald
Associate Editor: Valerie Witte
Production Editor: Lisa Brazieal
Copyeditor: Scout Festa
Proofreader: Patricia Pane
Composition: WolfsonDesign
Indexer: Valerie Haynes Perry
Cover Image: Rob Sylvan
Cover Design: Aren Straiger
Back Cover Author Photo: Rob Sylvan

Camera provided to author by B&H Photo
(www.bhphotovideo.com)

ISBN-13   978-0-321-79384-3
ISBN-10   0-321-79384-6

9 8 7 6 5 4 3 2 1
Printed and bound in the United States of America

DEDICATION

For all of the teachers I have had in the past, and all of the ones I have yet to meet.
Thank you.

ACKNOWLEDGMENTS

My deepest thanks go to Jeff Revell, the author of a number of books in the From Snapshots to Great Shots series, and specifically of the book on the D5000, which I had the honor and pleasure of updating for the D5100. Jeff is a tremendous photographer and gifted teacher. Thank you for providing such a sound foundation upon which to build.

Any book that has reached the final stage of being published is actually the work of many hands (eyes, brains, and hearts too) behind the scenes. I owe everyone at Peachpit a great deal of gratitude, but specifically Nikki McDonald, Ted Waitt, Valerie Witte, Lisa Brazieal, Scout Festa, Patricia Pane, Owen Wolfson, Valerie Haynes Perry, Aren Straiger, Sara Jane Todd, Scott Cowlin, and Nancy Aldrich-Ruenzel, who were instrumental in getting this book finished, making it look so darn fantastic, and putting it out into the world. Thank you all.

A special thanks to David Brommer and B&H Photo Video for help in securing the D5100 I used to write this book.

I am grateful for all that I have learned from my friends at the National Association of Photoshop Professionals, from the fantastic instructors at Photoshop World, and of course from my fellow photographers at iStockphoto. You all have taught and inspired me over the years.

I also want to thank my wife, Paloma, for being the love of my life and my number one supporter during this project; my son, Quinn, for assisting me on many shoots and being the model in many more; and my family, friends, and neighbors—Ea, Avery, Otis, Hayley, Mark, Adrienne, Emma, Julia, Paige, Kris, Gabby, Sabrina, Chris, Anna, Dan, Holden, Beth, and Brent—for being a part of the book in large and small ways.

Also, a big shout-out to Crackskull's Coffee & Books and the New Hampshire Media Makers. Thanks, guys!

Contents

Introduction

The D5100 is an amazing bit of technology and a very capable tool for creating photographs that you will be proud to show others. The intention of this book is not to be a rehash of the owner's manual that came with the camera, but rather to be a resource for learning how to improve your photography while specifically using your D5100. I am very excited and honored to help you in that process, and to that end I have put together a short Q&A to help you get a better understanding of just what you can expect from this book.

Q: IS EVERY CAMERA FEATURE GOING TO BE COVERED?

A: Nope, just the ones I felt you need to know about in order to start taking great photos. Believe it or not, you already own a great resource that covers every feature of your camera: the owner's manual. Writing a book that just repeats this information would have been a waste of my time and your money. What I did want to write about was how to harness certain camera features to the benefit of your photography. As you read through the book, you will also see callouts that point you to specific pages in your owner's manual that are related to the topic being discussed. For example, in Chapter 6, I discuss the use of the AE-L button, but there is more information available on this feature in the manual. I cover the function that applies to our specific needs, but I also give you the page numbers in the manual to explore this function even further.

Q: SO IF I ALREADY OWN THE MANUAL, WHY DO I NEED THIS BOOK?

A: The manual does a pretty good job of telling you how to use a feature or turn it on in the menus, but it doesn't necessarily tell you why and when you should use it. If you really want to improve your photography, you need to know the whys and whens to put all of those great camera features to use at the right time. To that extent, the manual just isn't going to cut it. It is, however, a great resource on the camera's features, and it is for that reason that I treat it like a companion to this book. You already own it, so why not get something of value from it?

Q: WHAT CAN I EXPECT TO LEARN FROM THIS BOOK?

A: Hopefully, you will learn how to take great photographs. My goal, and the reason the book is laid out the way it is, is to guide you through the basics of photography as they relate to different situations and scenarios. By using the features of your D5100 and this book, you will learn about aperture, shutter speed, ISO, lens selection, depth of field, and many other photographic concepts. You will also find plenty of full-page photos that include captions, shooting data, and callouts so you can see how all of the photography fundamentals come together to make great images. All the while, you will be learning how your camera works and how to apply its functions and features to your photography.

Q: WHAT ARE THE ASSIGNMENTS ALL ABOUT?

A: At the end of most of the chapters, you will find shooting assignments, where I give you some suggestions as to how you can apply the lessons of the chapter to help reinforce everything you just learned. Let's face it—using the camera is much more fun than reading about it, so the assignments are a way of taking a little break after each chapter and having some fun.

Q: SHOULD I READ THE BOOK STRAIGHT THROUGH OR CAN I SKIP AROUND FROM CHAPTER TO CHAPTER?

A: Here's the easy answer: yes and no. No, because the first four chapters give you the basic information that you need to know about your camera. These are the building blocks for using the camera. After that, yes, you can move around the book as you see fit because those chapters are written to stand on their own as guides to specific types of photography or shooting situations. So you can bounce from portraits to landscapes and then maybe to a little action photography. It's all about your needs and how you want to address them. Or, you can read it straight through. The choice is up to you.

Q: I DON'T SEE ANY CHAPTERS DEVOTED TO VIDEO. DO YOU COVER THAT?

A: I know that one of the reasons you probably bought the D5100 was its ability to capture HD video. I have covered some basic video setup information in Chapter 2, but I really wanted the focus of this book to be the photographic capabilities and possibilities. Don't worry, though; read the next Q&A and I think you'll be happy.

Q: IS THERE ANYTHING ELSE I SHOULD KNOW BEFORE GETTING STARTED?

A: In order to keep the book short and focused, I had to be pretty selective about what I put in each chapter. The problem is that there is a little more information that might come in handy after you've gone through all the chapters. So as an added value for you, there are two bonus chapters: Chapter 11, called "Pimp My Ride," and Chapter 12, "D5100 Video: Beyond the Basics." Chapter 11 is full of information on photo accessories that will assist you in making better photographs. You will find recommendations for things like filters, tripods, and much more. Chapter 12 will lead you through some video tips and techniques to make your D5100 videos even better. To access the bonus chapters, just log in to or join Peachpit.com (it's free) and enter the book's ISBN on this page: www.peachpit.com/store/register.aspx. After you register the book, a link to the bonus chapters will be listed on your Account page under Registered Products.

Q: IS THAT IT?

A: One last thought before you dive into the first chapter. My goal in writing this book has been to give you a resource that you can turn to for creating great photographs with your Nikon D5100. Take some time to learn the basics and then put them to use. Photography, like most things, takes time to master and requires practice. I have been a photographer for many years and I'm still learning. Always remember, it's not the camera but the person using it who makes beautiful photographs. Have fun, make mistakes, and then learn from them. In no time, I'm sure you will transition from a person who takes snapshots to a photographer who makes great shots.

1

ISO 200
1/30 sec.
f/8
60mm lens

The D5100 Top Ten List

TEN TIPS TO MAKE YOUR SHOOTING MORE PRODUCTIVE RIGHT OUT OF THE BOX

I'm going to go out on a limb here and guess that you've already taken your camera out of the box and played around with it a bit. I mean, who can resist that delicious smell of new electronics and the thrill of playing with a new toy? I usually find it easier to sit down and read the manual after having taken the camera for at least one spin around the proverbial block. Of course, it is totally fine if you are reading this book before you've got the camera in hand, and I applaud your restraint.

So, even if your camera is (slightly) out of the box, I've put together some tips to help you get the most out of your D5100 experience. It's never too late to start over and take it from the top. As I mentioned in the Introduction, the intention of this book is to extend the usefulness of your camera manual by expanding on subjects not covered in depth, or by calling your attention to certain aspects that deserve closer inspection, all the while taking you to places in your photographic education that are far beyond the boundaries of the manual. I want you to know not only how to use your camera, but how to use it while improving your ability to take the photos you want to take. To that end, there are some practical matters that should help you build the right foundation.

CAMERA FRONT

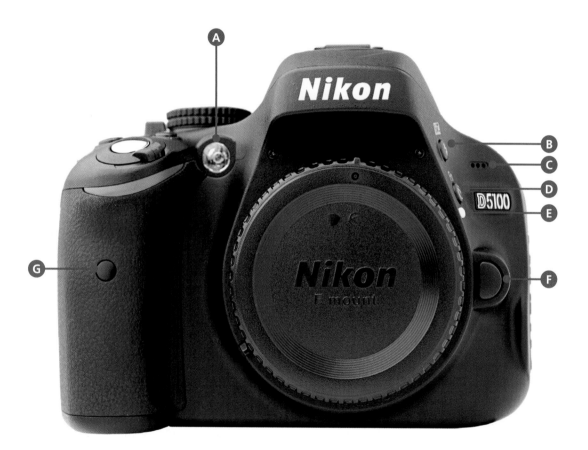

A AF-Assist Illuminator
B Flash Mode Button
C Microphone
D Function Button

E Lens Mounting Mark
F Lens Release Button
G Infrared Receiver

CAMERA BACK

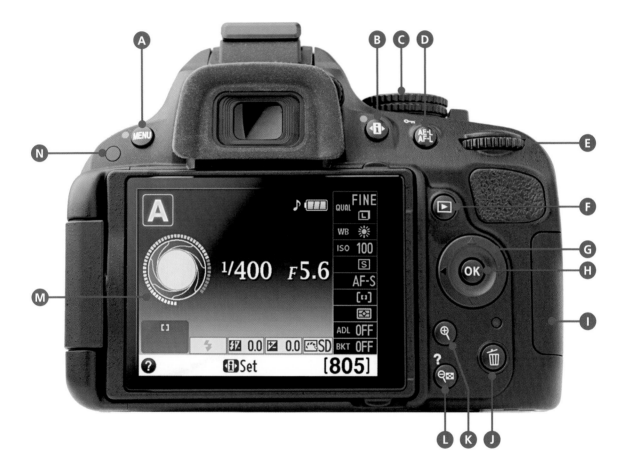

A	Menu	F	Playback Button	K	Playback Zoom In
B	Information Edit	G	Multi-Selector	L	Thumbnail/Playback Zoom Out
C	Mode Dial	H	OK Button	M	LCD/Information Screen
D	AutoExposure/AutoFocus Lock Button	I	Memory Card Door	N	Infrared Receiver
E	Command Dial	J	Delete Button		

CAMERA TOP

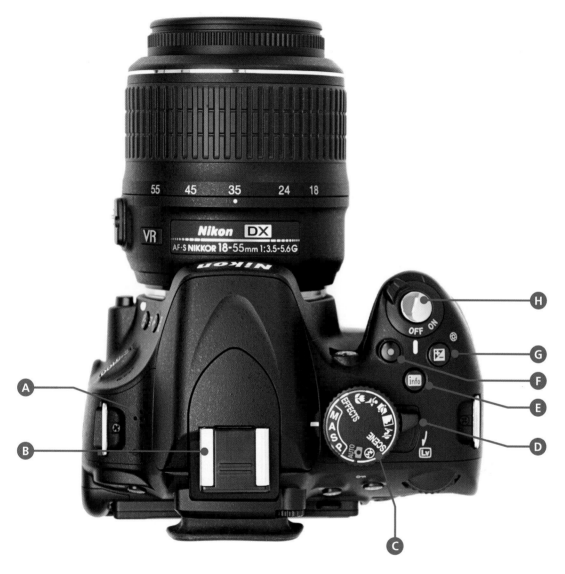

A Speaker
B Flash Hot Shoe
C Mode Dial
D Live View Switch

E Info Button
F Movie Record Button
G Exposure Compensation/Aperture Adjustment
H Shutter Release

1. CHARGE YOUR BATTERY

When you first open your camera and slide the battery into the battery slot, you will be pleased to find that there is probably juice in the battery and you can start shooting right away. What you should really be doing is getting out the battery charger and giving that power cell a full charge. Not only will this give you more time to shoot, it will start the battery off on the right foot. No matter what claims the manufacturers make about battery life and charging memory, I always get better life and performance when I charge my batteries fully and then use them right down to the point where they have nothing left to give. To check your battery level, insert the battery into the camera, turn on the camera, and look for the battery indicator in the upper-right section of the information screen (**Figure 1.1**).

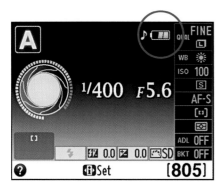

FIGURE 1.1
The LCD displays the amount of charge left on the battery.

KEEPING A BACKUP BATTERY

If I were to suggest just one accessory that you should buy for your camera, it would be a second battery. Nothing is worse than being out in the field and having your camera die. Keeping a fully charged battery in your bag will give you the confidence that you can keep on shooting without fail. Not only is this a great strategy to extend your shooting time, it also helps to lengthen the life of your batteries by alternating between them. No matter what the manufacturers say, batteries do have a life and using them half as much will only lengthen their usefulness. Trust me, thanks to the increased quality of the LCD display on the D5100 you will spend a lot of time gazing at your images (and eating up battery charge).

2. ADJUST YOUR AUTO OFF TIMER SETTING

One of the things that really bugged me when I first began shooting with the D5100 was the short duration that the playback and menu screens stayed on while I was working with the camera. This can be very frustrating when you are trying to learn about the camera and its features and you have to keep pressing the Menu or Info button to bring the screen back to life. This is also the case when reviewing images on the screen after taking a picture. The answer to this problem is to increase the timer setting to a longer duration. The D5100 has four different settings for the auto-off function: Short, Normal, Long, and Custom. To make things easy, I set my camera to the Long setting when first learning how it works, which gives one minute for playback/menus, 20 seconds for image review, ten minutes for live view, and one minute for auto-meter off. Once I've grown comfortable with the controls, I change the setting to Short to increase battery life. If you so choose, you can use the Custom setting to individually adjust each of these options.

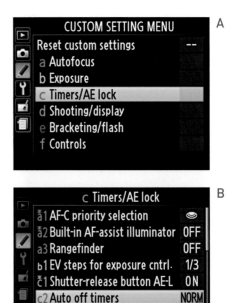

SETTING THE AUTO OFF TIMERS

1. Press the Menu button and navigate to the Custom Menu tab.

2. Select item c: Timers/AE lock and press the OK button (**A**).

3. Select item c2: Auto Off Timers and press OK again (**B**).

4. Highlight your choice of timer settings and press OK a final time to lock in your change (**C**).

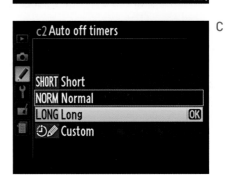

3. SET YOUR JPEG IMAGE QUALITY

Your new D5100 has a number of image-quality settings to choose from, and you can adjust them according to your needs. Most people shoot with the JPEG option because it allows them to capture a large number of photos on their memory cards. The problem is that unless you understand what JPEG is, you might be degrading the quality of your images without realizing it.

The JPEG format has been around since about 1994. JPEG stands for Joint Photographic Experts Group, and the format was developed by this group as a method of shrinking digital images down to a smaller size for the purpose of reducing large file sizes while retaining the original image information. (Technically, JPEG isn't even a file format—it's a mathematical equation for reducing image file sizes—but to keep things simple, we'll just refer to it as a file format.) The problem with JPEG is that, in order to reduce file size, it has to throw away some of the information. This is referred to as "lossy compression." This is important to understand because, while you can fit more images on your memory card by choosing a lower-quality JPEG setting, you will also be reducing the quality of your image. This effect becomes more apparent as you enlarge your pictures.

The JPEG file format also has one other characteristic: to apply the compression to the image before final storage on your memory card, the camera has to apply all of the image processing first. Image processing involves such factors as sharpening, color adjustment, contrast adjustment, noise reduction, and so on. Many photographers now prefer to use the RAW file format to get greater control over the image processing. We will take a closer look at this in Chapter 2, but for now let's just make sure that we are using the best-quality JPEG possible.

The D5100 has nine different settings for the JPEG format. There are three settings each for the Large, Medium, and Small image size settings. The three settings (Basic, Normal, and Fine) represent more or less image compression, based on your choice. The Large, Medium, and Small settings determine the actual physical size of your image in pixels. Let's work with the highest-quality setting possible. After all, our goal is to make big, beautiful photographs, so why start the process with a lower-quality image?

SETTING THE IMAGE QUALITY

1. Press the **i** button on the back of the camera to activate the cursor in the information screen.

2. Use the Multi-selector to select the image-quality setting, then press the OK button (**A**).

3. When the option screen appears, use the Multi-selector to choose the Fine setting, and press the OK button (**B**).

4. Now move the cursor down one step to choose the image size and press OK to get to the options (**C**).

5. Select the L option to use the largest image size available and press OK once more (**D**).

6. Press the **i** button again to return to shooting mode.

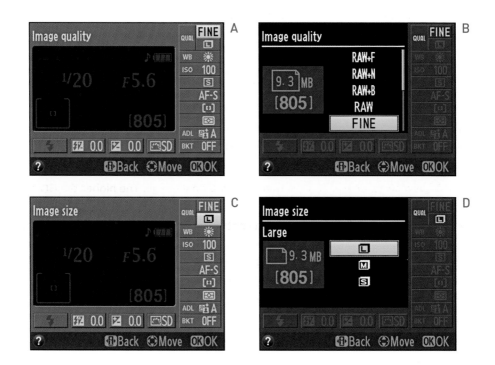

As you will see when scrolling through the quality settings, the higher the quality, the fewer pictures you will be able to fit on your card. If you have an 8 GB memory card, the quality setting we have selected will allow you to shoot about 844 photographs before you fill up your card. Always try to choose quality over quantity. Your pictures will be the better for it.

Manual Callout

For a complete chart that shows the image-quality settings with the number of possible shots for each setting, turn to page 218 in the Reference Manual on the companion CD that comes with the camera.

4. TURN OFF THE AUTO ISO SETTING

The ISO setting on your camera allows you to choose the level of sensitivity of the camera sensor to light. The ability to change this sensitivity is one of the biggest advantages to using a digital camera. In the days of film cameras, you had to choose the ISO by film type. This meant that if you wanted to shoot in lower light, you had to replace the film in the camera with one that had a higher ISO. So not only did you have to carry different types of film, but you also had to remove one roll from the camera to replace it with another, even if you hadn't used up the current roll. Now all you have to do is go to your information screen and select the appropriate ISO.

Having this flexibility is a powerful option, but just as with the Quality setting, the ISO setting has a direct bearing on the quality of the final image. The higher the ISO, the more digital noise the image will contain. Since our goal is to produce high-quality photographs, it is important that we get control over all of the camera controls and bend them to our will. When you turn your camera on for the first time, the ISO will be set to Auto. This means that the camera is determining how much light is available and will choose what it believes is the correct ISO setting. Since you want to use the lowest ISO possible, you will need to turn this setting off and manually select the appropriate ISO.

Which ISO you choose depends on your level of available or ambient light. For sunny days or very bright scenes, use a low ISO such as 100. As the level of light is reduced, raise the ISO level. Cloudy days or indoor scenes might require you to use ISO 400. Low-light scenes, such as when you are shooting at night, will mean you need to bump up that ISO to 1600. The thing to remember is to shoot with the lowest setting possible for maximum quality.

SETTING THE ISO

1. Press the **i** button on the back of the camera to activate the cursor in the information screen.

2. Use the Multi-selector to highlight the ISO Sensitivity option and press the OK button (**A**).

3. In the option screen, select the appropriate ISO for the level of light you are shooting in, and press the OK button to lock in the change (**B**).

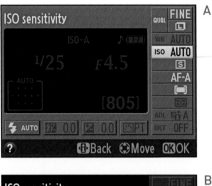

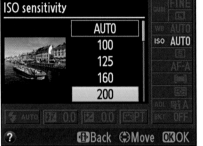

You should know that the Auto ISO option is only enabled as a default when using one of the automatic scene/effects modes. When using one of the professional modes (M, A, S, and P; we'll discuss these in Chapter 4), the Auto ISO feature will be automatically turned off. If you wish to use Auto ISO in one of these modes, you must activate it and set the auto parameters in the shooting menu. If you plan on shooting with the Auto mode, you cannot turn off the Auto ISO option at all.

NOISE

Noise is the enemy of digital photography, but it has nothing to do with the loudness of your camera operation. It refers to the electronic artifacts that appear as speckles in your image. They generally appear in darker shadow areas and are a result of the camera trying to amplify the signal to produce visible information. The more the image needs to be amplified—raising the sensitivity through higher ISOs—the greater the amount of noise there will be.

You can also change the ISO without taking your eye from the viewfinder. Although there is no dedicated ISO button on the D5100, you can still change this setting on the fly by setting the Function button to handle ISO sensitivity. Simply use Custom Setting Menu F to change the assignment of the Function button. Then, while you are looking through the viewfinder, just press and hold the Function button while turning the Command dial. You will see the ISO value change in your viewfinder display.

5. SET YOUR FOCUS POINT AND MODE

The Nikon focusing system is well known for its speed and accuracy. The automatic focus modes will give you a ton of flexibility in your shooting. There is, however, one small problem that is inherent with any focusing system. No matter how intelligent it is, the camera is looking at all of the subjects in the scene and determining which is closest to the camera. It then uses this information to determine where the proper focus point should be. It has no way of knowing what your main emphasis is, so it is using a "best guess" system. To eliminate this factor, you should set the camera to single-point focusing so that you can ensure that you are focusing on the most important feature in the scene.

The camera has 11 separate focus points to choose from. They are arranged in a diamond pattern with ten points around the outside of the diamond and one in the center. To start things off, you should select the focus point in the middle. Once you have become more familiar with the focus system, you can experiment with the other points, as well as the automatic point selection.

When possible, you should also change the focus mode to AF-S so that you can focus on your subject and then recompose your shot while holding that point of focus. Your camera has two different "zones" of shooting modes to choose from. These are located on the Mode dial, which is separated into automatic scene/effects modes and what might be referred to as the professional modes. The automatic modes, which are identifiable by small icons, do not allow for much, if any, customization, which includes focus mode. The professional modes, defined by the letter symbols M, A, S, and P, allow for much more control by the photographer (**Figure 1.2**).

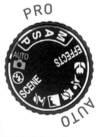

FIGURE 1.2
The camera's shooting modes are divided into the automatic scene/effects modes and the professional modes.

If the Mode dial is set to any of the automatic scene/effects modes, then it is best to leave the focus mode set to AF-A, which means the camera will automatically select either single-servo autofocus or continuous-servo autofocus, based on whether the subject is stationary or moving. If the Mode dial is set to one of the professional modes, then you will have the option to set the focus mode to AF-S (single-servo mode) if your subject is stationary.

SETTING THE FOCUS POINT AND FOCUS MODE

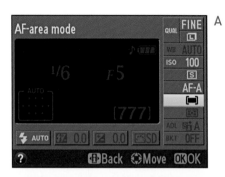

A

1. To choose a single point of focus, wake the camera (if necessary) by lightly pressing the shutter release button.

2. Press the **i** button on the back of the camera to activate the cursor in the information screen.

3. Use the Multi-selector to highlight the AF-area Mode option and press OK (**A**).

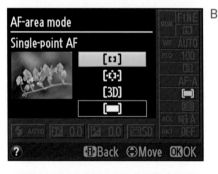

B

4. Select the top option, Single Point, and press OK (**B**).

5. With the cursor still active, move up one item to the Focus Mode option and press OK.

6. Select AF-A or AF-S, depending on the Mode dial setting, to configure the focus mode. Press the OK button to lock in your change (**C**).

7. Press the **i** button to return to the regular information screen.

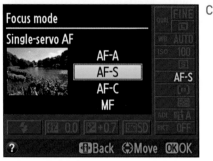

C

The camera is now ready for single focusing. You will hear a chirp when the camera has locked in and focused on the subject. To focus on your subject and then recompose your shot, just place the focus point in the viewfinder on your subject, depress the shutter release button halfway until the camera chirps, and without letting up on the shutter button, recompose your shot and then press the shutter button all the way down to make your exposure.

6. SET THE CORRECT WHITE BALANCE

Color balance correction is the process of rendering accurate colors in your final image. Most people don't even notice that light has different color characteristics because the human eye automatically adjusts to different color temperatures, so quickly, in fact, that everything looks correct in a matter of milliseconds.

When color film ruled the world, photographers would select which film to use according to what their light source was going to be. The most common film was balanced for daylight, but you could also buy film that was color balanced for tungsten light sources. Most other lighting situations had to be handled by using color filters over the lens. This process was necessary for the photographer's final image to show the correct color balance of a scene.

Your camera has the ability to perform this same process automatically, but you can also choose to override it and set it manually. Guess which method we are going to use? You are catching on fast! Once again, your photography should be all about maintaining control over everything that influences your final image.

Luckily, you don't need to have a deep understanding of color temperatures to control your camera's white balance. The choices are given to you in terms that are easy to relate to and that will make things pretty simple. Your white balance choices are:

- **Auto:** The default setting for your camera. It is also the setting used by all of the automatic scene/effects modes (see Chapter 3).

- **Incandescent:** Used for any occasion where you are using regular household-type bulbs for your light source. Incandescent (also called tungsten) is a very warm light source and will result in a yellow/orange cast if you don't correct for it.

- **Fluorescent:** Used to get rid of the green-blue cast that can result from using regular fluorescent lights as your dominant light source. Some fluorescent lights are actually balanced for daylight, which would allow you to use the Direct Sunlight white balance setting.

- **Direct Sunlight:** Most often used for general daylight/sunlit shooting.

- **Flash:** Used whenever you're using the built-in flash or a flash on the hot shoe. You should select this white balance to adjust for the slightly cooler light that comes from using a flash. (The hot shoe is the small bracket located on the top of your camera, which rests just above the eyepiece. This bracket is used for attaching a more powerful flash to the camera [see Chapter 8 and Chapter 11, which is one of the bonus chapters].)

- **Cloudy:** The choice for overcast or very cloudy days. This and the Shade setting will eliminate the blue color cast from your images.

- **Shade:** Used when working in shaded areas that are still using sunlight as the dominant light source.

- **Pre:** Indicates that you are using a customized white balance that is adjusted for a particular light source. This option can be adjusted using an existing photo you have taken or by taking a picture of something white or gray in the scene.

SETTING THE WHITE BALANCE

1. After turning on or waking the camera, select one of the professional shooting modes, such as P (you can't select the white balance when using any of the automatic modes).

2. Press the **i** button on the back of the camera to activate the cursor in the information screen.

3. Use the Multi-selector to highlight the White Balance mode and press the OK button (**A**).

4. Using the Multi-selector, select the appropriate white balance and then press the OK button (**B**).

5. Press the **i** button to return to the regular information screen.

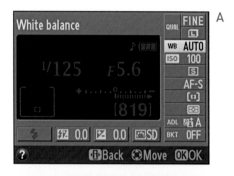

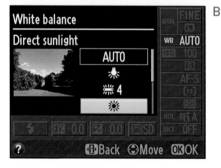

WHITE BALANCE AND THE TEMPERATURE OF COLOR

When you select different white balances in your camera, you will notice that underneath several of the choices is a number, e.g., 5200K, 7000K, or 3200K. These numbers refer to the Kelvin temperature of the colors in the visible spectrum. The visible spectrum is the range of light that the human eye can see (think of a rainbow or the color bands that come out of a spectrum). The visible spectrum of light has been placed into a scale called the Kelvin temperature scale, which identifies the thermodynamic temperature of a given color of light. Put simply, reds and yellows are "warm" and greens and blues are "cool." Even more confusing can be the actual temperature ratings. Warm temperatures are typically lower on the Kelvin scale, ranging from 3000 degrees to 5000 degrees, while cool temperatures run from 5500 degrees to around 10,000 degrees. Take a look at this list for an example of Kelvin temperature properties.

KELVIN TEMPERATURE PROPERTIES

Flames	1700K–1900K	Daylight	5000K
Incandescent bulb	2800K–3300K	Camera flash	5500K
White fluorescent	4000K	Overcast sky	6000K
Moonlight	4000K	Open shade	7000K

The most important thing to remember here is how the color temperature of light will affect the look of your images. If something is "warm," it will look reddish-yellow, and if something is "cool," it will have a bluish cast.

7. SET YOUR COLOR SPACE

The color space deals with how your images will ultimately be used. It is basically a set of instructions that tells your camera how to define the colors in your image and then output them to the device of your choice, be it your monitor or a printer. Your camera has a choice of two color spaces: sRGB and Adobe RGB.

The first choice, sRGB, was developed by Hewlett-Packard and Microsoft as a way of defining colors for the Internet. This space was created to deal with the way that computer monitors actually display images using red, green, and blue (RGB) colors. Because there are no black pixels in your monitor, the color space uses a combination of these three colors to display all of the colors in your image.

In 1998, Adobe Systems developed a new color space, Adobe RGB, which was intended to encompass a wider range of colors than was obtainable using traditional cyan, magenta, yellow, and black colors (called CMYK) but doing so using the primary red, green, and blue colors. It uses a more widely defined palette of colors (or gamut) than the sRGB space and, therefore, can contain some colors farther toward the more saturated end of the spectrum than sRGB.

A LITTLE COLOR THEORY

The visible spectrum of light is based on a principle called *additive color* and is based on three primary colors: red, green, and blue. When you add these colors together in equal parts, you get white light. By combining different amounts of them, you can achieve all the different colors of the visible spectrum. This is a completely different process than printing, where cyan, magenta, and yellow colors are combined to create various colors. This method is called *subtractive color* and has to do with the reflective properties of pigments or inks as they are combined.

The color space choice is applied only to the JPEG images produced by the camera. When shooting RAW, the color space is determined later when you are using software to process the photos. I typically use the Adobe RGB space when shooting JPEG because it has a wider gamut than sRGB, and it is always better to go from a wider color space to a narrower one when editing. That said, if you are shooting JPEG and sending photos straight to a printer or posting online without much (or any) editing, then sRGB is a good choice.

1. With the camera turned on, press the Menu button.

2. Using the Multi-selector, select the shooting menu and then highlight the Color Space option and press the OK button (**A**).

3. Highlight your desired color space and press the OK button once again (**B**).

4. Press the **i** button to return to the regular information screen.

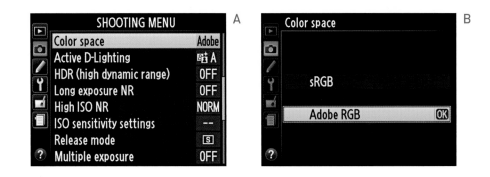

Note that if you choose Adobe RGB, the camera-generated file names will start with an underscore.

8. KNOW HOW TO OVERRIDE AUTOFOCUS

As good as the Nikon autofocus system is, there may be times when it just isn't doing the job for you. Many times this has to do with how you would like to compose a scene and where the actual point of focus should be. This can be especially true when you are using the camera on a tripod, where you can't prefocus and then recompose before shooting (as discussed earlier). To take care of this problem, you will need to manually focus the lens. I am only going to cover the kit lens that came with my D5100 (the 18–55mm VR), so if you have purchased a different lens be sure to check the accompanying instruction manual for the lens.

On the 18–55mm kit lens, you simply need to slide the switch at the base of the lens (located on the lens barrel near the body of the camera) from the A setting to the M setting (**Figure 1.3**). You can now turn the focus ring at the end of the lens to set your focus. Now that you're in manual focus mode, the camera will not give you an audible chirp when you have correctly focused.

We'll cover more manual focus situations in greater detail in future chapters.

FIGURE 1.3
Slide the focus
switch on the lens
to the M position to
manually focus.

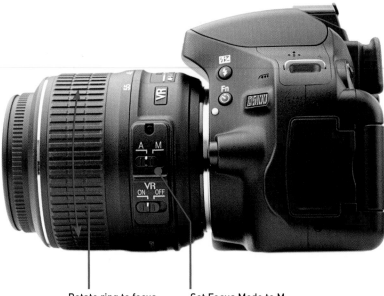

Rotate ring to focus   Set Focus Mode to M

9. REVIEW YOUR SHOTS

One of the greatest features of a digital camera is its ability to give us instant feed-back. By reviewing your images on the camera's LCD screen, you can instantly tell if you got your shot. This visual feedback allows you to make adjustments on the fly and make certain that all of your adjustments are correct before moving on.

When you first press the shutter release button, your camera quickly processes your shot and then displays the image on the LCD display. In addition, you can press the Playback button at any time to review your shots on the card. The default playback view displays your image along with the folder name, image file name, frame number/total number of images on the card, date, time, image size, and image quality setting.

There are other display options available that must be turned on using the camera menu. These options can be found in the Playback menu under the Playback dis-play options (**A**). With this menu option you can add display modes (**B**) such as None (image only), Highlights (**C**), RGB histogram (**D**), Shooting data (**E**), and Overview (**F**).

Once enabled, press the Playback button to display the default view and then press the Multi-selector up (or down) to cycle through each view. There is now a wealth of information—from shutter speed to the histogram (see the sidebar "The value of the histogram")—at your fingertips.

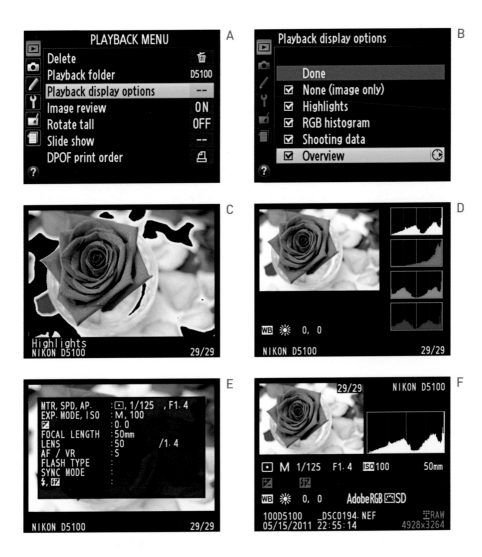

In fact, it may actually be information overload. I find the Highlights display (sometimes referred to as the "blinkies") to be very helpful for quickly finding out if I have blown out the highlights in a photo, and I turn to the Overview display for everything else I need to know about a capture. I turn off all the other options to make it faster to cycle through the options I do use. There's more on the Highlight display view and how to use it to improve your image quality in the "How I Shoot" section in Chapter 4. For now, I suggest enabling all display options to get a feel for what each one offers. Then you can circle back and keep only the ones you find helpful.

THE VALUE OF THE HISTOGRAM

Simply put, histograms are two-dimensional representations of your images in graph form. There are two different histograms that you should be concerned with: luminance and color. Luminance is referred to in your manual as "brightness" and is most valuable when evaluating your exposures. In **Figure 1.4**, you see what looks like a mountain range. The graph represents the entire tonal range that your camera can capture, from the whitest whites to the blackest blacks. The left side represents black, all the way to the right side, which represents white. The heights of the peaks represent the number of pixels that contain those luminance levels (the tall peak near the middle means the image contains a large amount of medium-dark pixels). Looking at this figure, it is hard to determine where all of the ranges of light and dark areas are and how much of each I have. If I look at the histogram, I can see that the largest peak of the graph is near the middle and trails off as it reaches the edges. In most cases, you would look for this type of histogram, indicating that you captured the entire range of tones, from dark to light, in your image. Knowing that is fine, but here is where the information really gets useful.

When you evaluate a histogram that has a spike or peak riding up the far left or right side of the graph, it means that you are clipping detail from your image. In essence, you are trying to record values that are either too dark or too light for your sensor to accurately record. This is usually an indication of over- or underexposure. It also means that you need to correct your exposure so that the important details will not record as solid black or solid white pixels (which is what happens when clipping occurs). There are times, however, when some clipping is acceptable. If you are photographing a scene where the sun will be in the frame, you can expect to get some clipping because the sun is just too bright to hold any detail. Likewise, if you are shooting something that has true blacks in it—think coal in a mineshaft at midnight—there are most certainly going to be some true blacks with no detail in your shot.

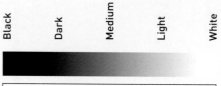

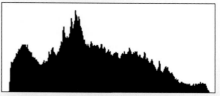

FIGURE 1.4

This is a typical histogram, where the dark to light tones run from left to right. The black to white gradient above the graph demonstrates where the tones lie on the graph and would not appear above your camera histogram display.

The main goal is to ensure that you aren't clipping any "important" visual information, and that is achieved by keeping an eye on your histogram. Take a look at **Figure 1.5**. The histogram displayed on the image shows a heavy skew toward the left with almost no part of the mountain touching the right side. This is a good example of what an underexposed image histogram looks like. Now look at **Figure 1.6** and compare the histogram for the image that was correctly exposed. Notice that even though there is a distinct peak on the graph, there is a distribution of tones across the entire histogram.

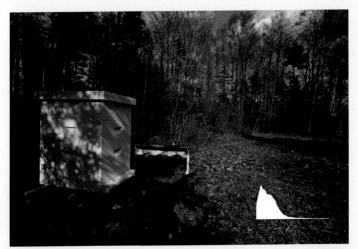

FIGURE 1.5
This image is about one stop underexposed. Notice the histogram is skewed to the left.

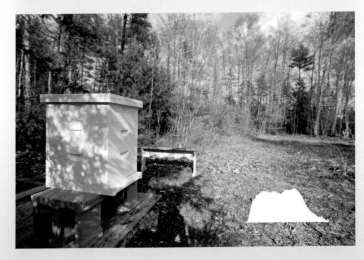

FIGURE 1.6
This histogram reflects a correctly exposed image.

Deleting or erasing images is a fairly simple process that is covered on page 27 of the printed user manual. To quickly get you on your way, simply press the Playback button and use the Multi-selector to find the picture that you want to delete. Then press the Delete button (it has a trash can icon on it) located on the back of the camera to the left of the eyepiece. When you see the confirmation screen, simply press the Delete button once again to complete the process.

Caution: Once you have deleted an image, it is gone for good. Make sure you don't want it before you drop it in the trash.

10. HOLD YOUR CAMERA FOR PROPER SHOOTING

You might think that this is really dumb, but I hope that you take a few seconds to read this over and make sure that you are giving yourself the best chance for great images. I can't begin to tell you how many times I see photographers holding their cameras in a fashion that is either unstable or just plain uncomfortable-looking. Much of this probably comes from holding point-and-shoot cameras. There is a huge difference between point-and-shoots and dSLR cameras, and learning the correct way to hold one now will result in great images later. The purpose of practicing correct shooting form is to provide the most stable platform possible for your camera (besides using a tripod, of course).

dSLR cameras are made to favor the right-handed and right-eyed individual. The basics of properly holding the camera begin with grasping the camera body with the right hand. You will quickly find that most of the important camera controls are within easy reach of your thumb and forefinger. The next step is to create a stable base for your camera to rest on. This is accomplished by placing the camera body on the up-facing palm of your left hand (**Figure 1.7**). Now you can curl your fingers around the lens barrel to quickly zoom or manually focus the lens.

When it comes to rotating the camera vertically to portrait orientation, most photographers favor rotating counter-clockwise (**Figure 1.8**) because it keeps all the controls easily accessible to the right hand, allows visibility in the left eye, and keeps your nose off the LCD screen. That said, it can fling your right elbow into the crowd, and the pressure of your right arm can create a tendency to rotate the camera too far. Some people find it more comfortable to rotate the camera clockwise, which pulls your right hand under the camera and your right elbow tight against your chest. It decreases visibility in your left eye and makes the controls a little more awkward to reach, but it can be more stable in a tight situation.

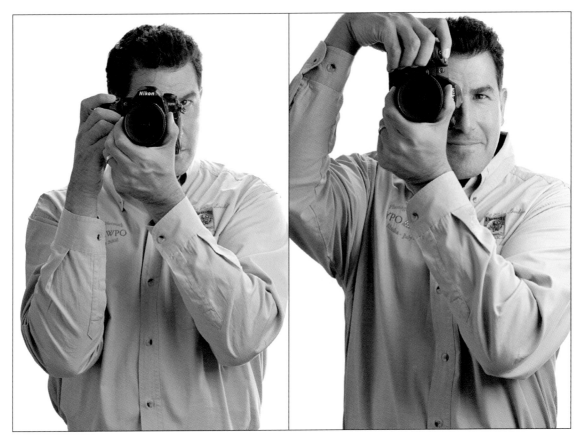

FIGURE 1.7
The proper way to hold your camera horizontally to ensure sharp, blur-free images.

FIGURE 1.8
The preferred way to hold your camera vertically. Practice rotating the camera each direction to find what is most comfortable and stable for you.

Now that you know where to put your hands, let's talk about what to do with the rest of your body parts. By using the underhand grip, your elbows will be drawn closer to your body. You should concentrate on pulling them in close to your body to stabilize your shooting position. You should also try to maintain proper upright posture. Leaning forward at the waist will begin to fatigue your back, neck, and arms. You can really ruin a day of shooting with a sore back, so make sure you stand erect with your elbows in. Finally, place your left foot in front of your right foot, and face your subject in a slightly wide stance. By combining all of these aspects into your photography, you will give yourself the best chance of eliminating self-imposed camera shake in your images, resulting in much sharper photographs.

Chapter 1 Assignments

Let's begin our shooting assignments by setting up and using all of the elements of the Top Ten list. Even though I have yet to cover the professional shooting modes, you should set your camera to the P (Program) mode. This will allow you to interact with the various settings and menus that have been covered thus far.

Basic camera setup

Charge your battery to 100% to get it started on a life of dependable service. Next, using your newfound knowledge, set up your camera to address the following: Image Quality, Auto ISO, and Color Space.

Selecting the proper white balance

Take your camera outside into a daylight environment and then photograph the same scene using different white balance settings. Pay close attention to how each setting affects the overall color cast of your images. Next, move indoors and repeat the exercise while shooting in a tungsten lighting environment. Finally, find a fluorescent light source and repeat one more time.

Focusing with single point and AF-S

Change your camera setting so that you are focusing using the single-point focus mode. Try using all of the different focus points to see how they work in focusing your scene. Then set your focus mode to AF-S and practice focusing on a subject and then recomposing before actually taking the picture. Try doing this with subjects at varying distances.

Evaluating your pictures with the LCD display

Set up your image display properties and then review some of your previous assignment images using the different display modes. Review your shooting information for each image and take a look at the histograms to see how the content of your photo affects the shape of the histograms.

Discovering the manual focus mode

Change your focus mode from autofocus to manual focus and practice a little manual focus photography. Get familiar with where the focus ring is and how to use it to achieve sharp images.

Get a grip: proper camera holding

This final assignment is something that you should practice every time you shoot: proper grip and stance for shooting with your camera. Use the described technique and then shoot a series of images. Try comparing it with improper techniques to compare the stability of the grip and stance.

Share your results with the book's Flickr group!

Join the group here: flickr.com/groups/nikond5100fromsnapshotstogreatshots/

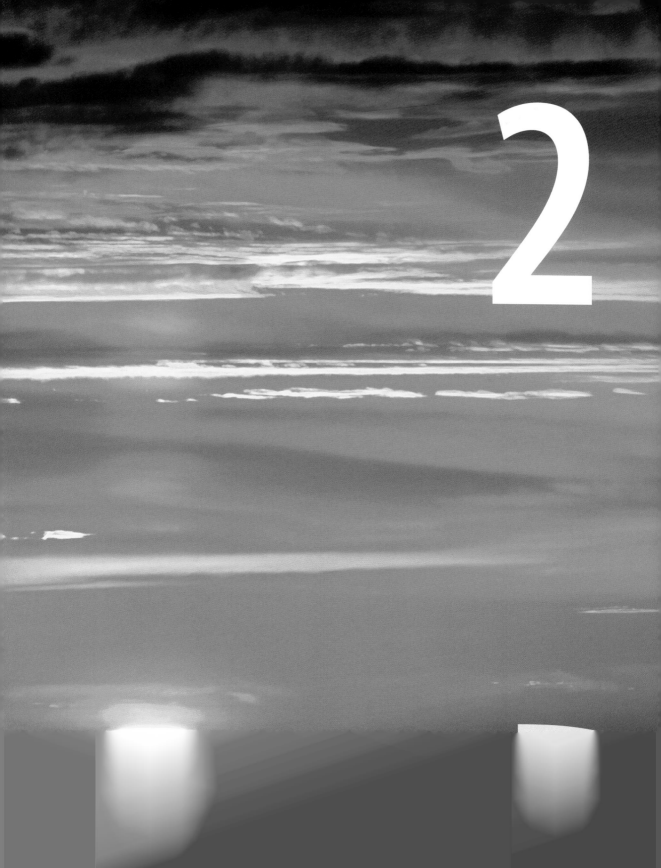

2

First Things First

A FEW THINGS TO KNOW AND DO
BEFORE YOU BEGIN TAKING PICTURES

Now that we've covered the top ten tasks to get you up and shooting, we should probably take care of some other important details. You must become familiar with certain features of your camera before you can take full advantage of it. Additionally, we will take some steps to prepare the camera and memory card for use. So to get things moving, let's start off with something that you will definitely need before you can take a single picture: a memory card.

PORING OVER THE PICTURE

Wild animals are some of my favorite subjects to capture. Whether they are in the wild, like these three brown bear cubs, or in captivity, they always present great opportunities and great challenges for improving your photographic skills.

ISO 800
1/500 sec.
f/5.6
400mm lens

The use of a telephoto lens allowed me to stay at a safe distance, but still fill the frame.

The aperture was at its widest setting for this lens to decrease depth of field.

The focus point was placed on the top cub.

The ISO was raised to allow for a shutter speed fast enough to stop motion.

CHOOSING THE RIGHT MEMORY CARD

Memory cards are the digital film that stores every shot you take until you move
them to a computer. The cards come in all shapes and
sizes, and they are critical for capturing all of your
photos. It is important not to skimp when it comes to
selecting your memory cards. The D5100 uses Secure
Digital (SD) memory cards (**Figure 2.1**).

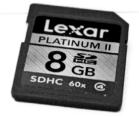

If you have been using a point-and-shoot camera,
chances are that you may already own an SD media
card. Which brand of card you use is completely up
to you, but here is some advice about choosing your
memory card:

FIGURE 2.1
Make sure you select an SD card
that has enough capacity to
handle your photography needs.

- Size matters, at least in memory cards. At 16.2
  megapixels, the D5100 will require a lot of storage space, especially if you shoot
  in the RAW or RAW+JPEG mode (more on this later in the chapter). You should
  definitely consider using a card with a storage capacity of at least 4 GB, but go
  with 8 GB if it is in your budget. If you plan on shooting high-definition video,
  be prepared for some large files. At five minutes, high-def video recording takes
  up approximately 700 MB of storage space. This means that you can fit about 30
  minutes of video on a 4 GB card.

- Consider buying High Capacity (SDHC) cards. These cards are generally much
  faster, both when writing images to the card and when transferring them to
  your computer. If you are planning on using the Continuous mode (see Chapter
  5) for capturing fast action, you can gain a boost in performance just by using an
  SDHC card with a class rating of at least 4 or 6. The higher the class rating, the
  faster the write speed. Class 6 or higher is
  recommended for video recording.

- Buy more than one card. If you have
  already purchased a memory card, consider
  getting another. You can quickly ruin your
  day of shooting by filling your card and
  then having to either erase shots or choose
  a lower-quality image format so that you
  can keep on shooting. With the cost of
  memory cards what it is, keeping a spare
  just makes good sense.

Manual Callout

For a list of Nikon-approved memory
cards for the D5100, you should
check out page 207 in the Reference
Manual on the companion CD that
comes with the camera.

FORMATTING YOUR MEMORY CARD

Now that you have your card, let's talk about formatting for a minute. When you purchase any new SD card, you can pop it into your camera and start shooting right away —and probably everything will work as it should. However, what you should do first is format the card in the camera. This process allows the camera to set up the card to record images from your camera. Just as a computer hard drive must be formatted, formatting your card ensures that it is properly initialized. The card may work in the camera without first being formatted, but chances of failure down the road are much higher.

As a general practice, I always format new cards or cards that have been used in different cameras. I also reformat cards after I have downloaded my images and want to start a new shooting session. Note that you should always format your card in the camera, not your computer. Using the computer could render the card useless. You should also pay attention to the card manufacturer's recommendations with respect to moisture, humidity, and proper handling procedures. It sounds a little cliché, but when it comes to protecting your images, every little bit helps.

Most people make the mistake of thinking that the process of formatting the memory card is equivalent to erasing it. Not so. The truth is that when you format the card all you are doing is changing the file management information on the card. Think of it as removing the table of contents from a book and replacing it with a blank page. All of the contents are still there, but you wouldn't know it by looking at the empty table of contents. The camera will see the card as completely empty so you won't be losing any space, even if you have previously filled the card with images. Your camera will simply write the new image data over the previous data.

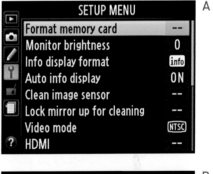

A

FORMATTING YOUR MEMORY CARD

1. Insert your memory card into the camera.

2. Press the Menu button and navigate to the Setup menu screen.

3. Use the Multi-selector on the back of the camera to highlight the Format Memory Card option and press OK (**A**).

4. The next screen will show you a warning, letting you know that formatting the card will delete images (**B**). Select Yes and press the OK button.

5. The card is now formatted and ready for use.

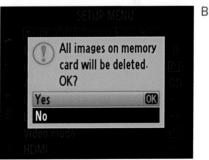

B

UPDATING THE D5100'S FIRMWARE

I know that you want to get shooting, but having the proper firmware can impact the way the camera operates. It can fix problems as well as improve operation, so you should probably check it sooner rather than later. Updating your camera's firmware is something that the manual completely omits, yet it can change the entire behavior of your camera operating systems and functions. The firmware of your camera is the set of computer operating instructions that control how your camera functions. Updating this firmware is a great way to not only fix little bugs but also gain access to new functionality. You will need to check out the information on the Nikon firmware update page (www.nikonusa.com/Service-And-Support/Download-Center.page) to see if a firmware update is available and how it will impact your camera, but it is always a good idea to be working with the most up-to-date firmware version available.

CHECKING THE CAMERA'S CURRENT FIRMWARE VERSION NUMBER

1. Press the Menu button and then navigate to the Setup menu.

2. Use the Multi-selector on the back of the camera to highlight the Firmware Version option and press OK (**A**).

3. Take note of the current version numbers (there are three of them) and then check the Nikon Web site to see if you are using the current versions (**B**).

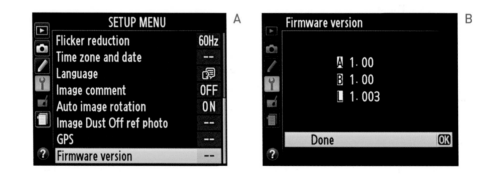

UPDATING THE FIRMWARE FROM YOUR SD CARD

1. Download the firmware update file from the Nikon Web site. (You can find the file by going to the Download Center section of the Nikon camera site and locating the firmware update for your camera and computer operating system.)

2. Once you have downloaded the firmware to your computer and extracted it, you will need to transfer it to your SD card. The card must be formatted in your camera prior to loading the firmware to it.

3. With a freshly charged camera battery, insert the card into the camera and turn it on.

4. Follow the instructions listed above for locating your firmware version, and you will now be able to update your firmware using the files located on the SD card.

When this book was being written, there were no firmware updates available for the D5100. After you check your camera firmware version and the Nikon site for updates, continue to check back periodically to see if there are updates available.

CLEANING THE SENSOR

Cleaning camera sensors used to be a nerve-racking process that required leaving the sensor exposed to scratching and even more dust. Now cleaning the sensor is pretty much an automatic function. Every time you turn the camera on and off, you can instruct the sensor in the camera to vibrate to remove any dust particles that might have landed on it.

There are five choices for cleaning in the camera Setup menu: Clean at Startup, Clean at Shutdown, Clean at Startup and Shutdown, Cleaning Off, and Clean Now. I'm kind of obsessive when it comes to cleaning my sensor, so I like to have it set to clean when I turn the camera on and off.

The one cleaning function that you will need to use via this menu is the Clean now feature. This should be done every time that you remove the lens from the camera body. That is because removing or changing a lens will leave the camera body open and susceptible to dust sneaking into the body. If you never change lenses, you shouldn't have too many dust problems. But the more often you change lenses, the more chances you are giving dust to enter the body. It's for this reason that I have added the Clean Now function to the custom My Menu list (see Chapter 10).

Every now and then, there will be a dust spot that is impervious to the shaking of the Auto Cleaning feature. This will require you to clean the sensor manually by raising the mirror and opening the camera shutter. When you activate this feature, it will move everything out of the way, giving you access to the sensor so that you can use a blower or other cleaning device to remove the stubborn dust speck. The camera will need to be turned off after cleaning to allow the mirror to reset.

If you choose to manually clean your sensor, use a device that has been made to clean sensors (not a cotton swab from your medicine cabinet). There are dozens of commercially available devices such as brushes, swabs, and blowers that will clean the sensor without damaging it. To keep the sensor clean, always store the camera with a body cap or lens attached.

The camera sensor is an electrically charged device. This means that when the camera is turned on, there is a current running through the sensor. This electric current can create static electricity, which will attract small dust particles to the sensor area. For this reason, it is always a good idea to turn off the camera prior to removing a lens. You should also consider having the lens mount facing down when changing lenses so that there is less opportunity for dust to fall into the inner workings of the camera.

USING THE CLEAN NOW FEATURE

1. Press the Menu button, then navigate to the Setup menu.

2. Use the Multi-selector on the back of the camera to highlight the Clean Image Sensor option and press OK (**A**).

3. Highlight the Clean Now option and press the OK button (**B**). The camera will clean the sensor for about two seconds and then return to the menu.

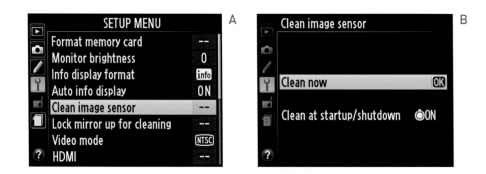

USING THE RIGHT FORMAT: RAW VS. JPEG

When shooting with your D5100, you have a choice of image formats that your camera will use to store the pictures on the memory card. JPEG is probably the most familiar format to anyone who has been using a digital camera. I touched on this topic briefly in Chapter 1, so you already have a little background on what JPEG and RAW files are.

There is nothing wrong with JPEG if you are taking casual shots. JPEG files are ready to use, right out of the camera. Why go through the process of adjusting RAW images of the kids opening presents when you are just going to email them to Grandma? Also, for journalists and sports photographers who are shooting multiple frames per second and who need to transmit their images across the wire, again, JPEG is just fine. So what is wrong with JPEG? Absolutely nothing—unless you care about having complete creative control over all of your image data (as opposed to what a compression algorithm thinks is important).

As I mentioned in Chapter 1, JPEG is not actually an image format. It is a compression standard, and compression is where things go bad. When you have your camera set to JPEG—whether it is Fine, Normal, or Basic—you are telling the camera to process the image based on the in-camera settings and then throw away enough image data to make it shrink into a smaller space. In doing so, you give up subtle image details that you will never get back in post-processing. That is an awfully simplified statement, but still fairly accurate.

SO WHAT DOES RAW HAVE TO OFFER?

First and foremost, RAW images are not compressed. (There are some cameras, like the D5100, that have a compressed RAW format, but it is lossless compression, which means there is no loss of actual image data.) Note that RAW image files will require you to perform post-processing on your photographs. This is not only necessary, it is the reason that most photographers use it.

RAW images have a greater dynamic range than JPEG-processed images. This means that you can recover image detail in the highlights and shadows that just isn't available in JPEG-processed images.

There is more color information in a RAW image because it is a 12- or 14-bit image (depending on the camera), which means it contains more color information than a JPEG, which is always an 8-bit image. More color information means more to work with and smoother changes between tones—kind of like the difference between performing surgery with a scalpel as opposed to a butcher's knife. They'll both get the job done, but one will do less damage.

IMAGE RESOLUTION

When discussing digital cameras, image resolution is often used to describe pixel resolution or the number of pixels used to make an image. This can be displayed as a dimension, such as 4928x3264. This is the physical number of pixels in the width and height of the image sensor. Resolution can also be referred to in megapixels (MP), such as 16.2 MP. This number represents the total number of pixels on the sensor and is commonly used to describe the amount of image data that a digital camera can capture.

Regarding sharpening, a RAW image offers more control because you are the one who is applying the sharpening according to the effect you want to achieve. Once again, JPEG processing applies a standard amount of sharpening that you cannot change after the fact. Once it is done, it's done.

Finally, and most importantly, a RAW file is your negative. No matter what you do to it, you won't change it unless you save your file in a different format. This means that you can come back to that RAW file later and try different processing settings to achieve differing results and never harm the original image. By comparison, if you make a change to your JPEG and accidentally save the file, guess what? You have a new original file, and you will never get back to that first image. That alone should make you sit up and take notice.

ADVICE FOR NEW RAW SHOOTERS

Don't give up on shooting RAW just because it means more work. Hey, if it takes up more space on your card, buy bigger cards or more small ones. Will it take more time to download? Yes, but good things come to those who wait. Don't worry about needing to purchase expensive software to work with your RAW files; you already own a program that will allow you to work with your RAW files. Nikon's ViewNX software comes bundled in the box with your camera and gives you the ability to work directly on the RAW files and then output the enhanced results. That said, you will have more control with dedicated RAW processing software such as Nikon's Capture NX2, Apple's Aperture, or Adobe's Photoshop and Lightroom.

My recommendation is to shoot in JPEG mode while you are using this book. This will allow you to quickly review your images and study the effects of the lessons. Once you have become comfortable with all of the camera features, you should switch to shooting in RAW mode so that you can start gaining more creative control over your image processing. After all, you took the photograph—shouldn't you be the one to decide how it looks in the end?

SHOOTING DUAL FORMATS

Your camera has the added benefit of being able to write two files for each picture you take, one in RAW and one in JPEG. If you have a RAW+JPEG setting selected, your camera will save your images in both formats on your card.

I think shooting RAW+JPEG is actually a good way to transition to shooting RAW. You get the ease and safety of the familiar JPEG, and the ability to compare the JPEG against your RAW processing experiences. Obviously this will take up more of the space on your memory card and hard drive, but think of it as a stepping-stone on the path to shooting only RAW in the future. It took me a little while to make the transition, and looking back there are some shots I took in JPEG mode that I now wish I had a RAW version of that I could try to improve. Live and learn.

SHOOTING IN RAW+JPEG

1. Press the **i** button to activate the cursor in the information screen.
2. Use the Multi-selector to highlight the Image Quality setting, located at the top right of the screen, and press OK (**A**).
3. Press up on the Multi-selector to highlight the RAW+JPEG option of your choice. The three options include RAW+B (Basic), RAW+N (Normal), and RAW+F (Fine) (**B**).
4. Press the OK button to lock in your changes.

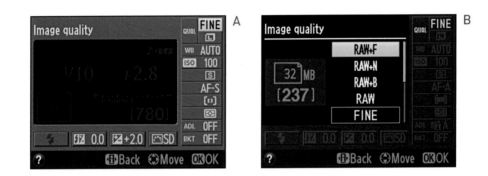

You will notice when you are in the selection screen that you will be able to see how much storage space each option will require on your SD card. The RAW+F option, which is the one I use, will take up approximately 32 MB of space for each photograph you take.

LENSES AND FOCAL LENGTHS

If you ask most professional photographers what they believe to be their most critical piece of photographic equipment, they would undoubtedly tell you that it is their lens. The technology and engineering that goes into your camera is a marvel, but it isn't worth a darn if it can't get the light from the outside onto the sensor. The D5100, as a digital single lens reflex (dSLR) camera, uses the lens for a multitude of tasks, from focusing on a subject, to metering a scene, to delivering and focusing the light onto the camera sensor. The lens is also responsible for the amount of the scene that will be captured (the frame). With all of this riding on the lens, let's take a more in-depth look at the camera's eye on the world.

Lenses are composed of optical glass that is both concave and convex in shape. The alignment of the glass elements is designed to focus the light coming in from the front of the lens onto the camera sensor. The amount of light that enters the camera is also controlled by the lens, the size of the glass elements, and the aperture mechanism within the lens housing. The quality of the glass used in the lens will have a direct effect on how well the lens can resolve details and on the contrast of the image (the ability to deliver great highlights and shadows). Most lenses now routinely include things like an autofocus motor and, in some cases, a vibration reduction mechanism.

One other aspect of the camera lens is often the first consideration of the photographer: lens length. Lenses are typically divided into three or four groups depending on the field of view they deliver.

Wide-angle lenses cover a field of view from around 110 degrees to about 60 degrees (**Figure 2.2**). There is also a tendency to get some distortion in your image when using extremely wide-angle lenses. This will be apparent toward the outer edges of the frame. As for which lenses would be considered wide angle, anything 35mm or smaller could be considered wide.

FIGURE 2.2
The 18mm lens setting provides a wide view of the scene but little detail of distant objects.

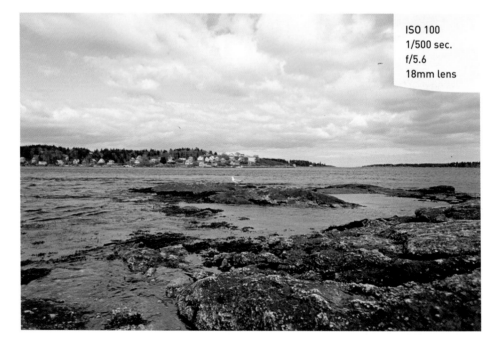

ISO 100
1/500 sec.
f/5.6
18mm lens

Wide-angle lenses can display a large depth of field, which allows you to keep the foreground and background in sharp focus. This makes them very useful for landscape photography. They also work well in tight spaces, such as indoors, where there isn't much elbow room available (**Figure 2.3**). They can also be handy for large group shots but, because of the amount of distortion, not so great for close-up portrait work.

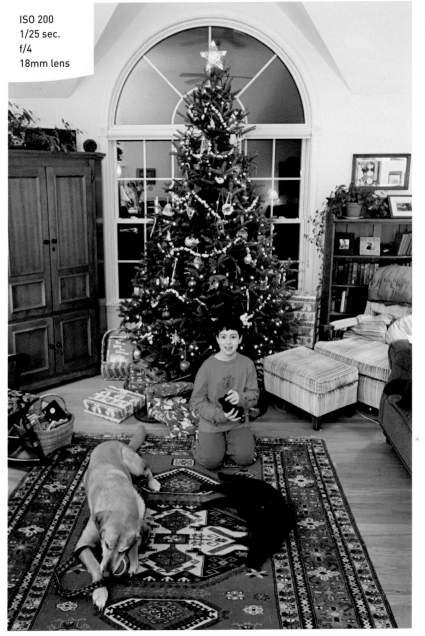

ISO 200
1/25 sec.
f/4
18mm lens

FIGURE 2.3
When shooting in tight spaces, such as indoors, a nice wide-angle lens helps capture more of the scene.

A *normal* lens has a field of view that is about 45 degrees and delivers approximately the same view as the human eye. The perspective is very natural and there is little distortion in objects. The normal lens for full-frame and 35mm cameras is the 50mm lens (**Figure 2.4**), but for the D5100 it is more in the neighborhood of a 35mm lens because of its sensor's 1.5x crop factor.

FIGURE 2.4
Long considered the "normal" lens for 35mm photography, the 50mm focal length can be considered somewhat of a telephoto lens on the D5100 because it has the same angle of view and magnification as an 80mm lens on a 35mm camera body.

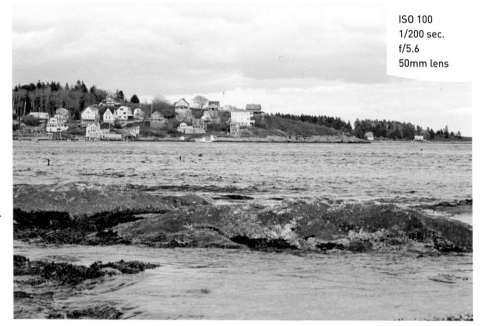

ISO 100
1/200 sec.
f/5.6
50mm lens

Normal focal length lenses are useful for photographing people and architecture and for most other general photographic needs. They create very little distortion and offer a moderate range of depth of field.

Most longer focal length lenses are referred to as *telephoto* lenses. They can range in length from 135mm up to 800mm or longer, and have a field of view that is about 35 degrees or smaller. These lenses have the ability to greatly magnify the scene, allowing you to capture details of distant objects, but the angle of view is greatly reduced (**Figure 2.5**). You will also find that you can achieve a much narrower depth of field. They also suffer from something called distance compression, which means they make objects at different distances appear to be much closer together than they really are.

Telephoto lenses are most useful for sports photography or any application where you need to get closer to your subject (**Figure 2.6**). They can have a compressing effect—making objects look closer together than they actually are—and a very narrow depth of field when shot at their widest apertures.

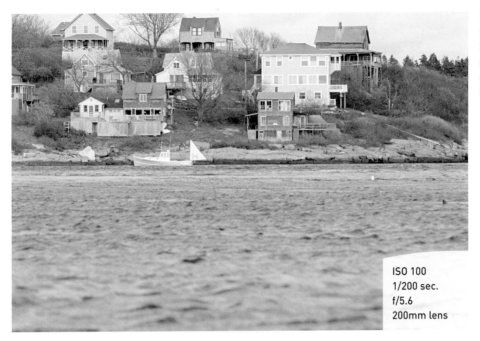

FIGURE 2.5
By switching to my
200mm lens, I was
able to bring the
opposite shore right
up close.

ISO 100
1/200 sec.
f/5.6
200mm lens

ISO 200
1/320 sec.
f/8
400mm lens

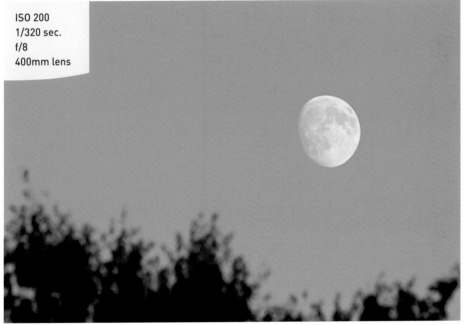

FIGURE 2.6
The long telephoto
lens makes the
moon appear close
to the treetop.

A *zoom* lens is a great compromise to carrying a bunch of single focal length lenses (also referred to as "prime" lenses). They can cover a wide range of focal lengths because of the configuration of their optics. However, because it takes more optical elements to capture a scene at different focal lengths, the light must pass through more glass on its way to the image sensor. The more glass, the lower the quality of the image sharpness. The other sacrifice that is made is in aperture. Zoom lenses typically have smaller maximum apertures than prime lenses, which means they cannot achieve a narrow depth of field or work in lower light levels without the assistance of image stabilization, a tripod, or higher ISO settings. (We'll discuss all this in more detail in later chapters.)

The D5100 can be purchased with the body only, but many folks will purchase it with a kit lens. The most common kit lens is the 18–55mm VR f/3.5–5.6. With my D5100, I have been working the 18–55mm as well as the 70–200mm VR AF-S lens.

Throughout the book, I will occasionally make reference to lenses that are wider or more telephoto than these, because I have a multitude of lenses that I use for my photography. This doesn't mean that you have to run out and purchase more lenses. It just means that if you do this long enough, you are sure to accumulate additional lenses that will expand your ability to be even more creative with your photography.

WHAT IS EXPOSURE?

In order for you to get the most out of this book, I need to briefly discuss the principles of exposure. Without this basic knowledge, it will be difficult for you to move forward in improving your photography. Granted, I could write an entire book on exposure and the photographic process—and many people have—but for our purposes I will just cover some of the basics. This will give you the essential tools to make educated decisions in determining how best to photograph a subject.

Exposure is the process whereby the light reflecting off a subject reflects through an opening in the camera lens for a defined period of time onto the camera sensor. The combination of the lens opening, shutter speed, and sensor sensitivity is used to achieve a proper exposure value (EV) for the scene. The EV is the sum of these components necessary to properly expose a scene. A relationship exists between these factors that is sometimes referred to as the "exposure triangle."

At each point of the triangle lies one of the factors of exposure:

- **ISO:** Determines the sensitivity of the camera sensor. ISO stands for the International Organization for Standardization, but the acronym is used as a term to describe the sensitivity of the camera sensor to light. The higher the sensitivity, the less light is required for a good exposure. These values are a carryover from the days of traditional color and black and white films.

- **Aperture:** Also referred to as the f-stop, this determines how much light passes through the lens at once.

- **Shutter Speed:** Controls the length of time that light is allowed to hit the sensor.

Here's how it works. The camera sensor has a level of sensitivity that is determined by the ISO setting. To get a proper exposure—not too much, not too little—the lens needs to adjust the aperture diaphragm (the size of the lens opening) to control the volume of light entering the camera. Then the shutter is opened for a relatively short period of time to allow the light to hit the sensor long enough for it to record on the sensor.

ISO numbers for the D5100 start at 100 and then double in sensitivity as you double the number. So 200 is twice as sensitive as 100. The camera can be set to use 1/2- or 1/3-stop increments, but for ISO just remember that the base numbers double: 100, 200, 400, 800, and so on. There are also a wide variety of shutter speeds that you can use. The speeds on the D5100 range from as long as 30 seconds to as short as 1/4000 of a second. When using the camera, you will not see the 1 over the number in the viewfinder, so you will need to remember that anything shorter than a second will be a fraction. Typically, you will be working with a shutter speed from around 1/30 of a second to about 1/2000 of a second, but these numbers will change depending on your circumstances and the effect that you are trying to achieve. The lens apertures will vary slightly depending on which lens you are using. This is because different lenses have different maximum apertures. The typical apertures that are at your disposal are f/4, f/5.6, f/8, f/11, f/16, and f/22.

When it comes to exposure, a change to any one of these factors requires changing one or more of the other two. This is referred to as reciprocal change. If you let more light in the lens by choosing a larger aperture, you will need to shorten the amount of time the shutter is open. If the shutter is allowed to stay open for a longer period of time, the aperture needs to be smaller to restrict the amount of light coming in.

HOW IS EXPOSURE CALCULATED?

We now know about the exposure triangle—ISO, shutter speed, and aperture—so it's time to put all three together to see how they relate to one another and how you can change them as needed.

STOP

You will hear the term *stop* thrown around all the time in photography. It relates back to the f-stop, which is a term used to describe the aperture of your lens. When you need to give some additional exposure, you might say that you are going to "add a stop." This doesn't just equate to the aperture; it could also be used to describe the shutter speed or even the ISO. So when your image is too light or dark or you have too much movement in your subject, you will probably be changing things by a "stop" or two.

When you point your camera at a scene, the light reflecting off your subject enters the lens and is allowed to pass through to the sensor for a period of time as dictated by the shutter speed. The amount and duration of the light needed for a proper exposure depends on how much light is being reflected and how sensitive the sensor is. To figure this out, your camera utilizes a built-in light meter that looks through the lens and measures the amount of light. That level is then calculated against the sensitivity of the ISO setting and an exposure value is rendered. Here is the tricky part: there is no single way to achieve a perfect exposure because the f-stop and shutter speed can be combined in different ways to allow the same amount of exposure. See, I told you it was tricky.

Here is a list of reciprocal settings that would all produce the same exposure result. Let's use the "sunny 16" rule, which states that, when using f/16 on a sunny day, you can use a shutter speed that is roughly equal to the ISO setting to achieve a proper exposure. For simplification purposes, we will use an ISO of 100.

RECIPROCAL EXPOSURES: ISO 100

F-STOP	2.8	4.0	5.6	8	11	16	22
SHUTTER SPEED	1/4000	1/2000	1/1000	1/500	1/250	1/125	1/60

If you were to use any one of these combinations, they would each have the same result in terms of the exposure (i.e., how much light hits the camera's sensor). Also take note that every time we cut the f-stop in half, we reciprocated by doubling our shutter speed. For those of you wondering why f/5.6 is half of f/8, it's because those numbers are actually fractions based on the opening of the lens in relation to its focal length. This means that a lot of math goes into figuring out just what the total area of a lens opening is, so you just have to take it on faith that f/5.6 is half of f/8 but twice as much as f/4. A good way to remember which opening is larger is to think of your camera lens as a pipe that controls the flow of water. If you had a pipe that was 1/2" in diameter (f/2) and one that was 1/8" (f/8), which would allow more water to flow through? It would be the 1/2" pipe. The same idea works here with the camera f-stops; f/2 is a larger opening than f/4 or f/8 or f/16.

Now that we know this, we can start using this information to make intelligent choices in terms of shutter speed and f-stop. Let's bring the third element into this by changing our ISO by one stop, from 100 to 200.

RECIPROCAL EXPOSURES: ISO 200

F-STOP	2.8	4.0	5.6	8	11	16	22
SHUTTER SPEED	–	1/4000	1/2000	1/1000	1/500	1/250	1/125

Notice that, since we doubled the sensitivity of the sensor, we now require half as much exposure as before. We have also reduced our maximum aperture from f/2.8 to f/4 because the camera can't use a shutter speed that is faster than 1/4000 of a second.

So why not just use the exposure setting of f/16 at 1/250 of a second? Why bother with all of these reciprocal values when this one setting will give us a properly exposed image? The answer is that the f-stop and shutter speed also control two other important aspects of our image: motion and depth of field.

MOTION AND DEPTH OF FIELD

There are distinct characteristics that are related to changes in aperture and shutter speed. Shutter speed controls the length of time the light has to strike the sensor; consequently, it also controls the blurriness (or lack of blurriness) of the image. The less time light has to hit the sensor, the less time your subjects have to move around and become blurry. This can let you control things like freezing the motion of a fast-moving subject (**Figure 2.7**) or intentionally blurring subjects to give the feel of energy and motion (**Figure 2.8**).

FIGURE 2.7
A fast shutter speed was used to freeze the action.

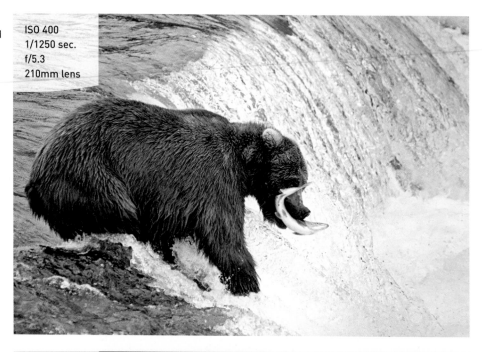

ISO 400
1/1250 sec.
f/5.3
210mm lens

FIGURE 2.8
The slower shutter speed relays a sense of motion as the globe spins around its axis.

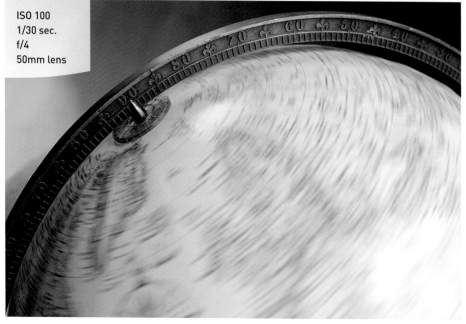

ISO 100
1/30 sec.
f/4
50mm lens

The aperture controls the amount of light that comes through the lens, but it also determines what areas of the image will be in focus. This is referred to as depth of field, and it is an extremely valuable creative tool. The smaller the opening (the larger the number, such as f/22), the greater the sharpness of objects from near to far (**Figure 2.9**). A large opening (or small number, like f/2.8) means more blurring of objects that are not at the same distance as the subject you are focusing on (**Figure 2.10**).

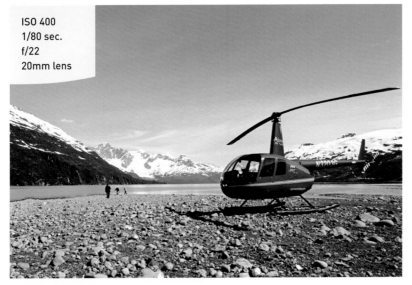

ISO 400
1/80 sec.
f/22
20mm lens

FIGURE 2.9
By using a small aperture, the area of sharp focus extends from a point that is near the camera all the way out to distant objects, which we can see by the level of detail in the foreground rocks, the helicopter, and even the distant mountains.

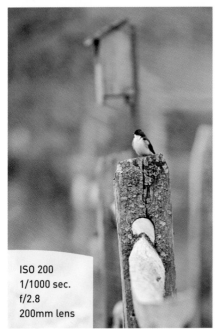

ISO 200
1/1000 sec.
f/2.8
200mm lens

FIGURE 2.10
Isolating a subject is accomplished by using a large aperture, which produces a narrow area of sharp focus, while blurring the foreground and everything in the background as well.

As we further explore the features of the camera, we will learn not only how to utilize the elements of exposure to capture properly exposed photographs, but also how we can make adjustments to emphasize our subject. It is the manipulation of these elements—motion and focus—that will take your images to the next level.

VIDEO AND THE D5100

Probably one of the reasons you purchased the D5100 instead of other competing camera models is its ability to capture video. Not just regular video, but full high-definition video. As I discussed in the book's introduction, I am going to keep the focus of this book on the photography aspects of the camera, but that doesn't mean I am going to simply ignore the video functions completely. In fact, I am dedicating a bonus chapter to some fun video tips, but I thought that I would at least cover the video basics here in Chapter 2 since we've already looked at a lot of other camera functions. First, let's cover some of the basic facts about the movie-making features.

Video recording is a feature of the Live View capabilities of the camera, so you'll have to put the camera into the active Live View mode to begin to capture video. This is accomplished by rotating the Live View switch (**Figure 2.11**) on the top of the camera, which activates the Live View on the rear display. If you want to control the aperture, you should set the aperture value to either Manual mode or Aperture Priority mode before switching to Live View. Otherwise, switch to one of the other modes and let the camera adjust it automatically.

Once Live View is active, press the **i** button and choose a focus mode. It is possible to use the full-time-servo (AF-F) mode while recording video, and you should try it out because it does a fine job in some situations, but I strongly urge you to refine your manual focus (MF) skills. Using manual focus not only gives you creative control of what is in focus, it also eliminates the sound of the lens trying to maintain autofocus.

Once your subject is in focus, you can push the Movie

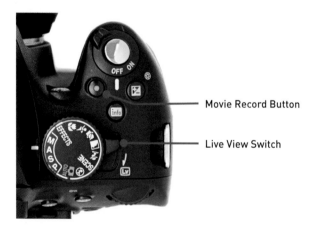

Movie Record Button

Live View Switch

FIGURE 2.11
Rotate the Live View switch to start.

Record button (Figure 2.11) to begin the recording process (there is no special movie mode). When the camera begins recording, you will notice a few new icons show up on the LCD (**Figure 2.12**). At the top left is a blinking red Record icon to let you know that the camera is in active recording mode, and just below that is the audio recording indicator. In the upper right, you'll notice the timer that is counting down your remaining recording time. This number is directly related to the quality you have selected for your video. To stop the video recording, simply press the OK button a second time. This will take you back to Live View mode.

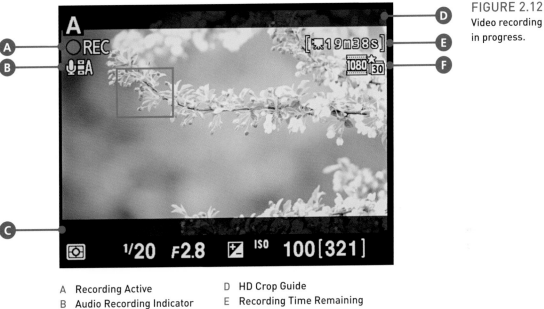

FIGURE 2.12
Video recording in progress.

A   Recording Active
B   Audio Recording Indicator
C   HD Crop Guide
D   HD Crop Guide
E   Recording Time Remaining
F   Movie Frame Size

VIDEO QUALITY

The highest-quality video setting on your D5100 will render high-definition video with a resolution of 1920x1080 pixels. This is also referred to as 1080p. The 1080 represents the height of the video image in pixels, and the "p" stands for progressive, which is how the camera actually records/draws the video on the screen. You can select lower-resolution video depending on your needs. The other two video resolutions are 1280x720 and 640x424. For high-definition TV and computer/media station viewing, you will be served best by using the 1920x1080 recording resolution. If you don't need full 1080p HD, such as when recording for the Internet, iPods, or portable video players, you might want to consider using the 1280x720 or 640x424 choices since they require less physical storage and take less time to upload to the Internet.

PROGRESSIVE SCAN

When it comes to video, there are usually two terms associated with the quality of the video and how it is captured and displayed on a monitor or screen: *progressive* and *interlaced*. The two terms describe how the video is drawn by line for each frame. Video frames are not displayed all at once like a photograph. In progressive video, the lines are drawn in sequence from top to bottom. Interlaced video draws all of the odd-numbered lines and then all of the even-numbered lines. This odd-even drawing can present itself as screen flicker, which is why the progressive video standard is preferred, especially when viewing higher-definition images.

SETTING THE MOVIE QUALITY

1. Start by pressing the Menu button.

2. Navigate to the Shooting menu using the Multi-selector, highlight the Movie Settings option, and press OK (**A**).

3. Highlight the Movie Quality setting and press OK (**B**).

4. Select the video quality of your choice and press the OK button (**C**).

5. Press the Menu button twice to exit the menu mode and return to shooting, or rotate the Live View switch to jump right into the Live View/video recording mode.

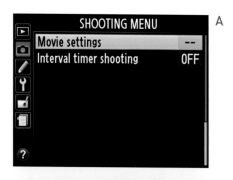

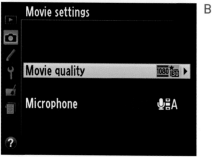

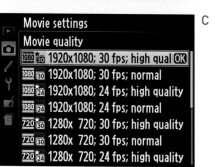

Manual Callout

Refer to page 53 of the printed user manual for a complete rundown of the video quality and frame rate settings.

SOUND

The D5100 can record audio to go along with your video, but there are a couple of things to keep in mind when using it. The first is to make sure you don't block the microphone. (If you look closely at the front of the camera body, you'll notice three small holes right above the silver D5100 nameplate). This should not be a problem if you are holding the camera as discussed in Chapter 1.

The next thing you need to know about the sound is that the built-in microphone records in mono, not stereo. This means that when you are watching the recorded video on your TV or computer, you might only hear the sound coming from one speaker. The D5100 does have an external microphone jack on the side panel (**Figure 2.13**), so you might want to consider investing in an external mic that is capable of recording in stereo (as well as of producing higher-quality audio recordings).

You do also have the option of turning off the audio altogether. This can be useful if the sound might be distracting or you plan on using your own soundtrack to be added to the video at a later time.

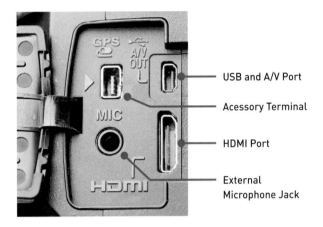

FIGURE 2.13
D5100 ports and mic jack

USB and A/V Port
Acessory Terminal
HDMI Port
External
Microphone Jack

TURNING OFF THE SOUND

1. Following the directions for setting the movie quality above, locate the Movie Settings menu and press the OK button.

2. Highlight the Microphone option and press OK again (**A**).

3. Select the Microphone Off option and press OK to lock in the change. Press the Menu button twice to return to shooting mode (**B**).

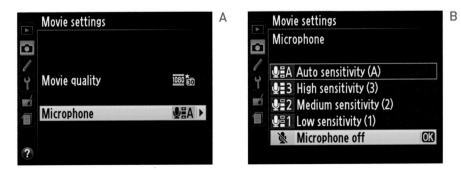

WATCHING YOUR VIDEOS

There are a couple of different ways you can review your video once you have fin-ished recording. The first, and probably the easiest, is to press the Playback button to bring up the recorded image on the rear LCD screen and then use the OK button to start playing the video. The Multi-selector acts as the video controller and allows you to rewind and fast-forward as well as stop the video altogether.

If you would like to get a larger look at things, you will need to either watch the video on your TV or move the video files to your computer. To watch on your TV, you can use the video cable that came with your camera and plug it into the small port on the side of the camera body (Figure 2.13). This lets you watch low-resolution video on your TV. To get the full effect from your HD videos, you will need to purchase an HDMI cable (your TV needs to support at least 720 HD and have an HDMI port to use this option). Once you have the cable hooked up to your TV, simply use the same camera controls that you used for watching the video on the rear LCD screen.

If you want to watch or use the videos on your computer, you will need to download the video using the Nikon software or by using an SD card reader attached to the computer. The video files will have the extension .mov at the end of the file name. These files should play on either a Mac or a PC using software that came with your operating system (QuickTime for Mac and Windows Media Player for the PC).

For even more information about using video with your D5100, be sure to download the Chapter 12 bonus chapter from Peachpit.com (as discussed in the introduction).

Chapter 2 Assignments

Formatting your card

Even if you have already begun using your camera, make sure you are familiar with formatting the Secure Digital card. If you haven't done so already, follow the directions given earlier in the chapter and format as prescribed (make sure you save any images that you may have already taken). Then perform the format function every time you have downloaded or saved your images or use a new card.

Checking your firmware version

Using the most up-to-date version of the camera firmware will ensure that your camera is functioning properly. Use the menu to find your current firmware version and then update as necessary using the steps listed in this chapter.

Cleaning your sensor

You probably noticed the sensor-cleaning message the first time you turned your camera on. Make sure you are familiar with the Clean Now command so you can perform this function every time you change a lens.

Exploring your image formats

I want you to become familiar with all of the camera features before using the RAW format, but take a little time to explore the format menu so you can see what options are available to you.

Exploring your lens

If you are using a zoom lens, spend a little time shooting with all of the different focal lengths, from the widest to the longest. See just how much of an angle you can cover with your widest lens setting. How much magnification will you be able to get from the telephoto setting? Try shooting the same subject with a variety of focal lengths to note the differences in how the subject looks, and also the relationship between the subject and the other elements in the photo.

Recording video clips

Take a little time to discover how the video function works on your camera. Set the video quality to high definition and record a short sequence, and then try it with some of the lower resolution settings. Open the video clips on your computer or hook up the camera to your TV, then review the different video clips to see how the quality setting affects the video.

Share your results with the book's Flickr group!

Join the group here: flickr.com/groups/nikond5100fromsnapshotstogreatshots/

3

ISO 100
1/30 sec.
f/8
80mm lens

The Auto Modes

GET SHOOTING WITH THE AUTOMATIC CAMERA MODES

The Nikon D5100 is an amazing camera that has some incredible features. In fact, with all of the technology built into it, it can be pretty intimidating for the person new to dSLR photography. For that reason, the folks at Nikon have made it a little easier for you to get some great-looking photographs without having to do a lot of thinking. Enter the scene modes. The camera modes on the automatic side of the Mode dial are simple, icon-labeled modes that are set up to use specific features of the camera for various shooting situations. In addition, a new feature of the D5100 is a collection of in-camera special effects. Let's take a look at the different modes and how and when to use them.

PORING OVER THE PICTURE

Don't let rainy days dampen your enthusiasm for shooting. As the rain starts to soften and the sky starts to lighten, I'll grab my tripod and head out to see what jewels I can find sparkling in the garden. Colors seem richer and flowers look fresh. The camera was set to Close-up mode for a good mix of aperture and shutter speed settings.

Wait for the wind to be still to reduce blurring caused by the subject moving.

The focus point was placed on the closest flower and moved off center for a stronger composition.

The use of a tripod gave a steady base when using a slower shutter speed.

The depth of field is shallow in close-up photography, which results in a softly blurred background.

ISO 100
1/40 sec.
f/5.6
55mm lens

AUTO MODE

 Auto mode is all about thought-free photography (**Figure 3.1**). There is little to nothing for you to do in this mode except point and shoot. Your biggest concern when using Auto mode is focusing. The camera will utilize the automatic focusing modes to achieve the best-possible focus for your picture. Naturally, the camera is going to assume that the object that is closest to the camera is the one that you want in sharpest focus. Simply press the shutter button down halfway while looking

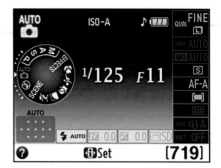

FIGURE 3.1
The Auto mode info screen.

through the viewfinder and you should see one of the focus points light up over the subject. Of course, you know that putting your subject in the middle of the picture is not the best way to compose your shot. So wait for the chirp to confirm that the focus has been set and then, while still holding down the button, recompose your shot. Now just press down the shutter button the rest of the way to take the photo. It's just that easy (**Figure 3.2**). The camera will take care of all your exposure decisions, including when to use the flash.

FIGURE 3.2
The Auto mode works great when you don't want to think too much and just want to snap some shots.

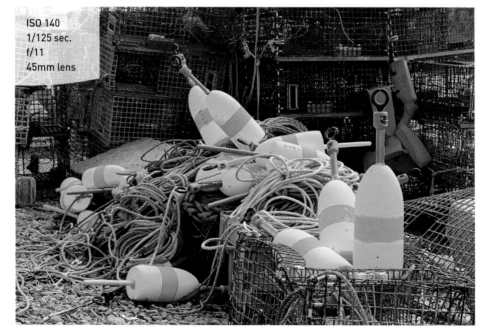

ISO 140
1/125 sec.
f/11
45mm lens

Let's face it: This is the lazy man's mode. But sometimes it's nice to be lazy and click away without giving thought to anything but preserving a memory. There are times, though, when you will want to start using your camera's advanced features to improve your shots.

AUTO (FLASH OFF) MODE

 Sometimes you will be in a situation where the light levels are low but you don't want to use the flash. It could be that you are shooting in a place that restricts flash photography, such as a museum, or it could be a situation where you want to capture the feel of the available light, such as an indoor scene lit by interesting lighting. This is where Auto (Flash Off) mode comes into play (**Figure 3.3**).

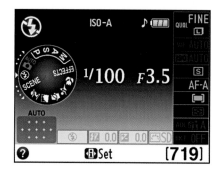

FIGURE 3.3
The Auto (Flash Off) mode info screen.

By keeping the flash from firing, you will be able to use just the available ambient light while the camera modifies the ISO setting to assist you in getting good exposures (**Figure 3.4**). If the camera feels that the shutter speed is going to be slow enough to introduce camera shake, it will give a warning on the rear information screen that reads "Subject is too dark." It will also list the shutter speed as "Lo" so that you know to check the camera settings. Despite what the camera may say, you'll want to either use a tripod or brace yourself really well if the shutter speed is 1/60 of a second or slower to avoid blurred images from camera movement.

Fortunately, most of the new Vibration Reduction (VR) lenses being sold today allow you to handhold the camera at much slower shutter speeds and still get great results. The two downfalls to this mode are the Auto ISO setting, which will quickly take your ISO setting up as high as 1600, and that there is still the possibility of getting blur from subject movement if the shutter speed is slow.

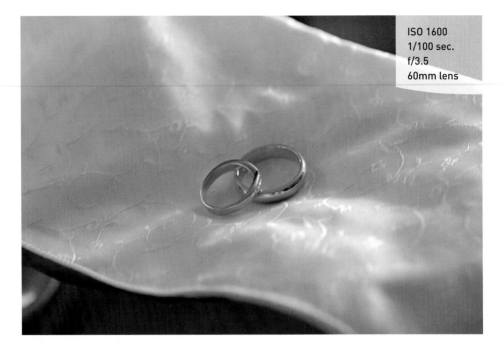

FIGURE 3.4
Auto (Flash Off) mode made sure the pop-up flash stayed disabled in the low-light environment.

ISO 1600
1/100 sec.
f/3.5
60mm lens

PORTRAIT MODE

One problem with Auto mode is that it has no idea what type of subject you are photographing and, therefore, uses the same settings for each situation. Shooting portraits is a perfect example. When you take a photograph of someone, you usually want the emphasis of the picture to be on the person, not necessarily the stuff going on in the background.

This is what Portrait mode is all about (**Figure 3.5**). When you set your camera to this mode, you are telling the camera to

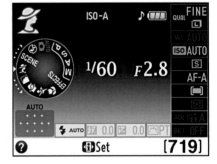

FIGURE 3.5
The Portrait mode info screen.

select a larger aperture so that the depth of field is much narrower and will give more blur to objects in the background. This blurry background places the attention on your subject (**Figure 3.6**). The other feature of this mode is the automatic selection of the D5100's built-in Portrait picture control (we'll go into more detail about picture controls in later chapters). This feature is optimized for skin tones and will also be a little softer to improve the look of skin.

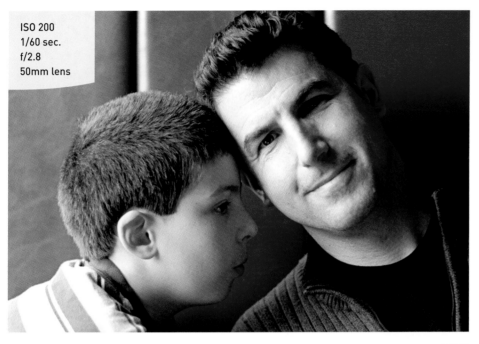

ISO 200
1/60 sec.
f/2.8
50mm lens

FIGURE 3.6
Portrait mode is useful for getting the right settings under the current lighting conditions for people photos. (Photo by Paloma Sylvan)

USING THE BEST LENS FOR GREAT PORTRAITS

When using Portrait mode, use a lens that is 50mm or longer. The longer lens will give you a natural view of the subject, as well as aid in keeping the depth of field narrow.

LANDSCAPE MODE

 As you might have guessed, Landscape mode has been optimized for shooting landscape images (**Figure 3.7**). Particular emphasis is placed on the picture control, with the camera trying to boost the greens and blues in the image (**Figure 3.8**). This makes sense, since the typical landscape would be outdoors where grass, trees, and skies should look more colorful. This picture control also boosts the sharpness that is applied during processing.

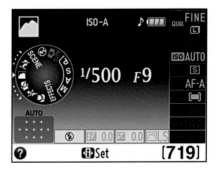

FIGURE 3.7
The Landscape mode info screen.

The camera also utilizes the lowest ISO settings possible in order to keep digital noise to a minimum. The downfall to this setting is that, once again, there is little control over the camera settings. The focus mode can be changed—but only from AF-A to Manual. Other changeable functions include image quality, ISO, and AF-area. Note that the flash cannot be used while in Landscape mode.

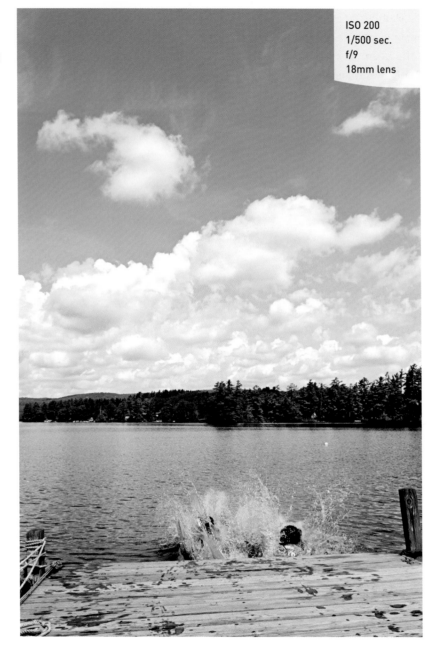

ISO 200
1/500 sec.
f/9
18mm lens

CHILD MODE

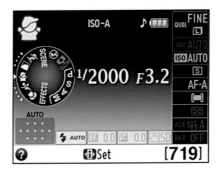

The Child mode (**Figure 3.9**) is like a blend of the Sports and Portrait modes. Understanding that children are seldom still, the camera will try to utilize a slightly faster shutter speed to freeze any movement. The picture control feature has also been optimized to render bright, vivid colors that one normally associates with pictures of children (**Figure 3.10**).

FIGURE 3.9
The Child mode info screen.

FIGURE 3.10
The Child mode tries to use a fast shutter speed, as well as make colors brighter and more vivid.

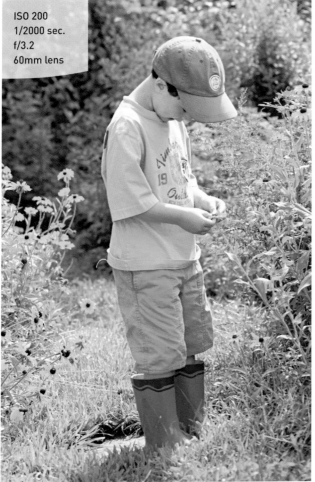

ISO 200
1/2000 sec.
f/3.2
60mm lens

SPORTS MODE

 While this is called Sports mode, you can use it for any moving subject that you are photographing (**Figure 3.11**). The mode is built on the principles of sports photography: continuous focusing, large apertures, and fast shutter speeds (**Figure 3.12**). To handle these requirements, the camera sets the focus mode to Dynamic, the aperture to a very large opening, and the ISO to Auto. Overall, these are sound settings that will capture most moving subjects well. We will take an in-depth look at all of these features, like Continuous shooting mode, in Chapter 5.

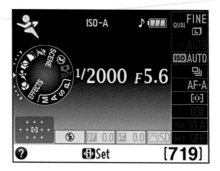

FIGURE 3.11
The Sports mode info screen.

FIGURE 3.12
This is the type of shot that was made for Sports mode, where action-freezing shutter speeds and continuous focusing capture the moment.

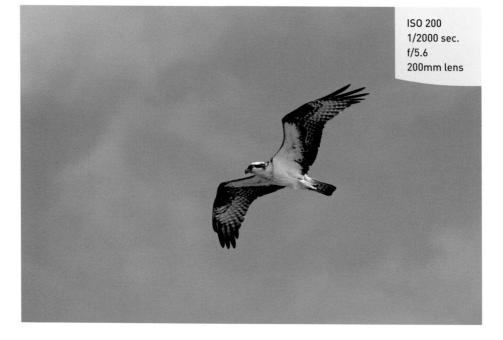

ISO 200
1/2000 sec.
f/5.6
200mm lens

You can, however, run the risk of too much digital noise in your picture if the camera decides that you need a very high ISO (such as 1600) because the available light is low. This is why you have the ability to change some options within the Sports mode, such as ISO and the Release mode (single or continuous). Also, when using Sports mode, you can change the focus mode from AF-A to Manual. This is especially handy if you know when and where the action will take place and want to prefocus the camera on a spot and wait for the right moment to take the photo.

CLOSE-UP MODE

 Although most zoom lenses don't support true "macro" settings, that doesn't mean you can't shoot some great close-up photos. The key here is to use your camera-to-subject distance to fill the frame and still achieve sharp focus. This means that you move yourself as close as possible to your subject while still being able to get a good, sharp focus. Oftentimes, your lens will be marked with the minimum focusing distance. On my 18–55mm zoom, it is about 6 inches with the lens set to 55mm.

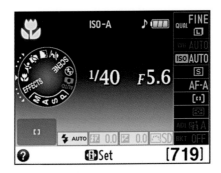

FIGURE 3.13
The Close-up mode info screen.

To help get the best focus in the picture, Close-up mode (**Figure 3.13**) will use the smallest aperture it can while keeping the shutter speed fast enough to get a sharp shot (**Figure 3.14**). It does this by raising the ISO or turning on the built-in flash—or a combination of the two. Fortunately, these are two of the settings that you can change in this mode. The flash will be set to Auto by default, but you can also change it to Auto-Redeye or Off, depending on your needs. The ISO can be changed from the Auto setting to one of your own choosing. This probably only needs to be done in low-light settings when the Auto-ISO starts to move up to maintain exposure values. Other settings that can be changed are the image quality, release mode, focus mode (AF-A or Manual), and AF-area.

FIGURE 3.14
Close-up mode
provided the proper
exposure to capture
the smallest of
details.

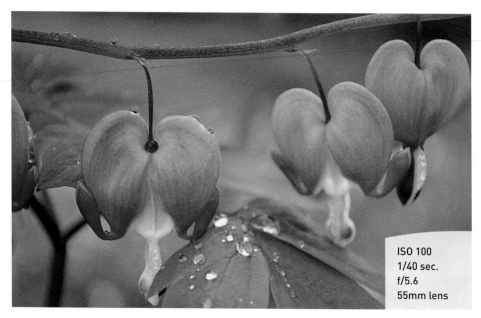

ISO 100
1/40 sec.
f/5.6
55mm lens

SCENE MODES

Most digital SLR cameras will have only seven or eight automatic modes
at their disposal, but the D5100 takes things to a whole new level with
11 additional scene modes to choose from (plus the seven effects modes
covered later in this chapter). Nikon has anticipated many of the typical shooting
scenarios that you will encounter and has created scene modes that are optimized
for those situations. Let's take a quick look at these modes, but first, here's how to
find them.

USING THE SCENE MODES

1. Set the Mode dial to the SCENE setting.
2. Rotate the Command dial until the appropriate scene appears on the
   information screen.

FOOD

Food photography is very popular as of late, and Nikon has provided you with a scene mode that is perfect for this type of photography (**Figure 3.15**). When you select this mode, the camera will use large apertures for fairly narrow depth of field, slightly overexposed settings to keep things bright, and a picture control that makes colors slightly more vivid.

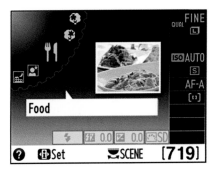

FIGURE 3.15
The Food scene mode.

NIGHT PORTRAIT

You're out on the town at night and you want to take a nice picture of someone, but you want to show some of the interesting scenery in the background as well. The solution is to use Night Portrait mode (**Figure 3.16**). When you set the dial to this mode, you are telling the camera that you want to use a slower-than-normal shutter speed so that the background is getting more time (and, thus, more light) to achieve a proper exposure.

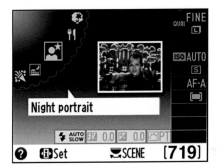

FIGURE 3.16
The Night Portrait scene mode.

The typical shutter speed for using flash is about 1/60 of a second or faster (but not faster than 1/200 of a second). By leaving the shutter open for a longer duration, the camera allows more of the background to be exposed so that you get a much more balanced scene. This is also a great mode for taking portraits during sunset. The camera uses an automatic ISO setting by default, so you will want to keep an eye on it to make sure that setting isn't so high that the noise levels ruin your photo.

NIGHT LANDSCAPE

A tripod or stable shooting surface is definitely recommended for the Night Landscape
mode (Figure 3.17). By using low ISOs, longer
shutter speeds, and noise reduction, you can
capture great cityscapes with more-accurate
colors. The flash and focus-assist functions are
turned off for this mode, so focusing might
be a little difficult. If so, try moving your
focus point to a different location or switch
to manual focus.

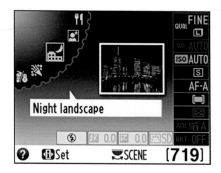

FIGURE 3.17
The Night Landscape scene mode.

PARTY/INDOOR

This mode is very much like the Night Portrait
mode except it is optimized for indoor use
(Figure 3.18). The flash is automatically set
to Auto+Red-eye Reduction and will use the
red-eye reduction lamp to help eliminate
the red-eye problem that often occurs when
using the flash indoors.

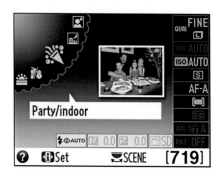

FIGURE 3.18
The Party/Indoor scene mode.

BEACH/SNOW

Shooting in a bright environment like the
beach or a ski resort can have a bad effect
on your images. The problem is that beaches
and snow often reflect a lot of light and can
fool the camera's light meter into underexposing. This means that the snow would
come out looking darker than it should. To
solve this problem, you can use the Beach/
Snow scene mode (Figure 3.19), which will
overexpose slightly, giving you much more
accurate tones.

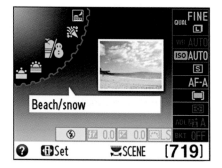

FIGURE 3.19
The Beach/Snow scene mode.

SUNSET

This mode is set to optimize the colors that are present in a sunset (**Figure 3.20**). It will utilize slightly longer exposures, so a tripod or steady shooting surface is advised. You also won't be able to use the flash in this mode since it would interfere with the settings necessary for capturing the sunset.

DUSK/DAWN

There are some great photo opportunities that take place both before the sun rises and after it sets. The only problem is that the typical camera settings don't truly capture the vibrancy of the colors. The Dusk/Dawn camera setting is optimized for low-light photography and helps boost colors and eliminate noise from longer exposures (**Figure 3.21**).

PET PORTRAIT

This mode is similar to the Portrait mode in that it uses larger apertures and faster shutter speeds (**Figure 3.22**). The difference is that the Portrait mode is optimized for human skin, with adjustments to the hues and color values. Pets don't normally have any skin showing, so the sharpness and hues are adjusted accordingly.

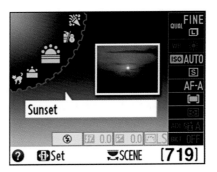

FIGURE 3.20
The Sunset scene mode.

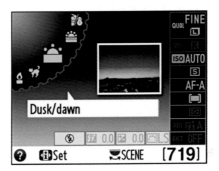

FIGURE 3.21
The Dusk/Dawn scene mode.

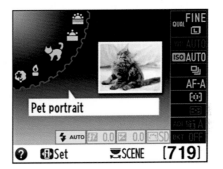

FIGURE 3.22
The Pet Portrait scene mode.

CANDLELIGHT

Sometimes it's pretty easy to know when to use a particular mode. This mode is similar to the Auto (Flash Off) mode, but it is tweaked for the color of candlelight and will give you much more pleasing results (**Figure 3.23**). If you are photographing people in candlelight, try using a tripod and have them hold fairly still to reduce image blur.

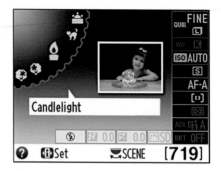

FIGURE 3.23
The Candlelight scene mode.

BLOSSOM

This mode is very similar to the Landscape setting but with a few slight adjustments. The color settings for Blossom have been optimized for use outdoors where there are many flowers in full bloom (**Figure 3.24**).

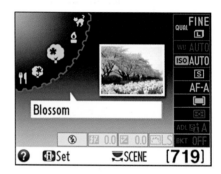

FIGURE 3.24
The Blossom scene mode.

AUTUMN COLORS

If you live in an area that has great fall color (like I do), you will want to give this mode a try (**Figure 3.25**). The big advantage to this scene mode is that it is optimized for the red and yellow hues that are present in autumn, and it really makes them pop. It also turns off the flash since the light from a flash can wash out the color in the leaves. Try using this mode when the leaves have turned and the skies are overcast. You will get some amazing color in your images.

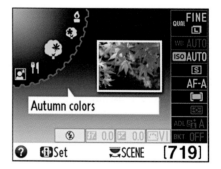

FIGURE 3.25
The Autumn Colors scene mode.

EFFECTS MODES

Beyond the scene-specific settings, there is a collection of in-camera special effects that are actually kind of fun to use. Remember, a digital camera is not only a light-capturing device but also a small computer in its own way. After an image is captured and saved to memory, these special effects modes give you the power to process your photos before they ever leave the camera. In fact, all of these effects can even be applied to video. Because the Night Vision, Color Sketch, Miniature Effect, and Selective Color effects require additional in-camera processing, it is not possible to shoot in RAW mode with them. In addition, due to the extra work the camera has to do to process these effects, be prepared to wait between exposures and expect the charge on the battery to be consumed faster.

I was a bit skeptical about these effects when I first heard about them. After all, one of the most important selling features of the D5100 is its stunning image quality, so it felt a bit risky to take the chance of capturing a good photo in, say, Color Sketch mode but not have any way to get the unprocessed original photo. But after giving each one a thorough test drive, I found some of them quite enjoyable to use. And once I started getting used to the effects, I started looking for specific instances that might be better suited to a given effect, and I found it much more satisfying.

USING THE EFFECTS MODES

1. Set the Mode dial to the EFFECTS setting.
2. Rotate the Command dial until the desired effect appears on the information screen.

SILHOUETTE

The Silhouette mode (**Figure 3.26**) does things like adjust the exposure for the brightest area of the scene as well as turn off the Active D-Lighting feature (see Chapter 10 for more on Active D-Lighting). This is necessary, since Active D-Lighting tries to boost exposure in shadow areas, which is the opposite of the effect you want when trying to get a nice silhouette. Look for situations with strong backlighting behind your subject.

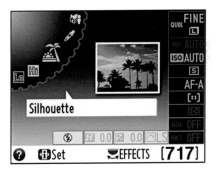

FIGURE 3.26
The Silhouette effects mode.

HIGH KEY

High-key photos are meant to have an overall bright, almost overexposed, look to them (**Figure 3.27**). Using the High Key setting forces the camera to overexpose a little and really lighten up those bright objects in your image. Subjects on bright backgrounds can work well with this effect. Note that the internal flash turns off in this mode to make full use of available light.

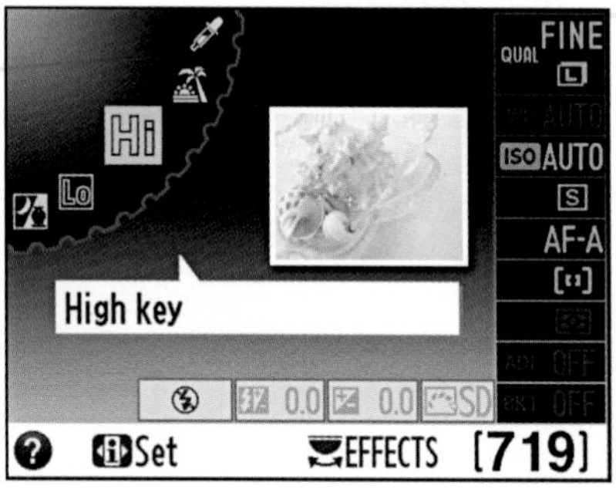

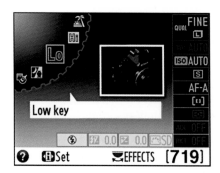

FIGURE 3.27
The High Key effects mode.

LOW KEY

Low-key photos are typically meant to have an overall dark look to them. Much like the beach/snow scenario in reverse, your camera's light meter will usually try to add some exposure when shooting a low-key scene to make everything brighter. If you want to keep things on the dark side, use the Low Key mode (**Figure 3.28**), which will keep the flash turned off and underexpose things just a little bit. Edgy and moody scenes can lend themselves more to this effect. Since the internal flash turns off and the scene may be dark, you'll want to have a solid base (or even a tripod) to avoid blur in your shots.

FIGURE 3.28
The Low Key effects mode.

NIGHT VISION

For times when it is so dark you're usually thinking it is time to put the camera away, the Night Vision (**Figure 3.29**) effect can be fun to experiment with. The internal flash and autofocus illumination assist turn off, and autofocus is only possible when in Live View (and it is on the slow side). You'll need a little light to see what you are doing, but this was my favorite effect to use. The camera will automatically adjust the ISO to the equivalent of 102,400 ISO

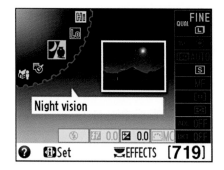

FIGURE 3.29
The Night Vision effects mode.

if needed, but the resulting JPEG images will be very noisy and only in grayscale. Think bad security camera footage. Since you're most likely to use this in extremely low-light situations, I do recommend a tripod or some other firm base.

COLOR SKETCH

Color Sketch (**Figure 3.30**) detects all the outlines in the scene and boosts the color to simulate a sketch-like effect. Turn on Live View to see a real-time updated preview of the effect in action. Bright and colorful scenes with recognizable shapes will benefit most from this effect.

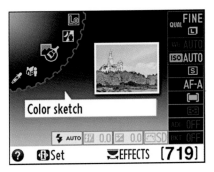
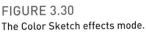

FIGURE 3.30
The Color Sketch effects mode.

MINIATURE EFFECT

A very popular effect seen in photography these days is achieved by using a tilt-shift lens to produce a narrow area of focus, which on certain scenes (typically taken from a high vantage point) can make the subjects appear miniaturized. There is something about the effect that is indeed very eye-catching. The D5100 simulates this with the Miniature Effect mode (**Figure 3.31**) without a special lens by simply allowing only a narrow band (which you can widen slightly while in Live View) of the image to be in focus and then gradually blurring the rest of the scene.

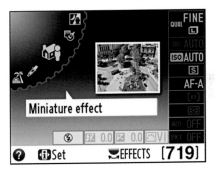

FIGURE 3.31
The Miniature Effect effects mode.

SELECTIVE COLOR

The Selective Color effect (**Figure 3.32**) can make a vibrantly colored object really stand out of the scene by desaturating all the colors in the scene except for the color you choose (up to three) to keep. The color selection process and a live preview is available when in Live View. It can be a little tricky selecting the color at first (use the image zoom button

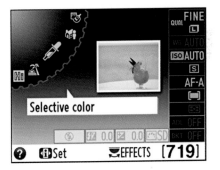
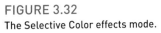

FIGURE 3.32
The Selective Color effects mode.

to zoom in on your color for easier selection), but it won't take long to get the hang of it. I'm more of a fan of doing this type of effect via software on my computer (to ensure I have a full-color original), but in a pinch (or for use in a video) it works pretty well.

Manual callout

You can learn more about the specific controls for each of these effects on page 58 of the printed user manual.

WHY YOU MAY NEVER WANT TO USE THE AUTO SCENE MODES AGAIN

With so many easy-to-use camera modes, why would anyone ever want to use anything else? Well, the first thing that comes to my mind is control. It is the number one reason for using a digital SLR camera. The ability to control every aspect of your photography will open up creative avenues that just aren't available in the automatic scene modes. Let's face it: There is a reason that the Mode dial is split into two different categories. Let's look at what we are giving up when we work in the scene modes.

- **White balance.** There is no choice available for white balance. You are simply stuck with the Auto setting. This isn't always a bad thing, but your camera doesn't always get it right. And in the scene modes, there is just no way to change it.

- **Picture control.** All of the automatic modes have specifically tuned picture controls. Some of them use the control presets, such as Landscape or Vivid, but there is no way to change the characteristics of the controls while in the auto modes.

- **Metering.** All of the auto scene modes use the Matrix metering mode to establish the proper exposure. This is generally not a bad thing, but if there are scenarios that would benefit from a center or spot metering solution (which we'll cover in later chapters), you're just out of luck.

- **Autofocus.** While each of the modes may use a specific focus area mode, such as Single or Dynamic, the actual focus mode for all of the scene modes is limited to either AF-A or Manual when shooting using the viewfinder. The problem is that you can't just use AF-S (single) or AF-C (continuous) as the default setting (unless you switch to Live View; see the sidebar "Live View").

- **Exposure compensation.** You will notice that in each and every automatic scene mode, the ability to adjust the exposure through the use of the exposure compensation feature has been completely turned off. This makes it very difficult to make the slight adjustments to exposure that are often needed.

- **Active D-Lighting.** This is another feature that is unavailable for changing in all of the auto modes. There are default settings for this feature that change from scene to scene, but there is no way for you to override the effect.

- **Flash compensation.** Just like the exposure compensation, there is no way to make any adjustments to the power output of the flash. This means that you are stuck with whatever the camera feels is correct, even if it is too weak or too strong for your particular subject.

- **Exposure bracketing.** One way to make sure that you have at least one good exposure is to use the bracketing feature of the camera, which takes images at varying exposures so you can get just the right look for your image. Unfortunately, this feature is also unavailable when using the scene modes.

Another thing you will find when using any of the automatic modes is that there are fewer choices in the camera menus for you to adjust. Each scene mode presents its own set of restrictions for the available menu items. These aren't the only restrictions to using the automatic scene modes, but they should be enough to make you want to explore the other side of the Mode dial, which I like to call the professional modes.

AUTOFOCUS MODES ON THE NIKON D5100

Four autofocus modes are available on the D5100. You can easily select the mode that will be most beneficial for the type of photography you are doing. The standard mode is called AF-S, which allows you to focus on one spot and hold the focus until you take the picture or release the shutter button. The AF-C mode will constantly refocus the camera on your subject the entire time you are depressing the shutter release button. This is great for sports and action photography. The AF-A mode is a combination of both of the previous modes, using AF-S mode unless it senses that the subject is moving, when it will switch to AF-C mode. When in Live View you will also have the fourth choice of AF-F, which is when the camera automatically attempts to keep a moving subject in focus without pressing the shutter, such as during video recording.

LIVE VIEW

Live View is the feature on your D5100 that allows you to see a real-time view of what the camera is looking at via the rear LCD display. Using Live View can be helpful when you want to see or shoot from an angle that doesn't allow you to place your eye to the viewfinder. It is also an excellent way of previewing any changes to white balance or the picture control because their effects will be visible on the screen. There's more on Live View in Chapters 6 and 7, but I want to mention that Live View does allow the AF-S autofocus mode while in the auto scene modes.

Chapter 3 Assignments

These assignments will have you shooting in the various automatic scene and effects modes so that you can experience the advantages and disadvantages of using them in your daily photography.

Shooting in Auto mode

It's time to give up complete control and just concentrate on what you see in the viewfinder. Set your camera to Auto and practice shooting in a variety of conditions, both indoors and outside. Take notice of the camera settings when you are reviewing your pictures. Try using the single-point autofocus area mode to pick a spot to focus on and then recompose before taking the picture.

Checking out Portrait mode

Grab your favorite photogenic person and start shooting in Portrait mode. Try switching between Auto and Portrait mode while photographing the same person in the same setting. You should see a difference in the sharpness of the background as well as the skin tones. If you are using a zoom lens, set it to about 55mm if available.

Capturing the scenery with Landscape and Close-up modes

Take your camera outside for some landscape and macro work. First, find a nice scene and then, with your widest available lens, take some pictures using Landscape mode and then switch back to Auto so that you can compare the settings used for each image as well as the changes to colors and sharpness. Now, while you are still outside, find something in the foreground—a leaf or a flower—and switch the camera to Close-up mode. See how close you can get and take note of the f-stop that the mode uses. Then switch to Auto and shoot the same subject.

Stopping the action with Sports mode

This assignment will require that you find a subject that is in motion. That could be the traffic in front of your home or your child at play. The only real requirement is that the subject be moving. This will be your opportunity to test out Sports mode. There isn't a lot to worry about here. Just point and shoot. Try shooting a few frames one at a time and then go ahead and hold down the shutter button and shoot a burst of about five or six frames. It will help if your subject is in good available light to start with so that the camera won't be forced to use high ISOs.

Having fun with the effects modes

Carve out some time to give each of the effects a good test run and have fun with it. It is all too easy to get hung up on getting the perfect shot, but with the effects modes you have permission to play. See how the world looks with just a single color; try envisioning things in miniature; check out your pets in Color Sketch mode. Just focus on being creative and exploring the results. You never know when one of these effects might come in handy down the road.

Share your results with the book's Flickr group!

Join the group here: flickr.com/groups/nikond5100fromsnapshotstogreatshots/

4

ISO 200
1/320 sec.
f/11
400mm lens

The Professional Modes

TAKING YOUR PHOTOGRAPHY TO THE NEXT LEVEL

If you talk to professional photographers, you will find that the majority of them are using a few selective modes that offer the greatest amount of control over their photography. To anyone who has been involved with photography for any period of time, these modes are known as the backbones of photography. They allow you to influence two of the most important factors in taking great photographs: *aperture* and *shutter speed.* To access these modes, you simply turn the Mode dial to one of the letter-designated modes and begin shooting. But wouldn't it be nice to know exactly what those modes control and how to make them do our bidding? Well, if you really want to take that next step in controlling your photography, it is essential that you understand not only how to control these modes, but why you are controlling them. So let's move that Mode dial to the first of our professional modes: Program mode.

I looked out my west-facing window one cold January morning to see the moon setting while the sun was rising in the east. I reached for my camera and put the 70–200 mm lens on as I noticed the crow in the branches above. Just as I framed the shot, the crow swooped down and the moment passed. It pays to always have the camera charged up and ready to go.

Increase ISO when you need a fast shutter speed to stop action and a smaller aperture for greater depth of field.

Look for frames within the frame to draw the eye to the subject.

The focus point was
placed on the tree
to keep detail in the
branches.

ISO 400
1/640 sec.
f/8
135 mm lens

I used the spot meter on the
tree bark to ensure I retained
the highlight detail.

P: PROGRAM MODE

 There is a reason that Program mode is only one click away from the automatic modes: With respect to apertures and shutter speeds, the camera is doing most of the thinking for you. So, if that is the case, why even bother with Program mode? First, let me say that it is very rare that I will use Program mode, because it just doesn't give as much control over the image-making process as the other professional modes. There are occasions, however, when it comes in handy, like when I am shooting in widely changing lighting conditions and don't have the time to think through all of my options, or when I'm not very concerned with having ultimate control of the scene. Think of a picnic outdoors in a partial shade/sun environment. I want great-looking pictures, but I'm not looking for anything to hang in a museum. If that's the scenario, why choose Program over one of the scene modes? Because it gives me choices and control that none of the scene modes can deliver.

Manual Callout

To see a comparison of all of the different modes, check out the table on page 216 of the reference manual on the CD that came with the camera.

WHEN TO USE PROGRAM (P) MODE INSTEAD OF THE AUTOMATIC SCENE MODES

• When shooting in a casual environment where quick adjustments are needed

• When you want more control over the ISO

• If you want to make corrections to the white balance

• When you want to change shutter speeds or the aperture to achieve a specific result

Let's go back to our picnic scenario. As I said, the light is moving from deep shadow to bright sunlight, which means that the camera is trying to balance our three photo factors (ISO, aperture, and shutter speed) to make a good exposure. From Chapter 1, we know that Auto ISO is just not a consideration, so we have already turned that feature off (you did turn it off, didn't you?). Well, in Program mode, you can choose which ISO you would like the camera to base its exposure on. The lower the ISO number, the better the quality of our photographs, but the less light sensitive the camera becomes. It's a balancing act with the main goal always being to keep the ISO as low as possible—too low an ISO, and we will get camera shake in our images from a long shutter speed; and too high an ISO means we will have an unacceptable amount of digital noise. For our purposes, let's go ahead and select ISO 400 so that we provide enough sensitivity for those shadows while allowing the camera to use shutter speeds that are fast enough to stop motion.

STARTING POINTS FOR ISO SELECTION

There is a lot of discussion concerning ISO in this and other chapters, but it might be helpful if you know where your starting points should be for your ISO settings. The first thing you should always try to do is use the lowest possible ISO setting. That being said, here are good starting points for your ISO settings:

- 100: Bright, sunny day
- 200: Hazy or outdoor shade on a sunny day
- 400: Indoor lighting at night or cloudy conditions outside
- 800: Late-night, low-light conditions or sporting arenas at night

These are just suggestions, and your ISO selection will depend on a number of factors that will be discussed later in the book. You might have to push your ISO even higher as needed, but at least now you know where to start.

With the ISO selected, we can now make use of the other controls built into Program mode. By rotating the Command dial, we now have the ability to shift the program settings. Remember, your camera is using the internal meter to pick what it believes are suitable exposure values, but sometimes it doesn't know what it's looking at and how you want those values applied (**Figures 4.1** and **4.2**). With the program shift, you can influence what the shot will look like. Do you need faster shutter speeds in order to stop the action? Just turn the Command dial to the right. Do you want a smaller aperture so that you get a narrow depth of field? Then turn the dial to the left until you get the desired aperture. The camera shifts the shutter speed and aperture accordingly in order to get a proper exposure, and you will get the benefit of your choice as a result. Just keep in mind that the camera is always trying to maintain the right exposure at every setting, and so the available light and the maximum and minimum aperture values of the attached lens will limit the range of shutter speeds at a given ISO value.

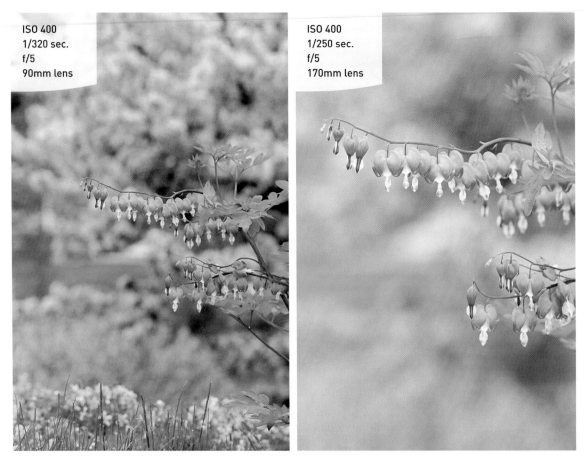

ISO 400
1/320 sec.
f/5
90mm lens

ISO 400
1/250 sec.
f/5
170mm lens

FIGURE 4.1

This is my first shot using Program mode. The camera settings are affected by the large area of white blossoms in the background.

FIGURE 4.2

By zooming in on the bleeding hearts in the foreground, the area of white blossoms was reduced, which reflected less light on the light meter and resulted in a reduction of shutter speed for proper exposure.

You will also notice that a small star will appear above the letter P in the viewfinder and the rear display if you rotate the Command dial. This star is an indication that you modified the exposure from the one the camera chose. To go back to the default Program exposure, simply turn the dial until the star goes away or switch to a different mode and then back to Program mode again.

Let's set up the camera for Program mode and see how we can make all of this come together.

1. Turn your camera on and then turn the Command dial to align the P with the indicator line.

2. Select your ISO by pressing the **i** button on the back of the camera.

3. Press up or down on the Multi-selector to highlight the ISO option, then select OK.

4. Press down on the Multi-selector to select a higher ISO setting and then press OK to lock in the change.

5. Point the camera at your subject and then activate the camera meter by depressing the shutter button halfway.

6. View the exposure information in the bottom of the viewfinder or by looking at the display panel on the back of the camera.

7. While the meter is activated, use your thumb to roll the Command dial left and right to see the changed exposure values.

8. Select the exposure that is right for you and start clicking. (Don't worry if you aren't sure what the right exposure is. We will start working on making the right choices for those great shots beginning with the next chapter.)

S: SHUTTER PRIORITY MODE

 S mode is what we photographers commonly refer to as Shutter Priority mode. Just as the name implies, it is the mode that prioritizes or places major emphasis on the shutter speed above all other camera settings.

Just as with Program mode, Shutter Priority mode gives us more freedom to control certain aspects of our photography. In this case, we are talking about shutter speed. The selected shutter speed determines just how long you expose your camera's sensor to light. The longer it remains open, the more time your sensor has to gather light. The shutter speed also, to a large degree, determines how sharp your photographs are. This is different from the image being sharply in focus. Two of the major influences on the sharpness of an image are camera shake and the subject's movement. Because a slower shutter speed means that light from your subject is hitting the sensor for a longer period of time, any movement by you or your subject will show up in your photos as blur.

WHEN TO USE SHUTTER PRIORITY (S) MODE

- When working with fast-moving subjects where you want to freeze the action (**Figure 4.3**); much more on this is in Chapter 5

- When you want to emphasize movement in your subject with motion blur (**Figure 4.4**)

- When you want to use a long exposure to gather light over a long period of time (**Figure 4.5**); more on this is in Chapter 8

- When you want to create that silky-looking water in a waterfall (**Figure 4.6**)

As you can see, the subject of your photo usually determines whether or not you will use Shutter Priority mode. It is important that you be able to visualize the result of using a particular shutter speed. The great thing about shooting with digital cameras is that you get instant feedback by viewing your shot on the LCD screen. But what if your subject won't give you a do-over? Such is often the case when shooting sporting events. It's not like you can go ask the quarterback to throw that touchdown pass again because your last shot was blurry from a slow shutter speed. This is why it's important to know what those speeds represent in terms of their capabilities to stop the action and deliver a blur-free shot.

FIGURE 4.3
Even the fastest
of subjects can be
frozen with the
right shutter speed.

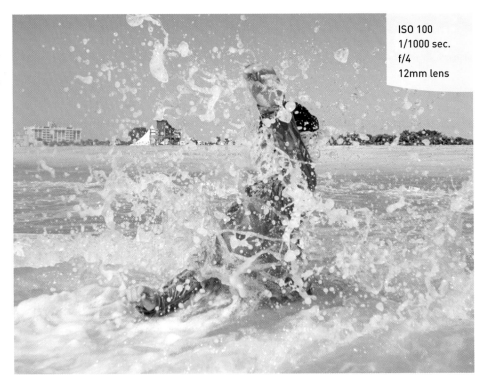

ISO 100
1/1000 sec.
f/4
12mm lens

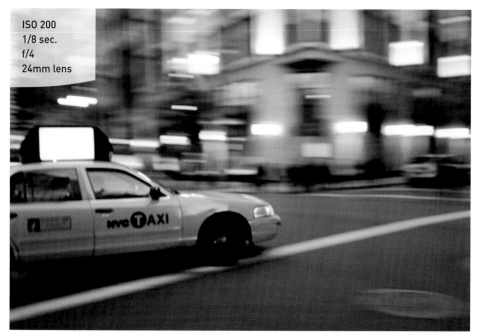

ISO 200
1/8 sec.
f/4
24mm lens

FIGURE 4.4
Slowing down the
shutter speed
and following the
motion conveys a
sense of movement
in the shot.

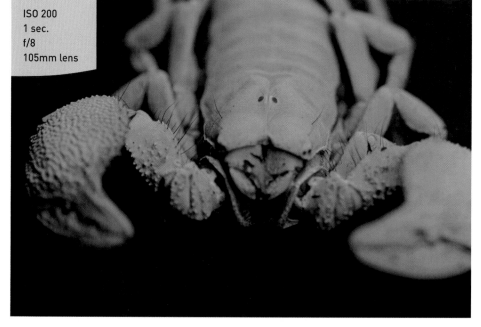

ISO 200
1 sec.
f/8
105mm lens

FIGURE 4.5
Long exposure
coupled with a
steady tripod
capture a portrait
of our pet scorpion
under a single
blacklight bulb.

FIGURE 4.6
Increasing the length of the expo-sure time gives falling water a silky look.

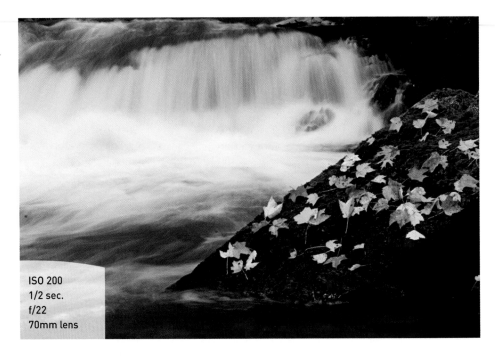

ISO 200
1/2 sec.
f/22
70mm lens

SHUTTER SPEEDS

A *slow* shutter speed refers to leaving the shutter open for a long period of time—like 1/30 of a second or less. A *fast* shutter speed means that the shutter is open for a very short period of time—like 1/250 of a second or more.

First, let's examine just how much control you have over the shutter speeds. The D5100 has a shutter speed range from 1/4000 of a second all the way down to 30 seconds. With that much latitude, you should have enough control to capture almost any subject. The other thing to think about is that Shutter Priority mode is considered a "semiautomatic" mode. This means that you are taking control over one aspect of the total exposure while the camera handles the other. In this instance, you are con-trolling the shutter speed and the camera is controlling the aperture. This is important, because there will be times that you want to use a particular shutter speed but your lens won't be able to accommodate your request.

For example, you might encounter this problem when shooting in low-light situations: If you are shooting a fast-moving subject that will blur at a shutter speed slower than 1/125 of a second but your lens's largest aperture is f/3.5, you might find that your aperture display in the viewfinder and the rear LCD panel will display the word "Lo."

This is your warning that there won't be enough light available for the shot—due to the limitations of the lens—so your picture will be underexposed.

Another case where you might run into this situation is when you are shooting moving water. To get that look of silky, flowing water, it's usually necessary to use a shutter speed of at least 1/15 of a second. If your waterfall is in full sunlight, you may get a message that reads "Hi" because the lens you are using only stops down to f/22 at its smallest opening. In this instance, your camera is warning you that you will be overexposing your image. There are workarounds for these problems, which we will discuss later (see Chapter 7), but it is important to know that there can be limitations when using Shutter Priority mode.

SETTING UP AND SHOOTING IN SHUTTER PRIORITY MODE

1. Turn your camera on and then turn the Mode dial to align the S with the indicator line.

2. Select your ISO by pressing the **i** button on the back of the camera.

3. Press up or down on the Multi-selector to highlight the ISO option and then press OK.

4. Press down on the Multi-selector to select a higher ISO setting, then press OK to lock in the change.

5. Point the camera at your subject and then activate the camera meter by depressing the shutter button halfway.

6. View the exposure information in the bottom area of the viewfinder or by looking at the rear LCD panel.

7. While the meter is activated, use your thumb to roll the Command dial left and right to see the changed exposure values. Roll the dial to the right for faster shutter speeds and to the left for slower speeds.

A: APERTURE PRIORITY MODE

 You wouldn't know it from its name, but Aperture Priority mode is one of the most useful and popular of all the professional modes. The mode is one of my personal favorites, and I believe that it will quickly become one of yours, as well. Aperture Priority mode is also deemed a semiautomatic mode because it allows you to once again control one factor of exposure while the camera adjusts for the other.

Why, you may ask, is this one of my favorite modes? It's because the aperture of your lens dictates depth of field. Depth of field, along with composition, is a major factor in how you direct attention to what is important in your image. It is the controlling factor of how much area in your image is sharp. If you want to isolate a subject from the background, such as when shooting a portrait, you can use a large aperture to keep the focus on your subject and make both the foreground and background blurry. If you want to keep the entire scene sharply focused, such as with a landscape scene, then using a small aperture will render the greatest amount of depth of field possible.

WHEN TO USE APERTURE PRIORITY (A) MODE

- When shooting portraits or wildlife (**Figure 4.7**)

- When shooting most landscape photography (**Figure 4.8**)

- When shooting macro, or close-up, photography (**Figure 4.9**)

FIGURE 4.7
A large aperture created a very blurry background, so all the emphasis was left on the subject.

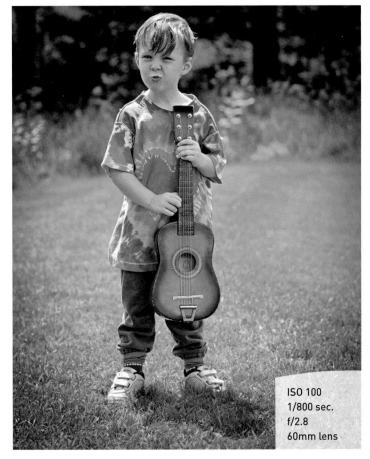

ISO 100
1/800 sec.
f/2.8
60mm lens

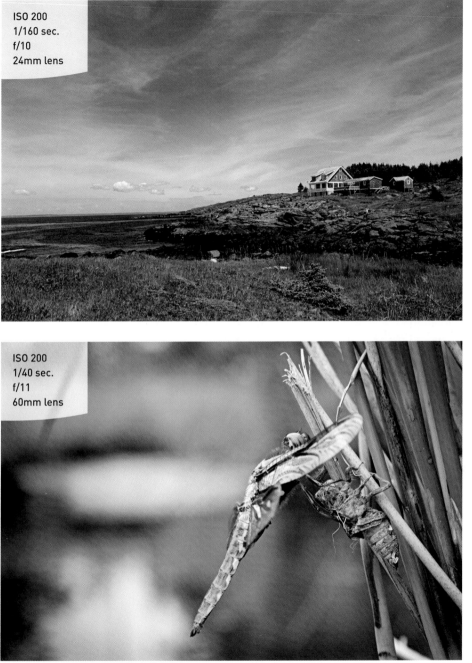

ISO 200
1/160 sec.
f/10
24mm lens

FIGURE 4.8
The smaller
aperture setting
brings sharpness
to near and far
objects.

ISO 200
1/40 sec.
f/11
60mm lens

FIGURE 4.9
Small apertures
give more
sharpness in
macro images.

F-STOPS AND APERTURE

As discussed earlier, when referring to the numeric value of your lens aperture, you will find it described as an *f-stop*. The f-stop is one of those old photography terms that, technically, relates to the focal length of the lens (e.g., 200mm) divided by the effective aperture diameter. These measurements are defined as "stops" and work incrementally with your shutter speed to determine proper exposure. Older camera lenses used one-stop increments to assist in exposure adjustments, such as 1.4, 2, 2.8, 4, 5.6, 8, 11, 16, and 22. Each stop represents about half the amount of light entering the lens iris as the larger stop before it. Today, most lenses don't have f-stop markings since all adjustments to this setting are performed via the camera's electronics. The stops are also now typically divided into 1/3-stop increments to allow much finer adjustments to exposures, as well as to match the incremental values of your camera's ISO settings, which are also adjusted in 1/3-stop increments.

So we have established that Aperture Priority (A) mode is highly useful in controlling the depth of field in your image. But it's also pivotal in determining the limits of available light that you can shoot in. Different lenses have different maximum apertures. The larger the maximum aperture, the less light you need in order to achieve an acceptably sharp image. You will recall that, when in Shutter Priority mode, there is a limit at which you can handhold your camera without introducing movement or hand shake, which causes blurriness in the final picture. If your lens has a larger aperture, you can let in more light all at once, which means that you can use faster shutter speeds. This is why lenses with large maximum apertures, such as f/1.4, are called "fast" lenses.

On the other hand, bright scenes require the use of a small aperture (such as f/16 or f/22), especially if you want to use a slower shutter speed. That small opening reduces the amount of incoming light, and this reduction of light requires that the shutter stay open longer.

SETTING UP AND SHOOTING IN APERTURE PRIORITY MODE

1. Turn your camera on and then turn the Mode dial to align the A with the indicator line.
2. Select your ISO by pressing the **i** button on the back of the camera.
3. Press up or down on the Multi-selector to highlight the ISO option, then select OK.
4. Press down on the Multi-selector to select a higher ISO setting, then press OK to lock in the change.

5. Point the camera at your subject and then activate the camera meter by depressing the shutter button halfway.

6. View the exposure information in the bottom area of the viewfinder or by looking at the rear display panel.

7. While the meter is activated, use your thumb to roll the Command dial left and right to see the changed exposure values. Roll the dial to the right for a smaller aperture (higher f-stop number) and to the left for a larger aperture (smaller f-stop number).

ZOOM LENSES AND MAXIMUM APERTURES

Some zoom lenses (like the 18–55mm kit lens) have a variable maximum aperture. This means that the largest opening will change depending on the zoom setting. In the example of the 18–55mm zoom, the lens has a maximum aperture of f/3.5 at 18mm and only f/5.6 when the lens is zoomed out to 55mm.

M: MANUAL MODE

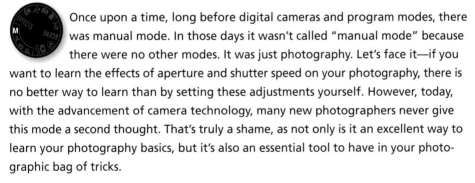 Once upon a time, long before digital cameras and program modes, there was manual mode. In those days it wasn't called "manual mode" because there were no other modes. It was just photography. Let's face it—if you want to learn the effects of aperture and shutter speed on your photography, there is no better way to learn than by setting these adjustments yourself. However, today, with the advancement of camera technology, many new photographers never give this mode a second thought. That's truly a shame, as not only is it an excellent way to learn your photography basics, but it's also an essential tool to have in your photographic bag of tricks.

When you have your camera set to Manual (M) mode, the camera meter will give you a reading of the scene you are photographing. It's your job, though, to set both the f-stop (aperture) and the shutter speed to achieve a correct exposure. If you need a faster shutter speed, you will have to make the reciprocal change to your f-stop. Using any other mode, such as Shutter Priority or Aperture Priority, would mean that you just have to worry about one of these changes, but Manual mode means you have to do it all yourself. This can be a little challenging at first, but after a while you will have a complete understanding of how each change affects your exposure, which will, in turn, improve the way that you use the other modes.

WHEN TO USE MANUAL (M) MODE

- When learning how each exposure element interacts with the others (**Figure 4.10**)

- When your environment is fooling your light meter and you need to maintain a certain exposure setting (**Figure 4.11**)

- When shooting silhouetted subjects, which requires overriding the camera's meter readings (**Figure 4.12**)

FIGURE 4.10
Using Manual mode allowed me to set the exposure for the bright detail in the leaf and let the background go dark.

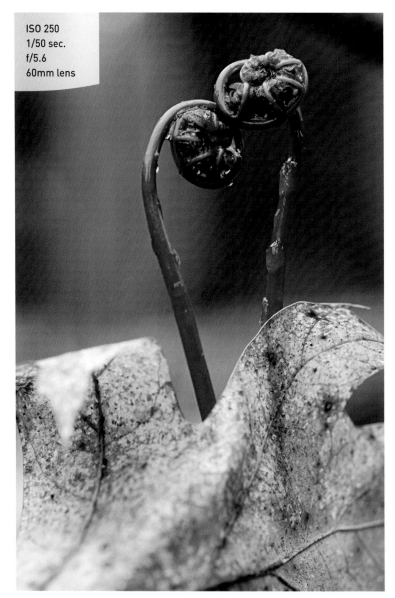

ISO 250
1/50 sec.
f/5.6
60mm lens

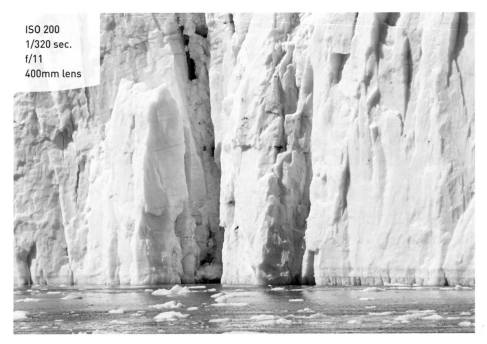

ISO 200
1/320 sec.
f/11
400mm lens

FIGURE 4.11
Beaches and
snow are always
a challenge for
light meters.
Using Manual
mode allowed
me to prevent the
scene from being
underexposed.

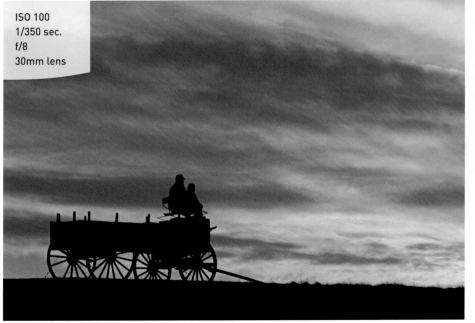

ISO 100
1/350 sec.
f/8
30mm lens

FIGURE 4.12
Although the
meter was doing
a pretty good job
of exposing for the
sky, I used Manual
mode to push the
foreground elements
into complete
black silhouette
and get richer color
in the sunset.

1. Turn your camera on and then turn the Mode dial to align the M with the indicator line.

2. Select your ISO by pressing the **i** button on the back of the camera.

3. Press up or down on the Multi-selector to highlight the ISO option, then select OK.

4. Press down on the Multi-selector to select a higher ISO setting, then press OK to lock in the change.

5. Point the camera at your subject and then activate the camera meter by depressing the shutter button halfway.

6. View the exposure information in the bottom area of the viewfinder or by looking at the display panel on the rear of the camera.

7. While the meter is activated, use your thumb to roll the Command dial left and right to change your shutter speed value until the exposure mark is lined up with the zero mark. The exposure information is displayed by a scale with marks that run from +2 to -2 stops. A proper exposure will line up with the arrow mark in the middle. As the indicator moves to the left, it is a sign that you will be overexposing (there is too much light on the sensor to provide adequate exposure). Move the indicator to the right and you will be providing less exposure than the camera meter calls for. This is underexposure.

8. To set your exposure using the aperture, depress the shutter release button until the meter is activated. Then, while holding down the Exposure Compensation/ Aperture button (located behind and to the right of the shutter release button), rotate the Command dial to change the aperture. Rotate right for a smaller aperture (large f-stop number) and left for a larger aperture (small f-stop number).

HOW I SHOOT: A CLOSER LOOK AT THE CAMERA SETTINGS I USE

The great thing about working with a dSLR camera is that I can always feel confident that some things will remain unchanged from camera to camera. For me, these are the Aperture Priority (A) and Shutter Priority (S) shooting modes. Regardless of the subject I am shooting—from landscape to portrait to macro—I am almost always going to be concerned with my depth of field. Whether it's isolating my subject with a large aperture or trying to maximize the overall sharpness of a sweeping landscape, I always keep an eye on my aperture setting. If I do have a need to control the action, I use Shutter Priority, my fallback mode. It's not really a fallback; it's more like the right tool for the right job. If I am trying to create a silky waterfall effect (**Figure 4.13**), I can depend on Shutter Priority mode to provide that long shutter speed that will deliver. Maybe I am shooting a soccer game; I definitely need the fast shutter speeds that will freeze the fast-moving action.

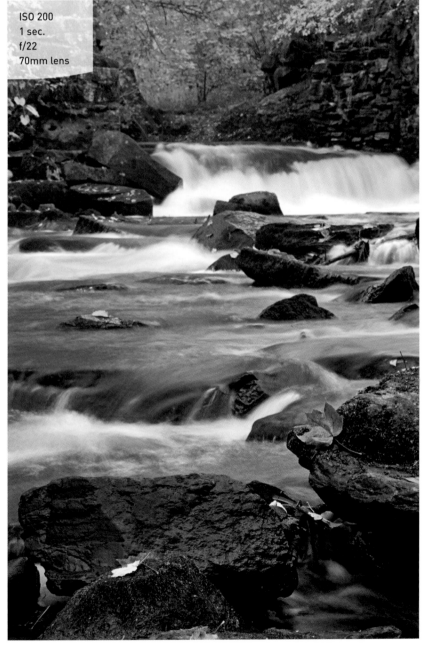

ISO 200
1 sec.
f/22
70mm lens

FIGURE 4.13
A small aperture decreases the light hitting the sensor and requires a longer shutter for proper exposure, which is the perfect combination for silky water and a wide depth of field.

While the other camera modes have their place, I think you will find that, like me and most other working pros, you will use the Aperture Priority and Shutter Priority modes for 90 percent of your shooting.

The other concern that I have when I am setting up my camera is just how low I can keep my ISO. This is always a priority for me because a low ISO will deliver the cleanest image. I raise the ISO only as a last resort because each increase in sensitivity is an opportunity for more digital noise to enter my image. To that end, I always have the High ISO Noise Reduction feature turned on (see Chapter 7).

To make quick changes while I shoot, I often use the Exposure Compensation feature (covered in Chapter 7) so that I can make small over- and underexposure changes. This is different than changing the aperture or shutter; it is more like fooling the camera meter into thinking the scene is brighter or darker than it actually is. To get to this function quickly, I simply press the Exposure Compensation/Aperture button, then dial in the desired amount of compensation. Truth be told, I usually have this set to –1/3 so that there is just a tiny bit of underexposure in my image. This usually leads to better color saturation. (Note: The Exposure Compensation feature does not work in the Manual shooting mode.)

One of the reasons I change my exposure is to make corrections when I see the "blinkies" in my rear LCD. Blinkies are the warning signal that part of my image has been overexposed to the point that I no longer have any detail in the highlights. When the Highlight Alert feature is turned on, the display will flash wherever the potential exists for overexposure. The black and white flashing will only appear in areas of your picture that are in danger of overexposure.

SETTING UP THE HIGHLIGHT ALERT FEATURE

1. Press the Menu button, then use the Multi-selector to access the Playback menu (**A**).

2. Once in the Playback menu, move the Multi-selector to Playback Display Options and press OK (**B**).

3. Move the Multi-selector down to select the Highlights option, then press OK to place a check mark next to the word Highlights (**C**).

4. Now move back up to select Done, and press OK again to lock in your change.

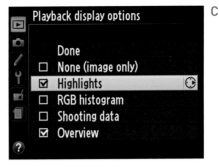

Once the highlight warning is turned on, I use it to check my images on the back of the LCD after taking a shot. If I see an area that is blinking, I will usually set the Exposure Compensation feature to an underexposed setting like –1/3 or –2/3 stops and take another photo, checking the result on the screen. I repeat this process until the warning is gone.

Sometimes, such as when shooting into the sun, the warning will blink no matter how much you adjust the exposure because there is just no detail in the highlight. Use your best judgment to determine if the warning is alerting you to an area where you want to retain highlight detail.

As you work your way through the coming chapters, you will see other tips and tricks I use in my daily photography, but the most important tip I can give is to understand the features of your camera so that you can leverage the technology in a knowledge-able way. This will result in better photographs.

Chapter 4 Assignments

This will be more of a mental challenge than anything else, but you should put a lot of work into these lesson assignments because the information covered in this chapter will define how you work with your camera from this point on. Granted, there may be times that you just want to grab some quick pictures and will resort to the automatic scene modes, but to get serious with your photography, you will want to learn the professional modes inside and out.

Starting off with Program mode

Set your camera on Program mode and start shooting. Become familiar with the adjustments you can make to your exposure by turning the Command dial. Shoot in bright sun, deep shade, indoors, anywhere that you have different types and intensities of light. While you are shooting, make sure that you keep an eye on your ISO and raise or lower it according to your environment.

Learning to control time with the Shutter Priority mode

Find some moving subjects and then set your camera to S mode. Have someone ride their bike back and forth or even just photograph cars as they go by. Start with a slow shutter speed of around 1/30 of a second and then start shooting with faster and faster shutter speeds. Keep shooting until you can freeze the action. Now find something that isn't moving, like a flower, and start with your shutter speed at something fast like 1/500 of a second and then work your way down. Don't brace the camera on a steady surface. Just try and shoot as slowly as possible, down to about 1/4 of a second. The point is to see how well you can handhold your camera before you start introducing hand shake into the image, making it appear soft and somewhat unfocused.

Controlling depth of field with the Aperture Priority mode

The name of the game with Aperture Priority mode is depth of field. Set up three items an equal distance from you. I would use chess pieces or something similar. Now focus on the middle item and set your camera to the largest aperture that your lens allows (remember, large aperture means a small number, like f/3.5). Now, while still focusing on the middle subject, start shooting with ever-smaller apertures until you are at the smallest f-stop for your lens. If you have a zoom lens, try doing this exercise with the lens at the widest and then the most telephoto settings. Now move up to subjects that are farther away, like telephone poles, and shoot them in the same way. The idea is to get a feel for how each aperture setting affects your depth of field.

Giving and taking with Manual mode

Manual mode is not going to require a lot of work, but you should pay close attention to your results. Go outside on a sunny day and, using the camera in Manual mode, set your ISO to 100, your shutter speed to 1/125 of a second, and your aperture to f/16. Now press your shutter release button to get a meter reading. You should be pretty close to that zero mark. If not, make small adjustments to one of your settings until it hits that mark. Now, this is where the fun begins. Start moving your shutter speed slower, to 1/60, and then set your aperture to f/22. Now go the other way. Set your aperture on f/8 and your shutter speed to 1/500. Now review your images. If all went well, all the exposures should look the same. This is because you balanced the light with reciprocal changes to the aperture and shutter speed. Now go back to our original setting of 1/125 at f/16 and try just moving the shutter speed without changing the aperture. Just make 1/3-stop changes (1/125 to 1/100 to 1/80 to 1/60), and then review your images to see what a 1/3 stop of overexposure looks like. Then do the same thing going in the opposite way. It's hard to know if you want to over- or underexpose a scene until you have actually done it and seen the results.

With each of the assignments, make sure that you keep track of your modes and exposures so that you can compare them with the image. If you are using software to review your images, you should also be able to check the camera settings that are embedded within the image's metadata.

Share your results with the book's Flickr group!

Join the group here: flickr.com/groups/nikond5100fromsnapshotstogreatshots/

5

ISO 100
1/400 sec.
f/9
24mm lens

Moving Target

THE TRICKS TO SHOOTING SUBJECTS IN MOTION

Now that you have learned about the professional modes, it's time to put your newfound knowledge to good use. Whether you are shooting the action at a professional sporting event, an osprey swooping for a fish, or a child on a merry-go-round, you'll learn techniques that will help you bring out the best in your photography when your subject is in motion.

The number one thing to know when trying to capture a moving target is that speed is king! I'm not talking about how fast your subject is moving, but rather how fast your shutter is opening and closing. Shutter speed is the key to freezing the moment in time—but also to conveying movement. It's all in how you turn the dial. There are also some other considerations for taking your shot to the next level: composition, lens selection, and a few more items that we will explore in this chapter. So strap on your seatbelt and hit the gas, because here we go!

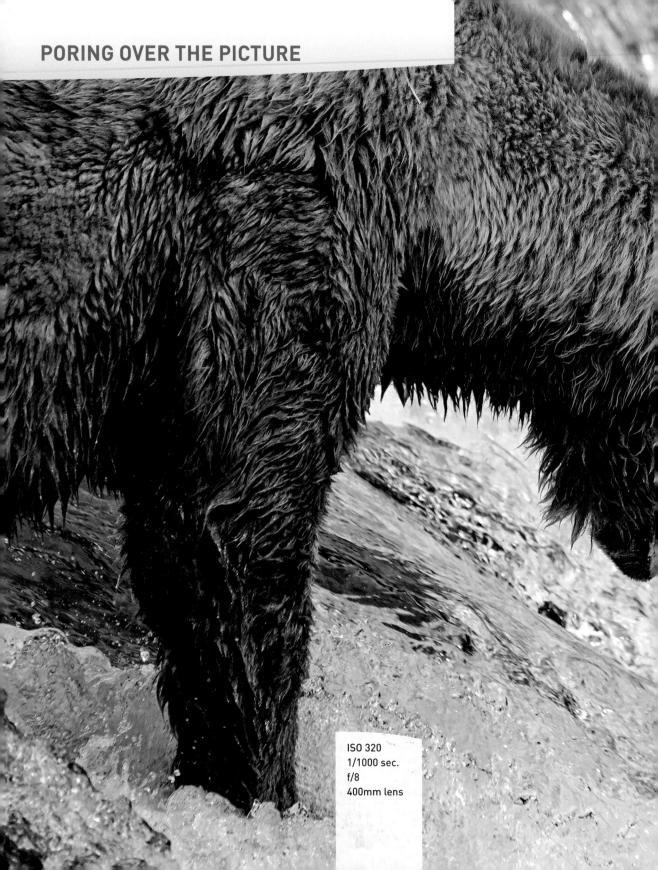

ISO 320
1/1000 sec.
f/8
400mm lens

Photographing brown bears during the salmon run is something I highly recommend adding to your bucket list. With the camera on a tripod and a manual exposure dialed in to freeze motion while giving the maximum depth of field without raising the ISO too high, I focused on the bear and used the continuous shooting mode as soon as I saw the salmon start to jump.

A close eye was kept on exposure to ensure detail was retained in the white water.

The aperture provided a wide enough depth of field to keep both the bear and the salmon in focus.

Flying water droplets and the salmon are frozen in midair by the fast shutter speed.

STOP RIGHT THERE!

Shutter speed is the main tool in the photographer's arsenal for capturing great action shots. The ability to freeze a moment in time often makes the difference between a good shot and a great one. To take advantage of this concept, you should have a good grasp of the relationship between shutter speed and movement. When you press the shutter release button, your camera goes into action by opening the shutter curtain and then closing it after a predetermined length of time. The longer you leave your shutter open, the more your subject will move across the frame, so common sense dictates that the first thing to consider is just how fast your subject is moving.

Typically, you will be working in fractions of a second. How many fractions depends on several factors. Subject movement, while simple in concept, is actually based on three factors. The first is the direction of travel. Is the subject moving across your field of view (left to right) or traveling toward or away from you? The second consideration is the actual speed at which the subject is moving. There is a big difference between a moving sports car and a child on a bicycle. Finally, the distance from you to the subject has a direct bearing on how fast the action seems to be taking place. Let's take a brief look at each of these factors to see how they might affect your shooting.

DIRECTION OF TRAVEL

Typically, the first thing that people think about when taking an action shot is how fast the subject is moving, but in reality the first consideration should be the direction of travel. Where you are positioned in relation to the subject's direction of travel is critically important in selecting the proper shutter speed. When you open your shutter, the lens gathers light from your subject and records it on the camera sensor. If the subject is moving across your viewfinder, you need a faster shutter speed to keep that lateral movement from being recorded as a streak across your image. Subjects that are moving perpendicular to your shooting location do not move across your viewfinder and appear to be more stationary. This allows you to use a slightly slower shutter speed (**Figure 5.1**). A subject that is moving in a diagonal direction—both across the frame and toward or away from you—requires a shutter speed in between the two.

SUBJECT SPEED

Once the angle of motion has been determined, you can then assess the speed at which the subject is traveling. The faster your subject moves, the faster your shutter speed needs to be in order to "freeze" that subject (**Figure 5.2**). A person walking across your frame might only require a shutter speed of 1/60 of a second, while a cyclist traveling in the same direction would call for 1/500 of a second. That same cyclist traveling toward you at the same rate of speed, rather than across the frame, might only require a shutter speed of 1/125 of a second. You can start to see how the relationship of speed and direction comes into play in your decision-making process.

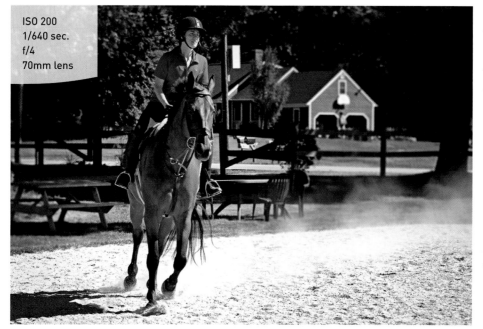

ISO 200
1/640 sec.
f/4
70mm lens

FIGURE 5.1
Action coming
toward the camera
can be captured
with slower
shutter speeds.

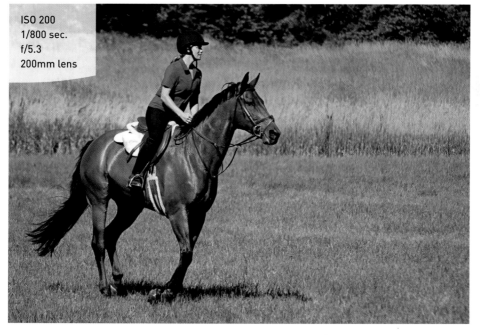

ISO 200
1/800 sec.
f/5.3
200mm lens

FIGURE 5.2
A fast-moving
subject that is
crossing your path
will require a faster
shutter speed.

SUBJECT-TO-CAMERA DISTANCE

So now we know both the direction and the speed of your subject. The final factor to address is the distance between you and the action. Picture yourself looking at a highway full of cars from up in a tall building a quarter of a mile from the road. As you stare down at the traffic moving along at 55 miles per hour, the cars and trucks seem to be slowly moving along the roadway. Now picture yourself standing in the median of that same road as the same traffic flies by at the same rate of speed.

Although the traffic is moving at the same speed, the shorter distance between you and the traffic makes the cars look like they are moving much faster. This is because your field of view is much narrower; therefore, the subjects are not going to present themselves within the frame for the same length of time. The concept of distance applies to the length of your lens as well (**Figure 5.3**). If you are using a wide-angle lens, you can probably get away with a slower shutter speed than if you were using a telephoto, which puts you in the heart of the action. It all has to do with your field of view. That telephoto gets you "closer" to the action—and the closer you are, the faster your subject will be moving across your viewfinder.

FIGURE 5.3
Because of the distance of the subject from the camera, a slower shutter speed could be used to capture this action.

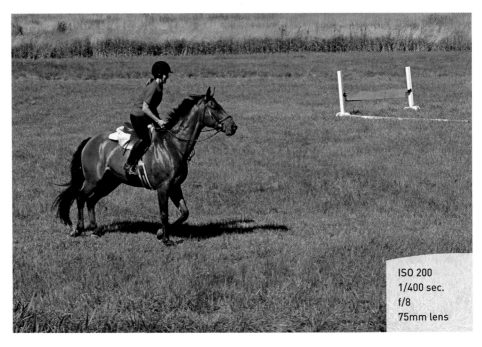

ISO 200
1/400 sec.
f/8
75mm lens

USING SHUTTER PRIORITY (S) MODE TO STOP MOTION

In Chapter 4, you were introduced to the professional shooting modes. You'll remember that the mode that gives you ultimate control over shutter speed is Shutter Priority, or S, mode, where you are responsible for selecting the shutter speed while handing over the aperture selection to the camera. The ability to concentrate on just one exposure factor helps you quickly make changes on the fly while staying glued to your viewfinder and your subject.

There are a couple of things to consider when using Shutter Priority mode, both of which have to do with the amount of light that is available when shooting. While you have control over which shutter speed you select in Shutter Priority mode, the range of shutter speeds that is available to you depends largely on how well your subject is lit.

Typically, when shooting fast-paced action, you will be working with very fast shutter speeds. This means that your lens will probably be set to its largest aperture. If the light is not sufficient for the shutter speed selected, you will need to do one of two things: select a lens that offers a larger working aperture, or raise the ISO of the camera. Working off the assumption that you have only one lens available, let's concentrate on balancing your exposure using the ISO.

Let's say that you are shooting a soccer game at night, and you want to get some great action shots. You set your camera to Shutter Priority mode and, after testing out some shutter speeds, determine that you need to shoot at 1/500 of a second to freeze the action on the field. When you place the viewfinder to your eye and press the shutter button halfway, you notice that the f-stop has been replaced by the word "Lo." This is your camera's way of telling you that the lens has now reached its maximum aperture and you are going to be underexposed if you shoot your pictures at the currently selected shutter speed. You could slow your shutter speed down until the Lo indicator goes away, but then you would get images with too much motion blur.

The alternative is to raise your ISO to a level that is fast enough for a proper exposure. The key here is to always use the lowest ISO that you can get away with. That might mean ISO 100 in bright, sunny conditions or ISO 5600 for an indoor or night situation (**Figure 5.4**). Just remember that the higher the ISO, the greater the amount of noise in your image. This is the reason that you see professional sports photographers using those mammoth lenses perched atop a monopod. They could use a smaller lens, but to get those very large apertures they need a huge piece of glass on the front of the lens. The larger the glass on the front of the lens, the more light it gathers and the larger the aperture for shooting. For the working pro, the large aperture translates into low ISO (and thus low noise), fast shutter speeds, and razor-sharp action.

FIGURE 5.4
The only way to stop action under the lights is to crank up your ISO.

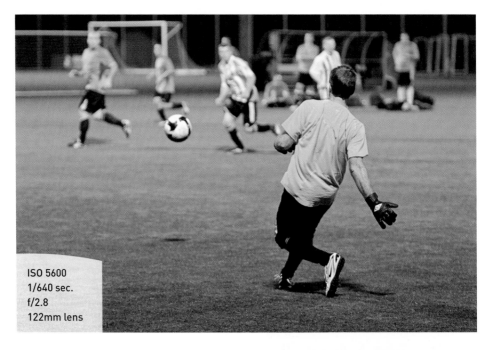

ISO 5600
1/640 sec.
f/2.8
122mm lens

ADJUSTING YOUR ISO ON THE FLY

1. Look at the exposure values (the shutter speed and aperture settings) in the lower portion of your viewfinder.

2. If the word "Lo" appears where the aperture normally is, press the **i** button on the back of the camera (if the camera's info screen is not visible, press the **i** button).

3. Press up or down on the Multi-selector button to highlight the ISO option and then press OK (**A**).

4. Press down on the Multi-selector to select a higher ISO setting, and press OK to lock in the change (**B**).

5. If you now see an aperture setting in the display, shoot away. If you still see the word "Lo," repeat steps 2–4 until it is set correctly.

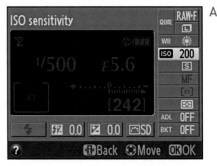

A

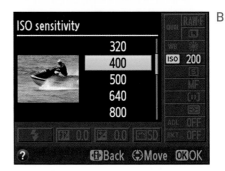

B

ZOOM IN TO BE SURE

When reviewing your shots on the LCD, don't be fooled by the display. The smaller your image is, the sharper it will look. To ensure that you are getting sharp, blur-free images, make sure that you zoom in on your LCD display.

To zoom in on your images, press the Playback button located on the rear of the camera and then press the Zoom In button (**Figure 5.5**). Continue pressing the Zoom In button to increase the zoom ratio.

To zoom back out, simply press the Zoom Out button (the magnifying glass with the minus sign on it) or press the Playback button again.

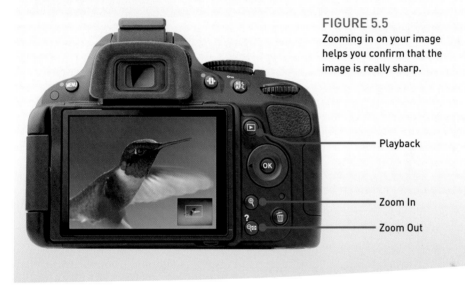

FIGURE 5.5
Zooming in on your image helps you confirm that the image is really sharp.

Playback

Zoom In

Zoom Out

USING APERTURE PRIORITY (A) MODE TO ISOLATE YOUR SUBJECT

One of the benefits of working in Shutter Priority mode with fast shutter speeds is that, more often than not, you will be shooting with the largest aperture available on your lens. Shooting with a large aperture allows you to use faster shutter speeds, but it also narrows your depth of field.

To isolate your subject in order to focus your viewer's attention on it, a larger aperture is required. The larger aperture reduces the foreground and background sharpness: The larger the aperture, the more blurred they will be.

The reason that I bring this up here is that when you are shooting most sporting events, the idea is to isolate your main subject by having it in focus while the rest of the image has some amount of blur. This sharp focus draws your viewer right to the subject. Studies have shown that the eye is drawn to sharp areas before moving on to the blurry areas. Also, depending on what your subject matter is, there can be a tendency to get distracted by a busy background if everything in the photo is equally sharp. Without a narrow depth of field, it might be difficult for the viewer to establish exactly what the main subject is in your picture.

Let's look at how to use depth of field to bring focus to your subject. In the previous section, I told you that you should use Shutter Priority mode for getting those really fast shutter speeds to stop action. Generally speaking, Shutter Priority mode will be the mode you most often use for shooting sports and other action, but there will be times when you want to ensure that you are getting the narrowest depth of field possible in your image. The way to do this is by using Aperture Priority mode.

So how do you know when you should use Aperture Priority mode as opposed to Shutter Priority mode? It's not a simple answer, but your LCD screen can help you make this determination. The best scenario for using Aperture Priority mode is a brightly lit scene where maximum apertures will still give you plenty of shutter speed to stop the action.

Let's say that you are shooting a game in the midday sun. If you have determined that you need something between 1/500 and 1/1250 of a second for stopping the action, you could just set your camera to a high shutter speed in Shutter Priority mode and start shooting. But you also want to be using an aperture of, say, f/4.5 to get that narrow depth of field. Here's the problem: If you set your camera to Shutter Priority mode and select 1/1000 of a second as a nice compromise, you might get that desired f/stop—but you might not. As the meter is trained on your moving subject, the light levels could rise or fall, which might actually change that desired f-stop to something higher, like f/5.6 or even f/8. Now the depth of field is extended, and you will no longer get that nice isolation and separation that you wanted.

To rectify this, switch the camera to Aperture Priority mode and select f/4.5 as your aperture. Now, as you begin shooting, the camera holds that aperture and makes exposure adjustments with the shutter speed. As I said before, this works well when you have lots of light—enough light so that you can have a high-enough shutter speed without introducing motion blur.

THE AUTO ISO SENSITIVITY CONTROL TRICK

There is a very cool trick that can get you the best of both worlds and that won't sacrifice your shutter speed or aperture. By setting up the Auto ISO sensitivity control feature, you can set the camera to automatically select an ISO that keeps you at your preferred shutter speed, while using the largest aperture and lowest ISO possible. It will also put an upper limit on the ISO to keep you from getting too much noise in your images.

Here's the way it works. If I am shooting an activity that requires a shutter speed of 1/250 of a second, I set that as the minimum in the auto control settings. Then I decide that I can deal with the noise that is produced with an ISO up to 1600, so I set that as my maximum sensitivity. Since I would always like to use the lowest ISO, I set the ISO Sensitivity setting to 100. Once everything is set, the camera will now adjust my ISO without any interaction from me, letting me shoot at my desired shutter speed at the lowest possible ISO and largest aperture setting possible. I used this feature when shooting the evening soccer game in Figure 5.5, and it allowed me to keep the shutter at 1/640 of a second on into the night.

SETTING UP THE AUTO ISO SENSITIVITY CONTROL FEATURE

1. Press the Menu button and then use the Multi-selector to get to the Shooting menu.

2. Press the Multi-selector to the right to enter the menu and then locate the ISO Sensitivity Settings feature (**A**).

3. Press the Multi-selector to the right to enter the set-up screen.

4. Press the Multi-selector to the right, select the lowest ISO that you wish to use (ISO Sensitivity), and press the OK button (**B**).

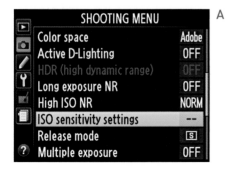 A

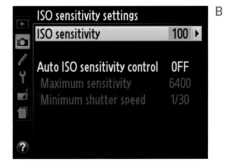 B

5. Press the Multi-selector down to highlight Auto ISO Sensitivity Control, and then move the selector to the right and select On to activate the feature (**C**).

6. Use the Multi-selector to choose the Maximum Sensitivity option (**D**). This allows you to set the upper limit of your ISO.

7. Finally, select the minimum shutter speed that you want to use while shooting (**E**). This will be completely dependent on the speed necessary to stop the action you are shooting.

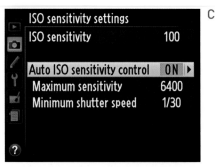

With everything set up, you can begin shooting without fear of constantly having to change the ISO. This technique is also quite helpful when working in varying light conditions. As you are shooting, you will notice the ISO AUTO warning in the lower portion of the viewfinder along with the adjusted ISO setting.

Manual callout

For more information about the Auto ISO sensitivity control, turn to page 155 in the reference manual on the companion CD that came with the camera.

KEEP THEM IN FOCUS WITH CONTINUOUS-SERVO FOCUS AND AF FOCUS POINT SELECTION

With the exposure issue handled for the moment, let's move on to an area that is equally important: focusing. If you have browsed your manual, you know that there are several focus modes to choose from in the D5100. To get the greatest benefit from each of them, it is important to understand how they work and the situations where each mode will give you the best opportunity to grab a great shot. Because we are discussing subject movement, our first choice is going to be Continuous-servo AF mode (AF-C). AF-C mode uses all of the focus points in the camera to find a moving subject and then lock in the focus when the shutter button is completely depressed.

SELECTING AND SHOOTING IN CONTINUOUS-SERVO AF FOCUS MODE

1. Press the **i** button on the back of the camera (if the camera's info screen is not visible, press the **i** button twice).

2. Press up or down on the Multi-selector to highlight the focus mode and then press the OK button.

3. Use the Multi-selector to select AF-C and press OK (**A**).

4. Locate your subject in the viewfinder, then press and hold the shutter button halfway to activate the focus mechanism.

5. The camera will maintain the subject's focus as long as it remains within one of the focus points in the viewfinder or until you release the shutter button or take a picture.

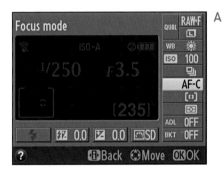

You should take note that holding down the shutter button for long periods of time will cause your battery to drain much faster because the camera will be constantly focusing on the subject.

When using the AF-C mode, you can use the AF point mode set to Dynamic area, which uses a focus point of your choosing as the primary focus, but uses information from the surrounding points if your subject happens to move away from the point.

SETTING THE AF-AREA MODE TO DYNAMIC

1. To set the AF-area mode, press the **i** button on the back of the camera.

2. Press up or down on the Multi-selector to highlight the AF-area mode and then press the OK button (**A**).

3. Use the Multi-selector to choose the Dynamic AF mode and press OK (**B**).

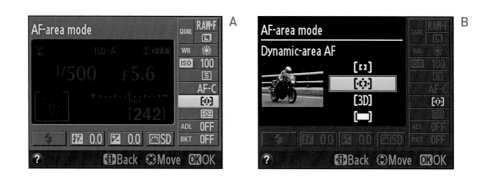

To select a focus point you want to use, simply move the Multi-selector up, down, left, or right until the desired point is highlighted in your viewfinder. Pressing the OK button in the center of the Multi-selector will reset your focus point to the center position.

Note that the AF mode is used to select the method with which the camera will focus the lens. This is different from the AF point, which is a cluster of small points that are visible in the viewfinder and are used to determine where you want the lens to focus (**Figure 5.6**). If you don't see Dynamic as an option, go back and choose the AF-C focus mode.

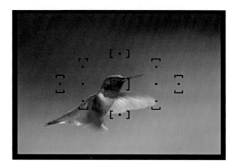

FIGURE 5.6
The Automatic Focus (AF) points are the 11 small boxes arranged in your viewfinder.

STOP AND GO WITH 3D-TRACKING AF

If you are going to be changing between a moving target and one that is still, you should consider using the 3D-tracking AF mode. This mode mixes both the AF-S and Dynamic modes for shooting a subject that goes from stationary to moving without having to adjust your focus mode.

When you have a stationary subject, simply place your selected focus point on your subject and the camera will focus on it. If your subject begins to move out of focus, the camera will track the movement, keeping a sharp focus.

For example, suppose you are shooting a football game. The quarterback has brought the team to the line and is standing behind the center, waiting for the ball to be hiked. If you are using the 3D-tracking AF mode, you can place your focus point on the quarterback and start taking pictures of him as he stands at the line. As soon as the ball is hiked and the action starts, the camera will switch to tracking mode and follow his movement within the frame. This can be a little tricky at first, but once you master it, it will make your action shooting effortless.

To select 3D-tracking, simply follow the same steps listed for selecting Dynamic AF-area mode on the previous page but instead select the 3D-tracking mode. It is important to know that the 3D-tracking AF mode uses color and contrast to locate and then follow the subject, so this mode might be less effective when everything is similar in tone or color.

CHOOSING A FOCUS MODE

Selecting the proper focus mode depends largely on what type of subject you are photographing. Single-point is typically best for stationary subjects. It allows you to determine exactly where you want your focus to be and then recompose your image while holding the focus in place. If you are taking pictures of an active subject that is moving quickly, trying to set a focus point with Single-point can be difficult, if not impossible. This is when you will want to rely on the Dynamic and 3D-tracking modes to quickly assess the subject distance and set your lens focus. This can be especially helpful if the subject distance is varying constantly.

MANUAL FOCUS FOR ANTICIPATED ACTION

While I utilize the automatic focus modes for the majority of my shooting, there are times when I like to fall back on manual focus. This is usually when I know when and where the action will occur and I want to capture the subject as it crosses a certain plane of focus. This is useful in sports like motocross or auto racing, where the subjects are on a defined track and I know exactly where I want to capture the action. I could try tracking the subject, but sometimes the view can be obscured by a curve. By pre-focusing the camera, all I have to do is wait for the subject to approach my point of focus and then start firing the camera.

Take a look at **Figure 5.7**. We have a hummingbird feeder set up outside one of our windows so that we can watch them come and go. They tend to follow a regular pattern as they approach the feeder, so I set up my camera on a tripod and trained it on a point where they tended to hover between feedings. I set focus to manual and fired in continuous mode each time one appeared. Not every shot was in focus on the right part of the bird, but it was easier than trying to follow a hummingbird around on its flight.

FIGURE 5.7
Pre-focus the camera to a point where you know the subject will be and start shooting right before they get there.

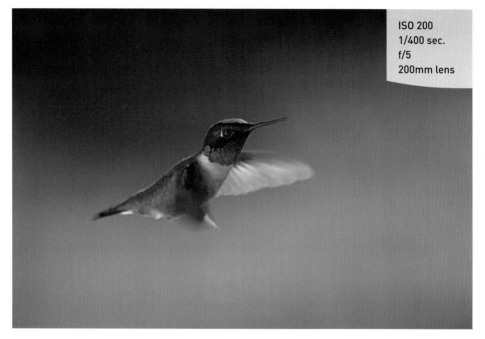

ISO 200
1/400 sec.
f/5
200mm lens

Here's another example (**Figure 5.8**), where I used manual focusing to determine where I wanted the subject to be critically focused. I stationed myself at a point where the rollercoaster came around a bend, so that it appeared to be coming right at me, and locked focused on the track. I would fire away in continuous shooting mode each time they came to that point in the track.

DRIVE MODES

The drive mode determines how fast your camera will take pictures. Single shot is for taking one photograph at a time. With every full press of the shutter release button, the camera will take a single image. The continuous mode allows for a more rapid capture rate. Think of it like a machine gun. When you are using the continuous mode, the camera will continue to take pictures as long as the shutter release button is held down.

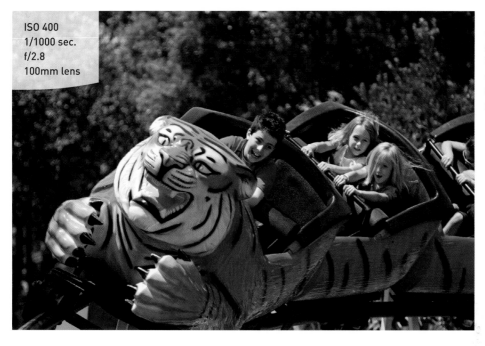

ISO 400
1/1000 sec.
f/2.8
100mm lens

FIGURE 5.8
Being able to
anticipate the
location of the
action gives you
time to get the best
composition.

KEEPING UP WITH THE CONTINUOUS SHOOTING MODE

Getting great focus is one thing, but capturing the best moment on the sensor can be difficult if you are shooting just one frame at a time. In the world of sports, and in life in general, things move pretty fast. If you blink, you might miss it. The same can be said for shooting in Single-frame mode. Fortunately, your D5100 comes equipped with a continuous shooting—or "burst"—mode that lets you capture a series of images at up to four frames a second (**Figure 5.9**).

Using the Continuous shooting mode causes the camera to keep taking images for as long as you hold down the shutter release button. In Single mode, you have to release the button and then press it again to take another picture.

FIGURE 5.9
Using the Continuous shooting mode means that you are sure to capture the peak of the action.

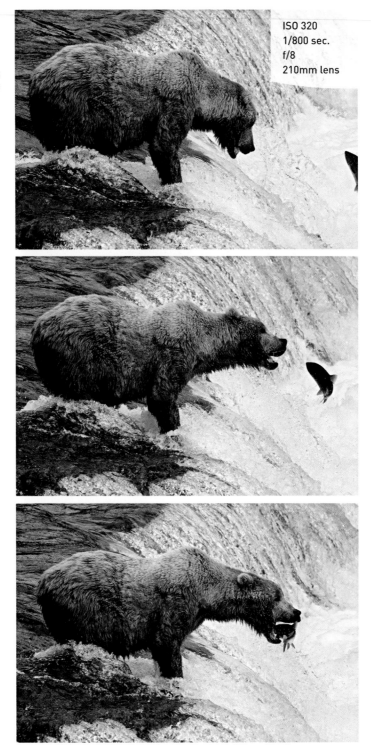

ISO 320
1/800 sec.
f/8
210mm lens

SETTING UP AND SHOOTING IN THE CONTINUOUS SHOOTING MODE

1. Press the **i** button on the back of the camera.

2. Press up or down on the Multi-selector to highlight the Release mode and then press OK (**A**).

3. Use the Multi-selector to choose the Continuous mode and press OK (**B**).

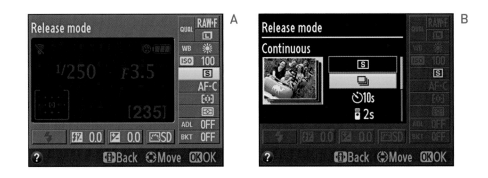

Your camera has an internal memory, called a "buffer," where images are stored while they are being processed prior to being moved to your memory card. Depending on the image format you are using, the buffer might fill up, and the camera will stop shooting until space is made in the buffer for new images. The camera readout in the viewfinder tells you how many frames you have available in burst mode. Just look in the viewfinder at the bottom right to see the maximum number of images for burst shooting. As you shoot, the number will go down and then back up as the images are written to the memory card.

A SENSE OF MOTION

Shooting action isn't always about freezing the action. There are times when you want to convey a sense of motion so that the viewer can get a feel for the movement and flow of an event. Two techniques you can use to achieve this effect are panning and motion blur.

PANNING

Panning has been used for decades to capture the speed of a moving object as it moves across the frame. It doesn't work well for subjects that are moving toward or away from you. Panning is achieved by following your subject across your frame, moving your camera along with the subject, and using a slower-than-normal shutter speed so that the background (and sometimes even a bit of the subject) has a sideways blur but the main portion of your subject is sharp and blur-free. The key to a great panning shot is selecting the right shutter speed: too fast and you won't get the desired blurring of the background; too slow and the subject will have too much blur and will not be recognizable. Practice the technique until you can achieve a smooth motion with your camera that follows along with your subject. The other thing to remember when panning is to follow through even after the shutter has closed. This will keep the motion smooth and give you better images.

In **Figure 5.10**, I used the panning technique to follow this horse as it ran in front of me. I set the camera to the Continuous shooting mode, and I used Shutter Priority mode to select a shutter speed of 1/40 of a second while the focus mode was on Dynamic. I wasn't worried about a narrow depth of field, because I knew that the movement of my camera at the slow shutter speed would blur the background.

FIGURE 5.10
Following the subject as it moves across the field of view allows for a slower shutter speed and adds a sense of motion.

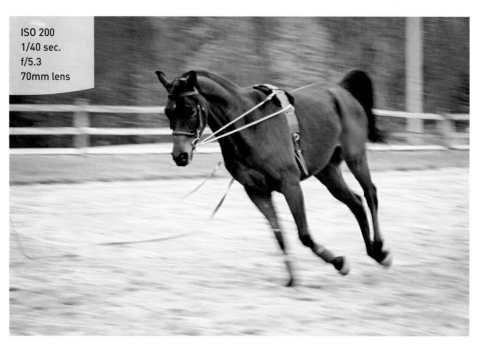

ISO 200
1/40 sec.
f/5.3
70mm lens

MOTION BLUR

Another way to let the viewer in on the feel of the action is to simply include some blur in the image. This isn't accidental blur from choosing the wrong shutter speed. This blur is more exaggerated, and it tells a story. In **Figure 5.11**, I was interested in capturing the sloshing of the water and the motion of the frog boots as my son jumped in our pond. A fast shutter speed would have surely frozen the action, but

I wanted the viewer to feel as though the water was still rippling around the pond and that the boot could break the surface at any moment.

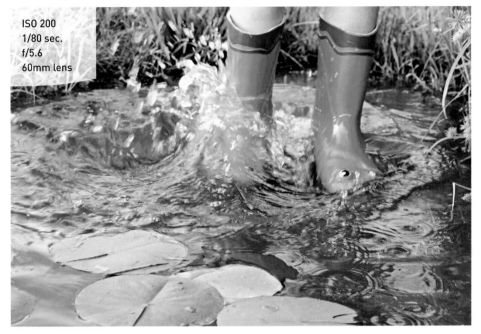

ISO 200
1/80 sec.
f/5.6
60mm lens

FIGURE 5.11
The movement of the boots and water, coupled with the slow shutter speed, conveys the sense of fluid motion.

Just as in panning, there is no preordained shutter speed to use for this effect. It is simply a matter of trial and error until you have a look that conveys the action. I try to get some area of the subject that is frozen. The key to this technique is the correct shutter speed combined with keeping the camera still during the exposure. You are trying to capture the motion of the subject, not of the photographer or the camera, so use a good shooting stance or even a tripod.

TIPS FOR SHOOTING ACTION

GIVE THEM SOMEWHERE TO GO

Whether you are shooting something as simple as your child's soccer match or as complex as the aerial acrobatics of a motorcycle jumper, where you place the subject in the frame is equally as important as how well you expose the image. A poorly composed shot can completely ruin a great moment by not holding the viewer's attention.

The one mistake I see many times in action photography is that the photographer doesn't use the frame properly. If you are dealing with a subject that is moving horizontally across your field of view, give the subject somewhere to go by placing them to the side of the frame, with their motion leading toward the middle of the frame (**Figure 5.12**). This offsetting of the subject will introduce a sense of direction and anticipation for the viewer. Unless you are going to completely fill the image with the action, try to avoid placing your subject in the middle of the frame. My dog was happy to catch as many snowballs as were required (and then some) to get the shot.

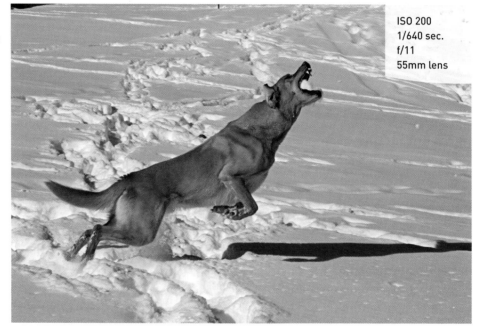

ISO 200
1/640 sec.
f/11
55mm lens

GET IN FRONT OF THE ACTION

Here's another one. When shooting action, show the action coming toward you (**Figure 5.13**). Don't shoot the action going away from you. People want to see faces. Faces convey the action, the drive, the sense of urgency, and the emotion of the moment. So if you are shooting action involving people, always position yourself so that the action is either coming at you or is at least perpendicular to your position.

PUT YOUR CAMERA IN A DIFFERENT PLACE

Changing your vantage point is a great way of finding new angles. Shooting from a low position with a wide-angle lens might let you incorporate some foreground to give depth to the image. Shooting from farther away with a telephoto lens will compress the elements in a scene and allow you to crop in tighter on the action. Don't be afraid to experiment and try new things.

The image in **Figure 5.14** is one of my favorite recent shots, and it all happened because I tried something different.

We started raising chickens for eggs this year and they have been a true joy to watch grow and to photograph. Talk about action photography—they never stop moving! On a recent evening I took advantage of Live View and the awesome swivel screen of the D5100 to put the camera at chicken-eye level and capture them strutting around their new coop. I also engaged the Auto ISO sensitivity control to ensure I kept a 1/250 of a second shutter speed in the waning light. AF focus mode was set to AF-A (since I was in Live View) and did a good job of following the hen as I fired away. This is not a shot I would have normally expected to be able to capture, but I was really pleased with the results and the performance of the D5100 under these unusual circumstances.

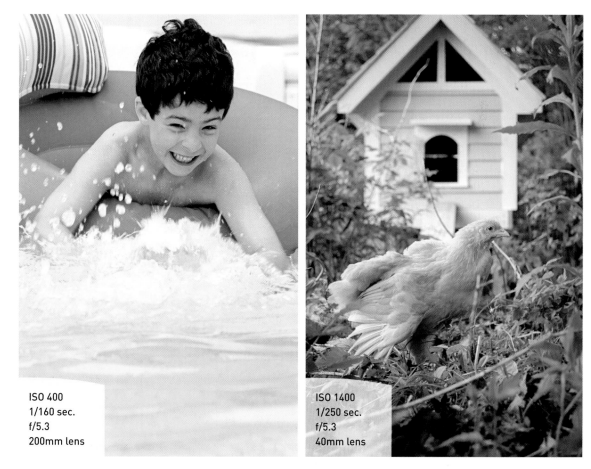

ISO 400
1/160 sec.
f/5.3
200mm lens

ISO 1400
1/250 sec.
f/5.3
40mm lens

FIGURE 5.13
Shooting from the front with a telephoto lens gives a feeling that the action is coming right at you.

FIGURE 5.14
Putting your camera in a different place can yield pleasing results.

Chapter 5 Assignments

The mechanics of motion

For this first assignment, you need to find some action. Explore the relationship between the speed of an object and its direction of travel. Use the same shutter speed to record your subject moving toward you and across your view. Try using the same shutter speed for both to compare the difference made by the direction of travel.

Wide vs. telephoto

Just as with the first assignment, photograph a subject moving in different directions, but this time, use a wide-angle lens and then a telephoto. Check out how the telephoto setting on the zoom lens will require faster shutter speeds than the lens at its wide-angle setting.

Getting a feel for focusing modes

We discussed two different ways to auto focus for action: Dynamic and 3D-tracking. Starting with Dynamic mode, find a moving subject and get familiar with the way the mode works.

Now repeat the process using the 3D-tracking AF mode. The point of the exercise is to become familiar enough with the two modes to decide which one to use for the situation you are photographing.

Anticipating the spot using manual focus

For this assignment, you will need to find a subject that you know will cross a specific line that you can pre-focus on. A street with moderate traffic works well for this. Focus on a spot on the street that the cars will travel across (don't forget to set your lens for manual focus). To do this right, you need to set the drive mode on the camera to the Continuous mode. Now, when a car approaches the spot, start shooting. Try shooting in three- or four-frame bursts.

Following the action

Panning is a great way to show motion. To begin, find a subject that will move across your path at a steady speed and practice following it in your viewfinder from side to side. Now, with the camera in Shutter Priority mode, set your shutter speed to 1/30 of a second and the focus mode to Dynamic. Now pan along with the subject and shoot as it moves across your view. Experiment with different shutter speeds and focal lengths. Panning is one of those skills that takes some time to get a feel for, so try it with different types of subjects moving at different speeds.

Feeling the movement

Instead of panning with the motion, use a stationary camera position and adjust the shutter speed until you get a blurred effect that gives the sense of motion while still being able to identify the subject. There is a big difference between a slightly blurred photo that looks like you just picked the wrong shutter speed and one that looks intentional for the purpose of showing motion. Just like panning, it will take some experimentation to find just the right shutter speed to achieve the desired effect.

Share your results with the book's Flickr group!

Join the group here: flickr.com/groups/nikond5100fromsnapshotstogreatshots/

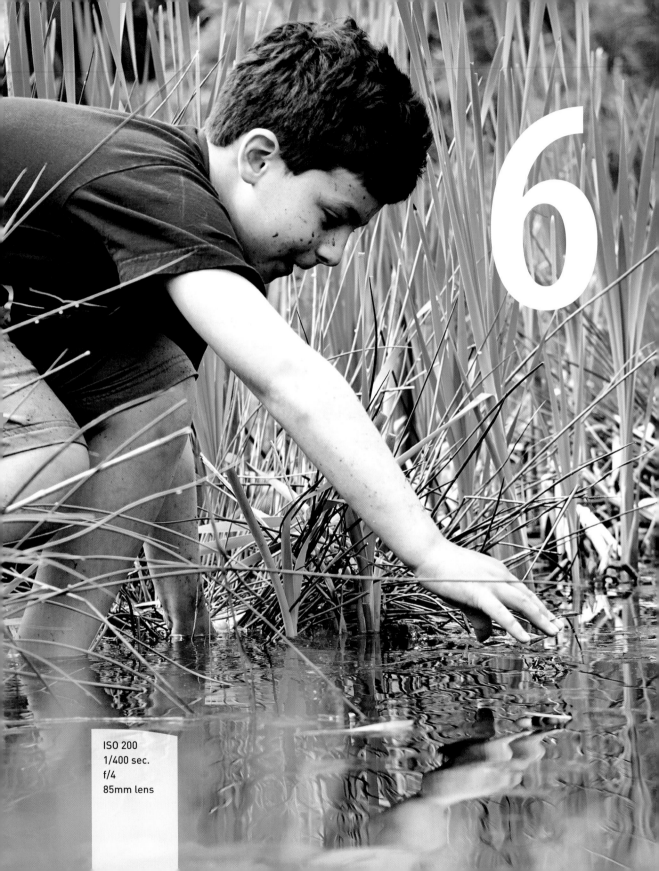

6

ISO 200
1/400 sec.
f/4
85mm lens

Say Cheese!

SETTINGS AND FEATURES TO MAKE GREAT PORTRAITS

Taking pictures of people is one of the great joys of photography. You will experience a great sense of accomplishment when you capture the spirit and personality of someone in a photograph. At the same time, you have a great responsibility because the person in front of the camera is depending on you to make them look good. You can't always change how someone looks, but you can control the way you photograph that individual. In this chapter, we will explore some camera features and techniques that can help you create great portraits.

I had the pleasure of shooting a senior portrait for my good friend's oldest daughter. It certainly helps when your subject is so photogenic, but I tried to put her in the best light possible by putting the sun and a backlit tree behind her, and a little bit of reflective material in front of her to bounce some of that great light back into her face. I added a tiny bit of fill light from an off-camera flash to wash out any shadows around the eyes.

Using a long zoom lens and a fairly wide-open aperture does a nice job of throwing the background into a beautiful wash of color.

Sharp focus on the eyes is critical in photographs of people. The bright sky behind us added a nice catchlight to her eyes.

Holding the camera in the portrait orientation allowed me to zoom in and fill the frame with the subject.

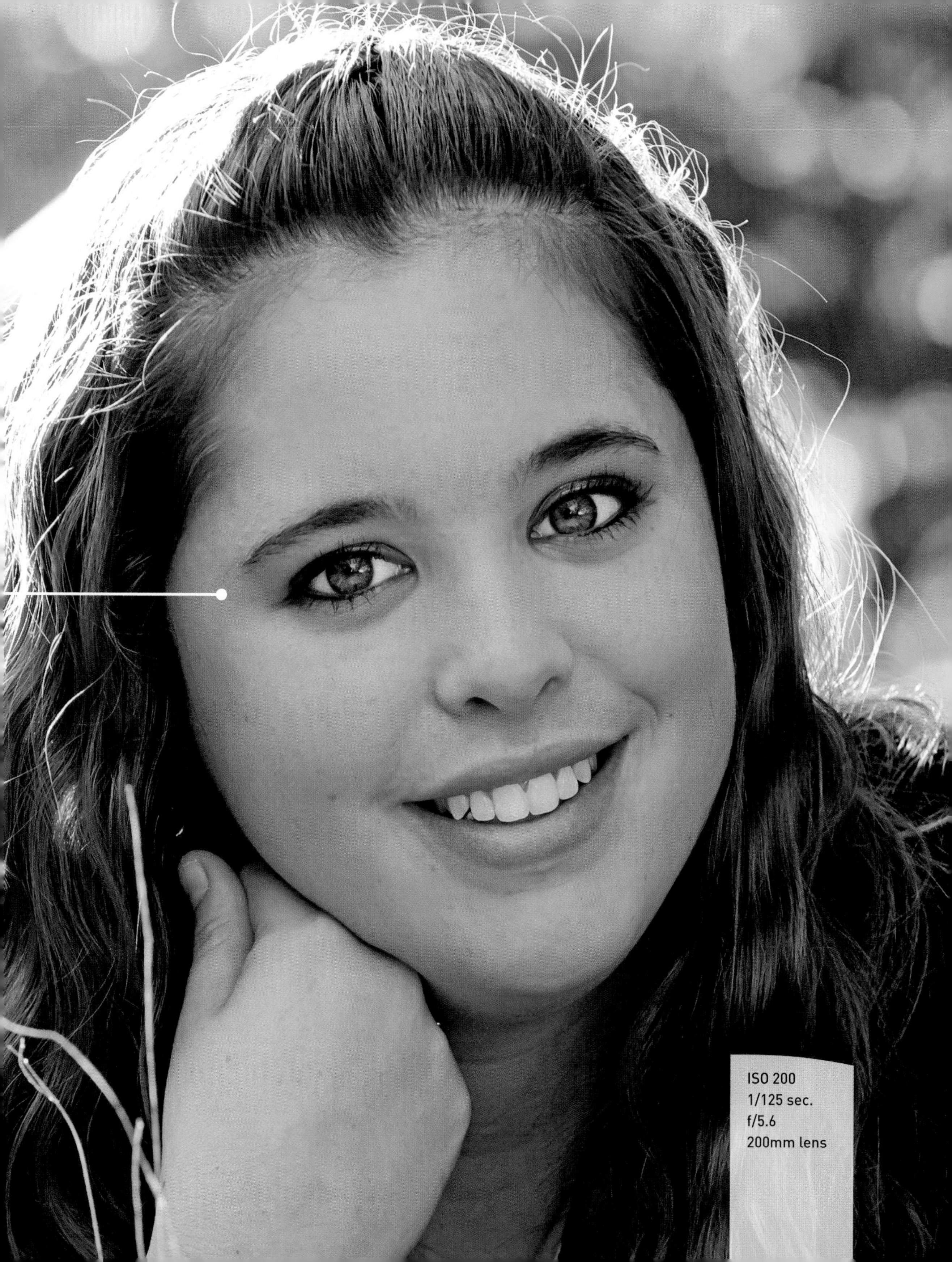

ISO 200
1/125 sec.
f/5.6
200mm lens

AUTOMATIC PORTRAIT MODE

In Chapter 3, we reviewed all of the automatic scene modes. One of them, Portrait mode, is dedicated to shooting portraits. While this is not my preferred camera setting, it is a great jumping-off point for those who are just starting out. The key to using this mode is to understand what is going on with the camera so that when you venture further into portrait photography, you can expand on the settings and get the most from your camera and, more importantly, your subject.

Whether you are photographing an individual or a group, the emphasis should always be on the subject. Portrait mode utilizes a larger aperture setting to keep the depth of field very narrow, which means that the background will appear slightly blurred or out of focus. To take full advantage of this effect, use a medium- to telephoto-length lens. Also, keep a pretty close distance to your subject. If you shoot from too far away, the narrow depth of field will not be as effective.

USING APERTURE PRIORITY MODE

If you took a poll of portrait photographers to see which shooting mode was most often used for portraits, the answer would certainly be Aperture Priority (A) mode. Selecting the right aperture is important for placing the most critically sharp area of the photo on your subject, while simultaneously blurring all of the distracting background clutter (**Figure 6.1**). Not only will a large aperture give the narrowest depth of field, it will also allow you to shoot in lower light levels at lower ISO settings.

This isn't to say that you have to use the largest aperture on your lens. A good place to begin is f/5.6. This will give you enough depth of field to keep the entire face in focus, while providing enough blur to eliminate distractions in the background. This isn't a hard-and-fast setting; it's just a good, all-around number to start with. Your aperture might change depending on the focal length of the lens you are using and on the amount of blur that you want for your foreground and background elements.

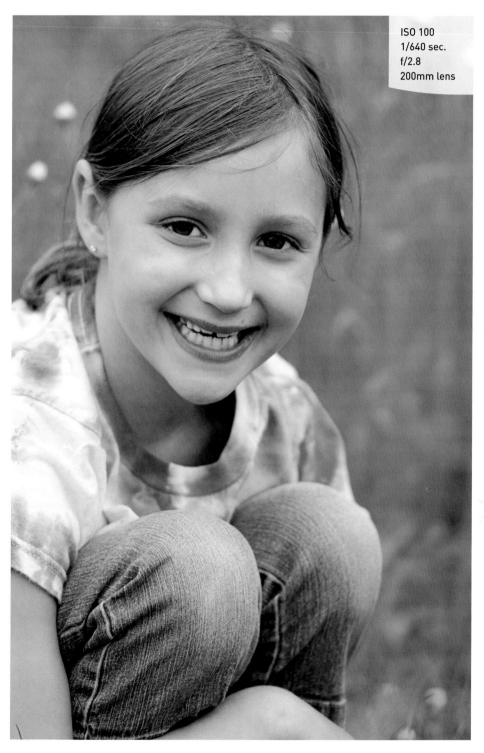

ISO 100
1/640 sec.
f/2.8
200mm lens

FIGURE 6.1
Using a wide aperture, especially with a longer lens, blurs distracting background details.

GO WIDE FOR ENVIRONMENTAL PORTRAITS

There will be times when your subject's environment is of great significance to the story you want to tell. This might mean using a smaller aperture to get more detail in the background or foreground. Once again, by using Aperture Priority mode, you can set your aperture to a higher f-stop, such as f/8 or f/11, and include the important details of the scene that surrounds your subject.

Using a wider-than-normal lens can also assist in getting more depth of field as well as showing the surrounding area. A wide-angle lens requires less stopping down of the aperture (making the aperture smaller) to achieve an acceptable depth of field. This is due to the fact that wide-angle lenses cover a greater area, so the depth of field appears to cover a greater percentage of the scene.

A wider lens might also be necessary to relay more information about the scenery (**Figure 6.2**). Select a lens length that is wide enough to tell the story but not so wide that you distort the subject. There's little in the world of portraiture quite as unflattering as giving someone a big, distorted nose (unless you are going for that sort of look). When shooting a portrait with a wide-angle lens, keep the subject away from the edge of the frame. This will reduce the distortion, especially in very wide focal lengths. As the lens length increases, distortion will be reduced. I generally don't like to go wider than about 24mm for portraits.

FIGURE 6.2
A wide-angle lens allows you to capture more of the environment in the scene without having to increase the distance between you and the subject.

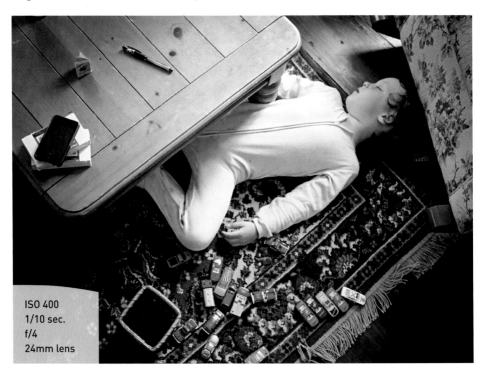

ISO 400
1/10 sec.
f/4
24mm lens

There are multiple metering modes in your camera, but the way they work is very similar. A light meter measures the amount of light being reflected off your subject and then renders a suggested exposure value based on the brightness of the subject and the ISO setting of the sensor. To establish this value, the meter averages all of the brightness values to come up with a middle tone, sometimes referred to as 18 percent gray. The exposure value is then rendered based on this middle gray value. This means that a white wall would be underexposed and a black wall would be overexposed in an effort to make each one appear gray. To assist with special lighting situations, the D5100 has three metering modes: Matrix (**Figure 6.3**), which uses the entire frame; Spot (**Figure 6.4**), which takes specific readings from small areas (often used with a gray card); and Center-weighted (**Figure 6.5**), which looks at the entire frame but places most of the exposure emphasis on the center of the frame.

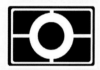

FIGURE 6.3
The Matrix metering mode uses the entire frame.

FIGURE 6.4
The Spot metering mode uses a very small area of the frame.

FIGURE 6.5
The Center-weighted metering mode looks at the entire frame but emphasizes the center of it.

METERING MODES FOR PORTRAITS

For most portrait situations, the Matrix metering mode is ideal. (For more on how metering works, see the "Metering Basics" sidebar.) This mode measures light values from all portions of the viewfinder and then establishes a proper exposure for the scene. The only problem that you might encounter when using this metering mode is when you have very light or dark backgrounds in your portrait shots.

In these instances, the meter might be fooled into using the wrong exposure information because it will be trying to lighten or darken the entire scene based on the prominence of dark or light areas (**Figure 6.6**). You can deal with this in one of two ways. You can use the Exposure Compensation feature, which we cover in Chapter 7, to dial in adjustments for over- and underexposure. Or you can change the metering mode to Center-weighted metering. The Center-weighted metering mode only uses the center area of the viewfinder (about 9 percent) to get its exposure information. This is the best way to achieve proper exposure for most portraits; metering off skin tones, averaged with hair and clothing, will often give a more accurate exposure (**Figure 6.7**). This metering mode is also great to use when the subject is strongly backlit.

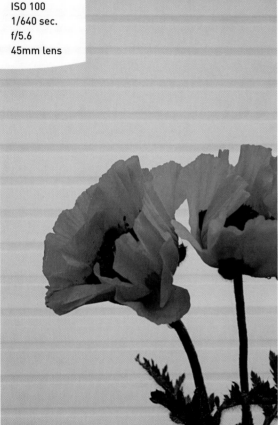

ISO 100
1/640 sec.
f/5.6
45mm lens

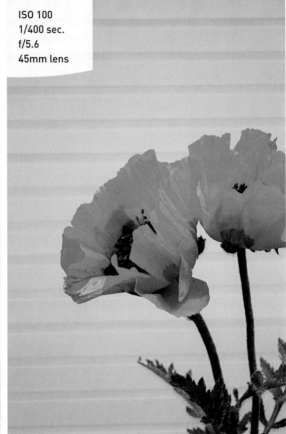

ISO 100
1/400 sec.
f/5.6
45mm lens

FIGURE 6.6
The light-colored background reflected a lot of light, which fooled the meter into choosing a slightly under-exposed setting for the photo.

FIGURE 6.7
When I switched to the Center-weighted metering mode, my camera was able to ignore much of the background and add a little more time to the exposure.

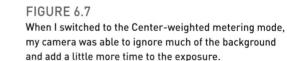

SETTING YOUR METERING MODE TO CENTER-WEIGHTED METERING

1. Press the **i** button to activate the cursor in the information screen.

2. Use the Multi-selector to move the cursor to the Metering icon and press the OK button (**A**).

3. Select the Center-weighted icon and press the OK button to lock in the change (**B**).

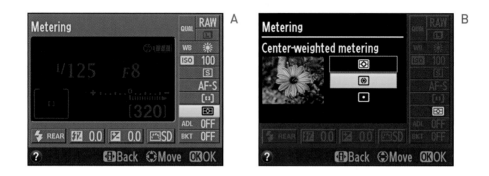

A   B

USING THE AE-L (AUTO EXPOSURE LOCK) FEATURE

There will often be times when your subject is not in the center of the frame but you still want to use the Center-weighted metering mode. So how can you get an accurate reading if the subject isn't in the center? Try using the AE-L (Auto Exposure Lock) feature to hold the exposure setting while you recompose.

AE Lock lets you use the exposure setting from any portion of the scene that you think is appropriate and then lock that setting in regardless of how the scene looks when you recompose. An example of this would be when you're shooting a photograph of someone and a large amount of blue sky appears in the picture. Normally, the meter might be fooled by all that bright sky and try to reduce the exposure. Using AE Lock, you can establish the correct metering by zooming in on the subject (or even pointing the camera toward the ground), taking the meter reading and locking it in with the AE-L feature, and then recomposing and taking your photo with the locked-in exposure.

SHOOTING WITH THE AE LOCK FEATURE

1. Find the AE Lock button on the back of the camera and place your thumb on it.

2. While looking through the viewfinder, place the focus point on your subject, press the shutter release button halfway to get a meter reading, and focus the camera.

3. Press and hold the AE Lock button to lock in the meter reading. You should see the AE-L indicator in the viewfinder.

4. While pressing in the AE-L button, recompose your shot and take the photo.

5. To take more than one photo without having to take another meter reading, just hold down the AE Lock button until you are done using the meter setting.

Manual Callout

There is a way to lock in your AE-L reading so that you can continue shooting without having to hold in the AE-L button. This involves changing the button function in the custom menu, but I prefer to leave this feature turned off because I would, more often than not, forget that it is on and end up using the wrong metering for a new subject. If you want to learn more about this feature, check out pages 69 and 166 of the reference manual on the companion CD that came with the camera.

FOCUSING: THE EYES HAVE IT

It has been said that the eyes are the windows to the soul, and nothing could be truer when you are taking a photograph of someone (**Figure 6.8**). You could have the perfect composition and exposure, but if the eyes aren't sharp the entire image suffers. While there are many different focusing modes to choose from on your D5100, for portrait work you can't beat AF-S (Single-servo AF) mode using a single focusing point. AF-S focusing will establish a single focus for the lens and then hold it until you take the photograph; the other focusing modes continue focusing until the photograph is taken. The single-point selection lets you place the focusing point right on your subject's eye and set that spot as the critical focus spot. Using AF-S mode lets you get that focus and recompose all in one motion.

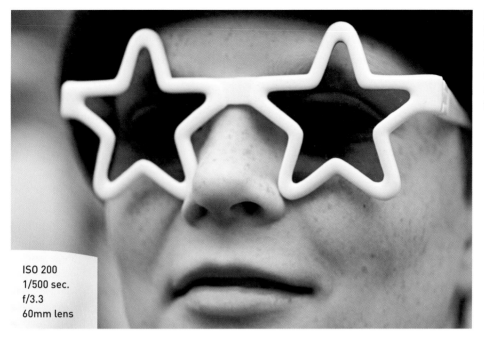

FIGURE 6.8
When photograph-
ing people, you
should almost
always place the
emphasis on
the eyes.

ISO 200
1/500 sec.
f/3.3
60mm lens

SETTING UP FOR AF-S FOCUS MODE

1. Press the **i** button to activate the cursor in the information screen.

2. Use the Multi-selector to move the cursor to the Focus mode icon and press the OK button (**A**).

3. Select the AF-S setting and then press the OK button (**B**).

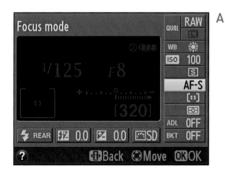

A

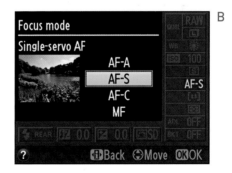

B

1. Press the **i** button to activate the cursor in the information screen.

2. Use the Multi-selector to move the cursor to the AF-area mode icon and press the OK button (**A**).

3. Select the Single-point AF icon and press the OK button (**B**).

4. When you are back in shooting mode, use the Multi-selector to move the focus point to one of the 11 available positions. This is visible while looking through the viewfinder but also on the information screen.

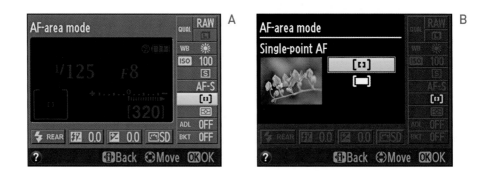

Now, to shoot using this focus point, place that point on your subject's eye and press the shutter button halfway until focus locks (you will hear the chirp if the audible beep is turned on). While still holding the shutter button down halfway, recompose if necessary and take your shot.

I typically use the center point for focus selection. I find it easier to place that point directly on the location where my critical focus should be established and then recompose the shot. Even though the single point can be selected from any of the focus points, it typically takes longer to figure out where that point should be in relation to my subject. By using the center point, I can quickly establish focus and get on with my shooting.

CLASSIC BLACK AND WHITE PORTRAITS

There is something timeless about a black and white portrait. It eliminates the distraction of color and puts all the emphasis on the subject. To get great black and whites without having to resort to any image-processing software, set your picture control to Monochrome (**Figure 6.9**). You should know that the picture controls are automatically applied when shooting with the JPEG file format. If you are shooting in RAW, the picture that shows up on your rear LCD display will look black and white, but it will appear as a color image if you open it in non-Nikon RAW processing software (like Adobe Photoshop Lightroom or Apple Aperture). This is because the nature of RAW data is that it hasn't been processed by the camera. If using Nikon's ViewNX 2 or Capture NX 2 software, you'll see the assigned picture control when you first open the photo, but you can use the software to apply any picture control to your RAW image.

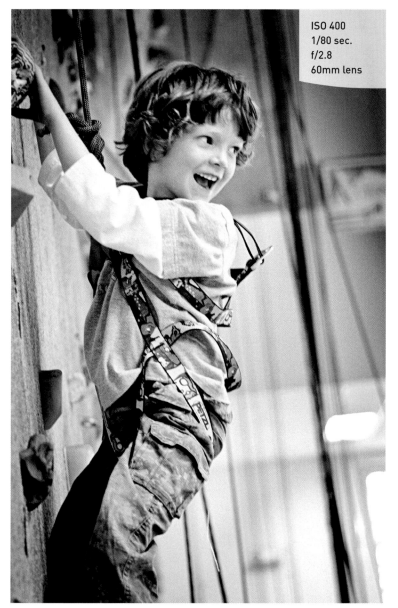

ISO 400
1/80 sec.
f/2.8
60mm lens

FIGURE 6.9
Getting high-quality black and white portraits is as simple as setting the picture control to Monochrome.

The real key to using the Monochrome picture control is to customize it for your portrait subject. The control can be changed to alter the sharpness and contrast. For women, children, puppies, and anyone else who should look somewhat soft, set the Sharpness setting to 0 or 1. For old cowboys, longshoremen, and anyone else who you want to look really detailed, try a setting of 6 or 7. I typically like to leave Contrast at a setting of around –1 or –2. This gives me a nice range of tones throughout the image.

The other adjustment that you should try is to change the picture control's Filter effect from None to one of the four available settings (Yellow, Orange, Red, and Green). Using the filters will have the effect of either lightening or darkening the skin tones. The Red and Yellow filters usually lighten skin, while the Green filter can make skin appear a bit darker. Experiment to see which one works best for your subject.

SETTING YOUR PICTURE CONTROL TO MONOCHROME

1. Press the **i** button to activate the cursor in the information screen.

2. Use the Multi-selector to move the cursor to the Set Picture Control icon and press the OK button (**A**).

3. Select the MC setting, then press the OK button.

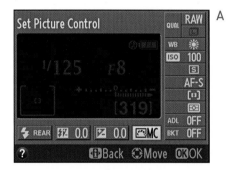

CUSTOMIZING YOUR MONOCHROME PICTURE CONTROL

1. Start by pressing the Menu button.

2. Navigate to the Shooting menu, select Manage Picture Control, and press OK (**B**).

3. Select Save/Edit and press OK again.

4. Scroll down to Monochrome and then press the Multi-selector to the right to enter the customization screen (**C**). Don't hit the OK button here or it will go right to the Save As screen.

5. Now that you are in the customize screen, make the desired changes to each of the different items (move the Multi-selector up or down to select the item you want to change and left to right to change the settings) (**D**).

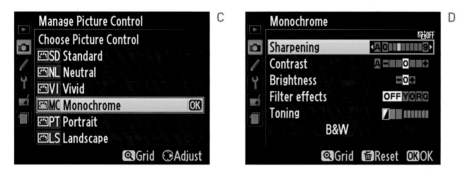

6. When you have everything set the way you want, press the OK button to save your new custom settings. Select the first available slot (C1) and press right on the Multi-selector (**E**). You can now use the default name or type in one of your own. To delete the current name, use the Command dial to select the letter location and hit the Delete (trashcan) button. Then use the Multi-selector to spell the new name (**F**). When done, press the OK button.

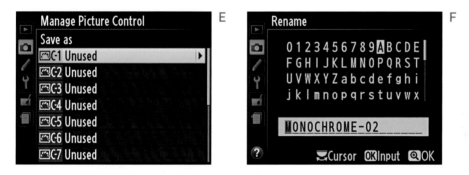

7. To use the new setting, follow the previous set of directions for selecting a picture control except this time, choose C1 instead of MC.

THE PORTRAIT PICTURE CONTROL FOR BETTER SKIN TONES

As long as we are talking about picture controls for portraits, there is another control on your D5100 that has been tuned specifically for this type of shooting. Oddly enough, it's called Portrait. To set this control on your camera, simply follow the same directions as earlier, except this time, select the Portrait control (PT) instead of Monochrome. There are also individual options for the Portrait control that, like the Monochrome control, include sharpness and contrast. You can also change the saturation (how intense the colors will be) and the hue, which lets you change the skin tones from more reddish to more yellowish. I prefer brighter colors, so I like to boost the Saturation setting to +2 and leave everything else at the defaults. You won't be able to use the same adjustments for everyone, especially when it comes to color tone, so do some experimenting to see what works best.

DETECT FACES WITH LIVE VIEW

Face detection in digital cameras has been around for a few years, but it's still a new concept in the world of the dSLR. Your D5100 has four different autofocus area modes for Live View: Wide-area, Normal-area, Subject-tracking, and Face-priority. Face-priority mode is probably the slowest of the Live View focusing modes, so I use it mostly when I am working with a tripod or my subjects are going to remain fairly still. When you turn on Live View with Face-priority focusing, the camera does an amazing thing: It zeroes in on any face appearing on the LCD and places a box around it (**Figure 6.10**). I'm not sure how it works; it just does.

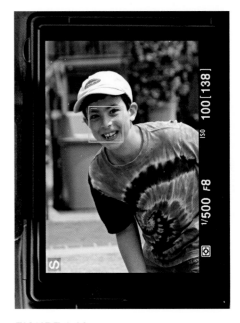

FIGURE 6.10
The Live View Face-priority mode can lock in on your subject's face for easy focusing.

If there is more than one face in the frame, a box will appear over each of them, but it will only use one to focus. The box that has the small inside corners outlined is the one the camera is currently using for focus (this is usually the face closest to the camera).

SETTING UP AND SHOOTING WITH LIVE VIEW AND FACE PRIORITY FOCUSING

1. Activate the Live View function by moving the Lv switch under the Mode dial on top of the camera.

2. Press the **i** button to enter the Information screen and use the Multi-selector to navigate to the AF-area mode icon (**A**).

3. Press the OK button to enter the AF-area mode selection screen.

4. Use the Multi-selector to choose Face-priority AF and press the OK button (**B**).

5. Press the shutter release button to exit the menu mode and get ready for shooting.

6. Point your camera at a person and watch as the frame appears over the face in the LCD.

7. Depress and hold the shutter release button halfway to focus on the face and wait until you hear the confirmation chirp.

8. Press the shutter button fully to take the photograph.

> ## Manual Callout
>
> There is a complete chapter in the printed user manual that is dedicated to using Live View mode. It starts on page 44.

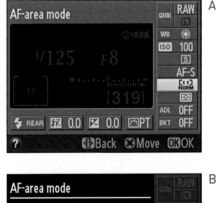

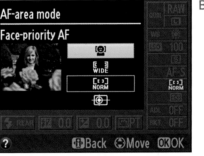

Live View can be used with any of the professional modes, or you can combine it with the Portrait scene mode.

USING LIVE VIEW'S GRID OVERLAY

There is another benefit to using Live View: the Grid overlay. This is a feature that actually places a grid over your image, dividing it into sectors, which can be of great benefit in properly composing your image for portraits (**Figure 6.11**). Check out Chapter 7 for full instructions on setting up and using this feature.

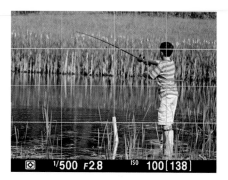

FIGURE 6.11
Using Live View's Grid option can help you compose your shots.

USE FILL FLASH FOR REDUCING SHADOWS

A common problem when taking pictures of people outside, especially during the midday hours, is that the overhead sun can create dark shadows under the eyes and chin. You could have your subject turn his or her face to the sun, but that is usually considered cruel and unusual punishment. So how can you have your subject's back to the sun and still get a decent exposure of the face? Try turning on your flash to fill in the shadows. This also works well when you are photographing someone with a ball cap on. The bill of the hat tends to create heavy shadows over the eyes, and the fill flash will lighten up those areas while providing a really nice catchlight in the eyes.

Another scenario where this is useful is when photographing people at sunset. At a recent dinner out with friends, I just had to capture them with the sun setting in the background as the lights of the city started to come on (**Figure 6.12**). I popped up the flash, set it to Rear Curtain Sync (more on that in Chapter 8), and reduced the flash power a little. The longer exposure captured the colors of the sky, and the fill flash provided enough light to brighten the faces and add a little catchlight.

CATCHLIGHT

A *catchlight* is that little sparkle that adds life to the eyes. When you are photographing a person with a light source in front of them, you will usually get a reflection of that light in the eye, be it your flash, the sun, or something else brightly reflecting in the eye. The light is reflected off the surface of the eyes as bright highlights and serves to bring attention to the eyes.

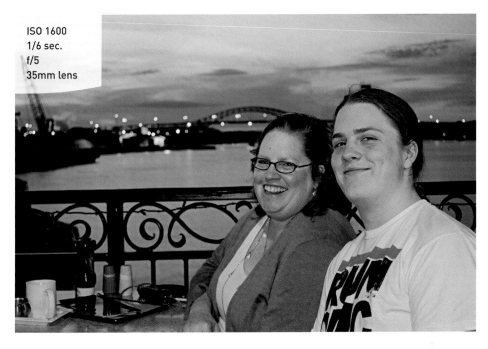

ISO 1600
1/6 sec.
f/5
35mm lens

FIGURE 6.12
I used fill flash to brighten the faces and add a little catchlight to the eyes.

The key to using the flash as a fill is to not use it on full power. If you do, the camera will try to balance the flash with the available light, and you will get a very flat and featureless face.

SETTING UP AND SHOOTING WITH FILL FLASH

1. Press the pop-up flash button to raise your pop-up flash into the ready position.

2. Press the **i** button to activate the cursor in the information screen.

3. Use the Multi-selector to navigate to the Flash Compensation icon located along the bottom of the screen and press the OK button (**A**).

4. Select a flash compensation setting of –0.3 and press OK (**B**).

5. Take a photograph and check your playback LCD to see if it looks good. If not, try reducing power in one-third stop increments.

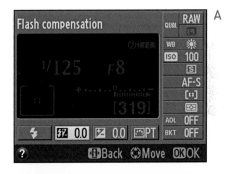

A

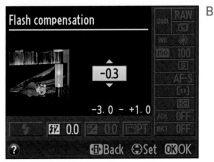

B

One problem that can quickly surface when using the on-camera flash is red-eye. Not to worry, though—we will talk about that in Chapter 8.

PORTRAITS ON THE MOVE

Not all portraits are shot with the subject sitting in a chair, posed and ready for the picture. Sometimes you might want to get an action shot that says something about the person, similar to an environmental portrait. Children, especially, just like to move. Why fight it? Set up an action portrait instead.

For the photo in **Figure 6.13**, I set my camera to Manual mode. My son was having his first ski lesson and I wanted to be sure to capture the event. I used a high shutter speed to freeze the action and a wide-open aperture to blur the background. I set the focus mode to AF-C and the drive mode to Continuous, and I fired away. I had hundreds of shots from the day, but this one of him giving me a thumbs-up despite being covered in snow from a few falls is one of my favorites.

FIGURE 6.13
I used a fast shutter speed to stop the action, along with a large aperture to decrease depth of field.

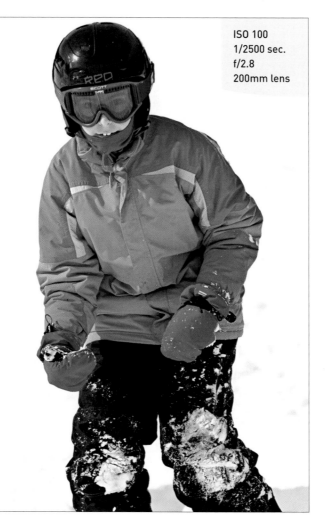

ISO 100
1/2500 sec.
f/2.8
200mm lens

TIPS FOR SHOOTING BETTER PORTRAITS

Before we get to the assignments for this chapter, I thought it might be a good idea to leave you with a few extra pointers on shooting portraits that don't necessarily have anything specific to do with your camera. There are entire books that cover things like portrait lighting, posing, and so on. But here are a few pointers that will make your people pics look a lot better.

AVOID THE CENTER OF THE FRAME

This falls under the category of composition. Place your subject to the side of the frame (**Figure 6.14**)—it just looks more interesting than plunking them smack dab in the middle (**Figure 6.15**).

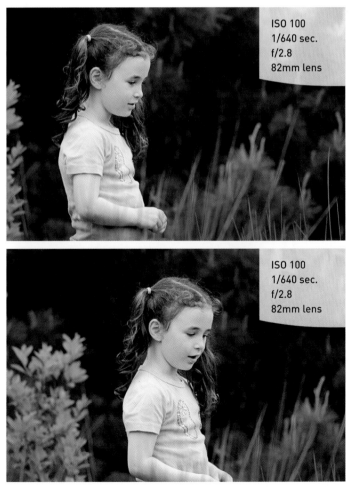

ISO 100
1/640 sec.
f/2.8
82mm lens

FIGURE 6.14
Try cropping in a bit, and place the subject's face off center to improve the shot.

ISO 100
1/640 sec.
f/2.8
82mm lens

FIGURE 6.15
Having the subject in the middle of the frame with so much empty space on the sides can make for a less-than-interesting portrait.

CHOOSE THE RIGHT LENS

Choosing the correct lens can make a huge impact on your portraits. A wide-angle lens can distort the features of your subject, which can lead to an unflattering portrait (**Figure 6.16**). Select a longer focal length if you will be close to your subject (**Figure 6.17**).

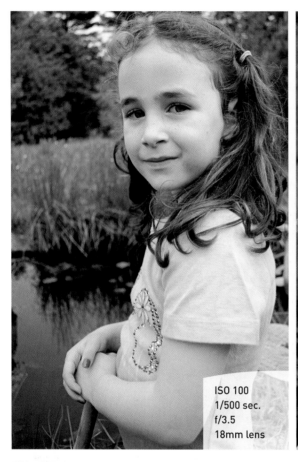

ISO 100
1/500 sec.
f/3.5
18mm lens

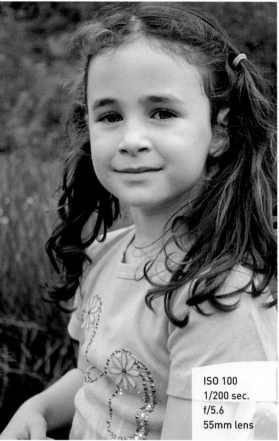

ISO 100
1/200 sec.
f/5.6
55mm lens

FIGURE 6.16
At this close distance, the 18mm lens is distorting the subject's face.

FIGURE 6.17
By zooming out to 55mm, I was able to remove the distortion for a much better photo.

DON'T CUT THEM OFF AT THE JOINT

There is an old rule about photographing people: never crop the picture at a joint. This means no cropping at the ankles, knees, elbows, or wrists (**Figure 6.18**). If you need to crop at the legs, the proper place to crop is mid-shin or mid-thigh. For the arms, try and keep it all in the frame (**Figure 6.19**), or crop just above or below the elbow.

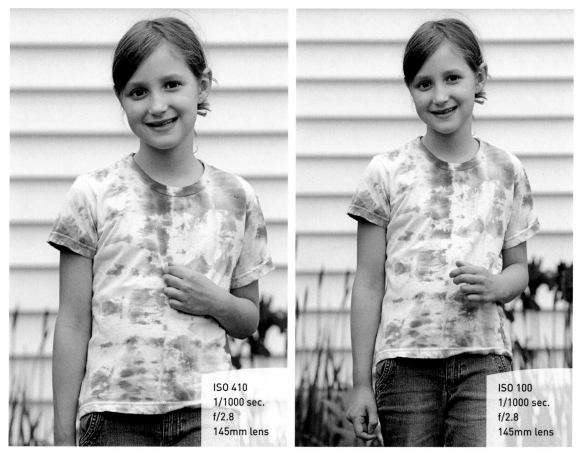

ISO 410
1/1000 sec.
f/2.8
145mm lens

ISO 100
1/1000 sec.
f/2.8
145mm lens

FIGURE 6.18
Cutting a person off at the joints, such as at the wrist, looks a bit unnatural.

FIGURE 6.19
Keep the hands in the frame when you can, as they communicate a lot about the subject.

USE THE FRAME

Turn your camera vertically for a more pleasing composition (**Figure 6.20**). Get in the habit of rotating the camera vertically after every shot you take in the horizontal position.

SUNBLOCK FOR PORTRAITS

The midday sun can be harsh and can do unflattering things to people's faces. If you can, find a shady spot out of the direct sunlight (**Figure 6.21**). You will get softer shadows, smoother skin tones, and better detail. This holds true for overcast skies as well. Just be sure to adjust your white balance accordingly.

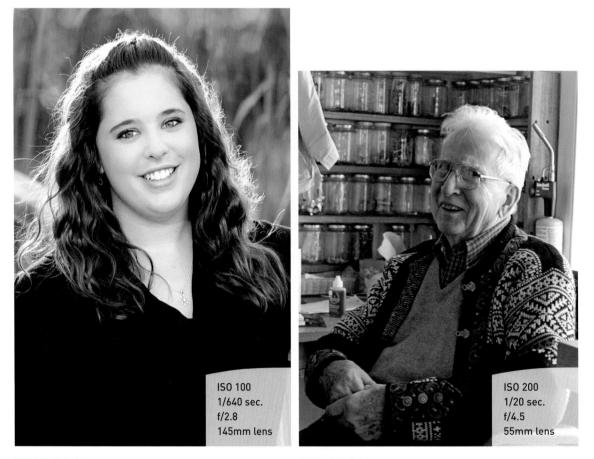

ISO 100
1/640 sec.
f/2.8
145mm lens

ISO 200
1/20 sec.
f/4.5
55mm lens

FIGURE 6.20
Get in the habit of turning your camera to a vertical position when shooting portraits. This is also referred to as portrait orientation.

FIGURE 6.21
Stepping into the open garage, where the light streaming in from a back window made for much nicer light than the midday sun outside.

FRAME THE SCENE

Using elements in the scene to create a frame around your subject is a great way to draw the viewer in. You don't have to use a window frame to do this. Just look for elements in the foreground that could be used to force the viewer's eye toward your subject (**Figure 6.22**).

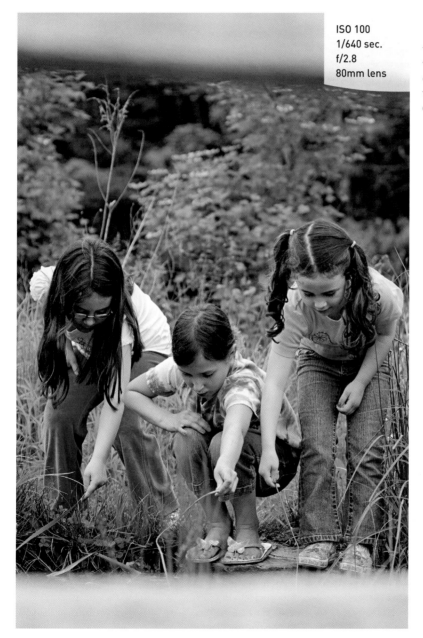

ISO 100
1/640 sec.
f/2.8
80mm lens

FIGURE 6.22
I stepped over the fence to frame the shot through the rails. Learn to use the elements of the scene to frame your subject and draw in the viewer's eyes.

KEEP AN EYE ON YOUR BACKGROUND

Sometimes it's so easy to get caught up in taking a great shot that you forget about the smaller details. Try to keep an eye on what is going on behind your subject so they don't end up with things popping out of their heads (**Figures 6.23** and **6.24**).

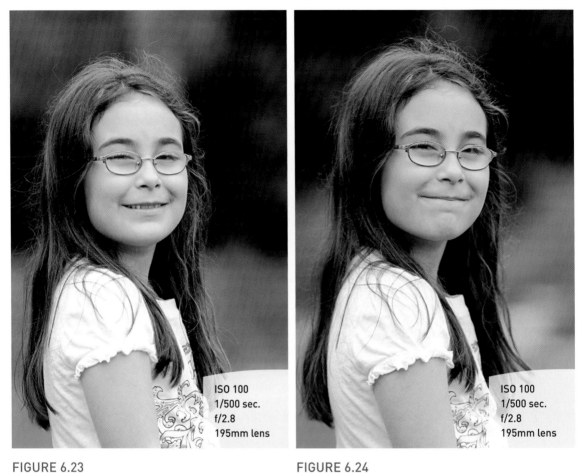

ISO 100
1/500 sec.
f/2.8
195mm lens

ISO 100
1/500 sec.
f/2.8
195mm lens

FIGURE 6.23
A fence post in the background is going right into the subject's head.

FIGURE 6.24
By moving the camera a little to the left, I was able to remove the distracting post from the photo.

GIVE THEM A HEALTHY GLOW

Nearly everyone looks better with a warm, healthy glow. Some of the best light of the day happens just a little before sundown, so shoot at that time if you can (**Figure 6.25**).

MORE THAN JUST A PRETTY FACE

Most people think of a portrait as a photo of someone's face. Don't ignore other aspects of your subject that reflect their personality—hands, especially, can go a long way to describing someone (**Figure 6.26**) and capturing the moment.

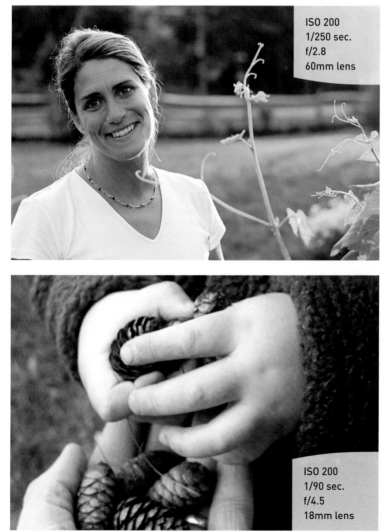

ISO 200
1/250 sec.
f/2.8
60mm lens

ISO 200
1/90 sec.
f/4.5
18mm lens

FIGURE 6.25
You just can't beat the glow of the late afternoon sun for adding warmth to your portraits.

FIGURE 6.26
There's more to a person than just their face. Hands can tell a lot about what is happening in the scene.

GET DOWN ON THEIR LEVEL

If you want better pictures of children, don't shoot from an adult's eye level. Getting the camera down to the child's level will make your images look more personal (**Figure 6.27**).

FIGURE 6.27
Sometimes taking photographs of children means lying on the floor, but the end result is a much better image.

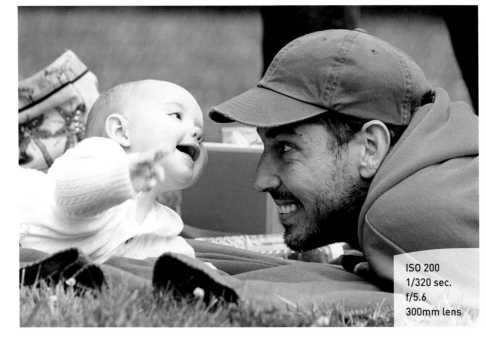

ISO 200
1/320 sec.
f/5.6
300mm lens

ELIMINATE SPACE BETWEEN YOUR SUBJECTS

One of the problems you can encounter when taking portraits of more than one person is that of personal space. What feels like a close distance to the subjects can look impersonal to the viewer. Have your subjects move close together, eliminating any open space between them (**Figure 6.28**).

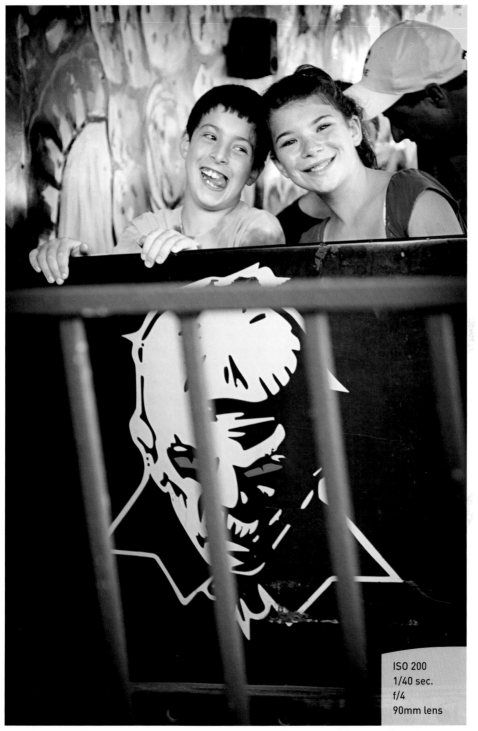

ISO 200
1/40 sec.
f/4
90mm lens

DON'T BE AFRAID TO GET CLOSE

When you are taking someone's picture, don't be afraid of getting close and filling the frame (**Figure 6.29**). This doesn't mean you have to shoot from a foot away; try zooming in and capture the details.

FIGURE 6.29
Filling the frame with the subject's face can lead to a much more intimate portrait.

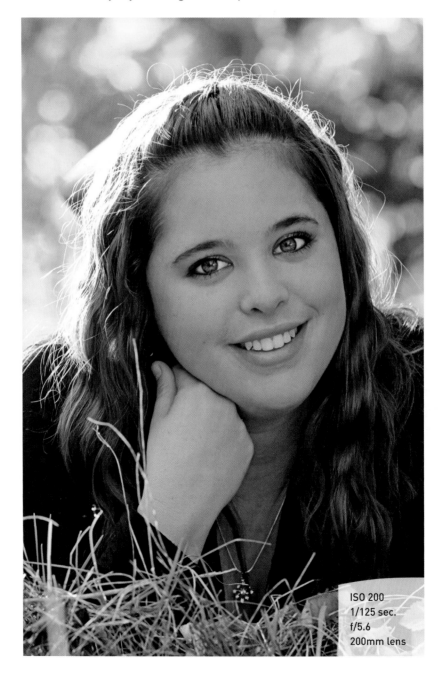

ISO 200
1/125 sec.
f/5.6
200mm lens

Chapter 6 Assignments

Depth of field in portraits

Let's start with something simple. Grab your favorite person and start experimenting with using different aperture settings. Shoot wide open (the widest your lens goes, such as f/3.5 or f/5.6) and then really stopped down (like f/22). Look at the difference in the depth of field and how it plays an important role in placing the attention on your subject. (Make sure you don't have your subject standing against the background. Give some distance so that there is a good blurring effect of the background at the wide f-stop setting.)

Discovering the qualities of natural light

Pick a nice sunny day and try shooting some portraits in the midday sun. If your subject is willing, have them turn so the sun is in their face. If they are still speaking to you after blinding them, have them turn their back to the sun. Try this with and without the fill flash so you can see the difference. Finally, move them into a completely shaded spot and take a few more.

Picking the right metering method

Find a very dark or light background and place your subject in front of it. Now take a couple of shots, giving a lot of space around your subject for the background to show. Now switch metering modes and use the AE Lock feature to get a more accurate reading of your subject. Notice the differences in exposure between the metering methods.

Picture controls for portraits

Have some fun playing with the different picture controls. Try the Portrait control as compared to the Standard. Then try out Monochrome and play with the different color filter options to see how they affect skin tones.

Share your results with the book's Flickr group!

Join the group here: flickr.com/groups/nikond5100fromsnapshotstogreatshots/

7

Landscape Photography

TIPS, TOOLS, AND TECHNIQUES TO GET THE MOST OUT OF YOUR LANDSCAPE PHOTOGRAPHY

There has always been something about shooting landscapes that has brought a sense of joy to my photography. It might have something to do with being outdoors and working at the mercy of Mother Nature. Maybe it's the way it challenges me to visualize the landscape and try to capture it with my camera. It truly is a celebration of light, composition, and the world we live in.

In this chapter, we will explore some of the features of the D5100 that not only improve the look of your landscape photography, but also make it easier to take great shots. We will also explore some typical scenarios and discuss methods to bring out the best in your landscape photography.

I've always loved snow, and I guess that is a good thing for living in the Northeast. I also think snow scenes are some of the most photogenic landscapes possible. Snowscapes are very evocative, but they also enhance contrasts and can transform even the most mundane scenery into something magical.

Waiting until there was just a little color to the sky added an element of warmth to this cold scene.

Using a wide-open aperture and focusing on the barn throws the foreground into soft focus, adding depth to the image.

Keeping the barn off center created a stronger composition.

ISO 200
1/40 sec.
f/2.8
70mm lens

A tripod was essential for eliminating camera-shake blur at the slow shutter speed.

SHARP AND IN FOCUS: USING TRIPODS

Throughout the previous chapters we have concentrated on using the camera to create great images. We will continue that trend through this chapter, but there is one additional piece of equipment that is crucial in the world of landscape shooting: the tripod. There are a couple of reasons why tripods are so critical to your landscape work, the first of which involves the time of day that you will be working. For reasons that will be explained later, the best light for most landscape work happens at sunrise and just before sunset. While these are the best times to shoot, they're also kind of dark. That means you'll be working with slow shutter speeds. Slow shutter speeds mean camera shake. Camera shake equals bad photos.

The second reason is also related to the amount of light that you're gathering with your camera. When taking landscape photos, you will usually want to be working with very small apertures, as they give you lots of depth of field. This also means that, once again, you will be working with slower-than-normal shutter speeds.

Slow shutter = camera shake = bad photos.

Do you see the pattern here? The one tool in your arsenal that will truly defeat the camera shake issue and ensure tack-sharp photos is a good tripod (**Figure 7.1**).

FIGURE 7.1
A sturdy tripod is the key to sharp landscape photos. (Photo: istockphoto/ sculpies)

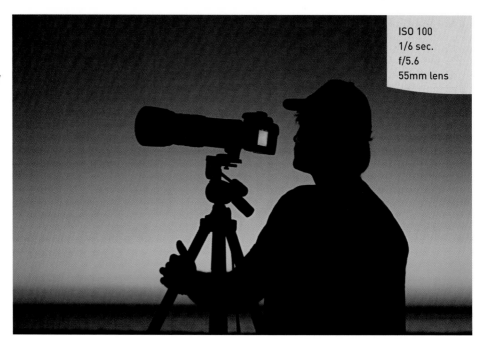

ISO 100
1/6 sec.
f/5.6
55mm lens

So what should you look for in a tripod? Well, first make sure it is sturdy enough to support your camera and any lens that you might want to use. Next, check the height of the tripod. Bending over all day to look through the viewfinder of a camera on a short tripod can wreak havoc on your back. Finally, think about getting a tripod that utilizes a quick-release head. This usually employs a plate that screws into the bottom of the camera and then quickly snaps into place on the tripod. This will be especially handy if you are going to move between shooting by hand and using the tripod. There's more information about tripods in bonus Chapter 11.

TRIPOD STABILITY

Most tripods have a center column that allows the user to extend the height of the camera above the point where the tripod legs join together. This might seem like a great idea, but the reality is that the further you raise that column, the less stable your tripod becomes. Think of a tall building that sways near the top. To get the most solid base for your camera, always try to use it with the center column at its lowest point so that your camera is right at the apex of the tripod legs.

VR LENSES AND TRIPODS DON'T MIX

If you are using Vibration Reduction (VR) lenses on your camera, you need to remember to turn this feature off when you use a tripod (**Figure 7.2**). This is because the Vibration Reduction can, while trying to minimize camera movement, actually create movement when the camera is already stable. To turn off the VR feature, just slide the VR selector switch on the side of the lens to the Off position.

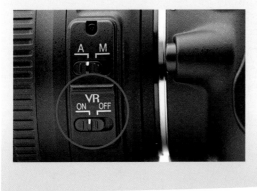

FIGURE 7.2
Turn off the Vibration Reduction feature when using a tripod.

SELECTING THE PROPER ISO

When shooting most landscape scenes, the ISO should only be increased as a last resort. While it is easy to select a higher ISO to get a smaller aperture, the noise that it can introduce into your images can be quite harmful. The noise is not only visible as large grainy artifacts, but it can also be multi-colored, which further degrades the image quality.

Take a look at **Figures 7.3** and **7.4**, which show a photograph taken with an ISO of 1600. The purpose was to shorten the shutter speed and still use a small aperture setting of f/11. The problem is that the noise level is so high that, in addition to being distracting, it is obscuring fine details in the plants and trees.

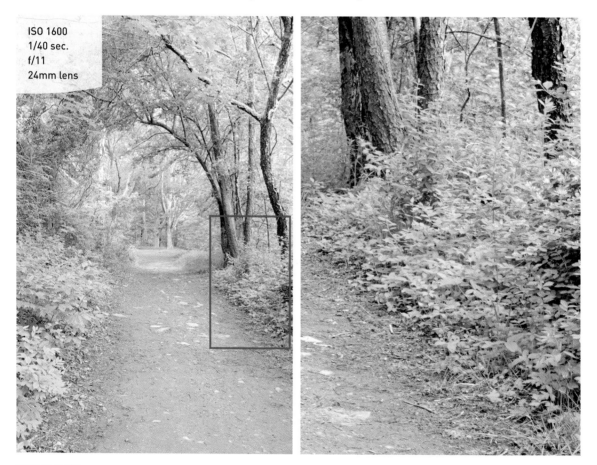

ISO 1600
1/40 sec.
f/11
24mm lens

FIGURE 7.3
A high ISO setting created a lot of digital noise in the shadows.

FIGURE 7.4
When the image is enlarged, the noise is even more apparent. It is most noticeable as the grainy texture in the shadows.

Now check out another image that was taken in the same dim light on the trail, but with a much lower ISO setting (**Figures 7.5** and **7.6**). As you can see, the noise levels are much lower, which means that my blacks look black, and the fine details are beautifully captured.

When shooting landscapes, set your ISO to the lowest possible setting at all times. Between the use of Vibration Reduction lenses (if you are shooting handheld) and a good tripod, there should be few circumstances where you would need to shoot landscapes with anything above an ISO of 400.

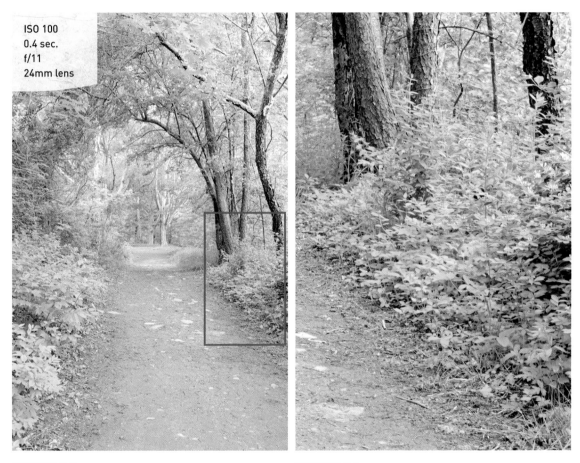

ISO 100
0.4 sec.
f/11
24mm lens

FIGURE 7.5
By lowering the ISO to 100, I was able to avoid the noise and capture a clean image.

FIGURE 7.6
Zooming in shows that the noise levels for this image are almost nonexistent.

USING NOISE REDUCTION

Both of the trail images were taken with a tripod, but the image set to an ISO of 100 required a much longer shutter speed (4/10 of a second at ISO 100) compared to the high ISO image (1/40 of a second at ISO 1600). The temptation to use higher ISOs should always be avoided, as the end result will be more image noise and less detail.

There can be an issue when using a low ISO setting: the sometimes-lengthy shutter speeds can also introduce noise. This noise is a result of the heating of the camera sensor as it is being exposed to light. This effect is not visible in short exposures, but as you start shooting with shutter speeds that exceed one second, the level of image noise can increase. Your camera has a couple of features that you can turn on to combat noise from long exposures and high ISOs.

SETTING UP NOISE REDUCTION

1. Press the Menu button, then use the Multi-selector to get to the Shooting menu.

2. Using the Multi-selector, select Long Exposure NR and then press OK (**A**). Change this option to On and press the OK button.

3. Now use the Multi-selector to get to the High ISO NR setting in the Shooting menu (it's located just under Long Exposure NR) and press OK (**B**).

4. ISO noise reduction comes in four flavors: High, Normal, Low, and Off. Set this to Normal for everyday shooting or to High for those instances where you have to significantly raise your ISO (**C**).

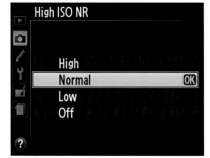

A

SHOOTING MENU	
Color space	Adobe
Active D-Lighting	OFF
HDR (high dynamic range)	OFF
Long exposure NR	ON
High ISO NR	NORM
ISO sensitivity settings	--
Release mode	S
Multiple exposure	OFF

B

SHOOTING MENU	
Color space	Adobe
Active D-Lighting	OFF
HDR (high dynamic range)	OFF
Long exposure NR	ON
High ISO NR	NORM
ISO sensitivity settings	--
Release mode	S
Multiple exposure	OFF

C

High ISO NR

High
Normal   OK
Low
Off

SELECTING A WHITE BALANCE

This probably seems like a no-brainer. If it's sunny, select Daylight. If it's overcast, choose the Shade or Cloudy setting. Those choices wouldn't be wrong for those circumstances, but why limit yourself? Sometimes you can actually change the mood of the photo by selecting a white balance that doesn't quite fit the light for the scene that you are shooting.

Figure 7.7 is an example of a correct white balance. It was late afternoon and the sun was starting to move low in the sky, giving everything that warm afternoon glow. The white balance for this image was set to Daylight.

But what if I want to make the scene look like it was shot in the early morning hours? Simple, I just change the white balance to Fluorescent, which is a much cooler setting (**Figure 7.8**).

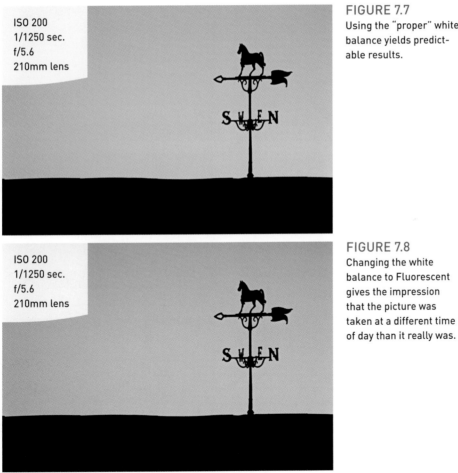

ISO 200
1/1250 sec.
f/5.6
210mm lens

FIGURE 7.7
Using the "proper" white balance yields predictable results.

ISO 200
1/1250 sec.
f/5.6
210mm lens

FIGURE 7.8
Changing the white balance to Fluorescent gives the impression that the picture was taken at a different time of day than it really was.

You can select the most appropriate white balance for your shooting conditions in a couple of ways. The first is to just take a shot, review it on the LCD, and keep the one you like. Of course, you would need to take one for each white balance setting, which means that you will have to take about seven different shots to see which is most pleasing.

The second method, and my personal favorite, doesn't require taking a single shot. Instead, it uses Live View to get perfectly selected white balances. Live View gives instant feedback as you scroll through all of the white balance settings and displays them for you right on the LCD. Even better, you can choose a custom setting that will let you dial in exactly the right look for your image.

To use Live View to preview the white balance, first you have to customize the Function button.

CUSTOMIZING THE FUNCTION BUTTON FOR WHITE BALANCE

1. Press the Menu button and use the Multi-selector to access the Custom Setting menu (**A**).

2. Now highlight menu item f: Controls and press OK.

3. Select item f1: Assign Fn Button and press OK (**B**).

4. Now select WB: White Balance and press OK (**C**). This will give you quick access to the white balance options by pressing the Function button.

USING LIVE VIEW TO PREVIEW DIFFERENT WHITE BALANCE SETTINGS

1. Rotate the Live View switch located under the Mode dial on top of the camera.

2. With Live View activated, press the Function button on the front of the camera (it's located between the lens release and flash buttons).

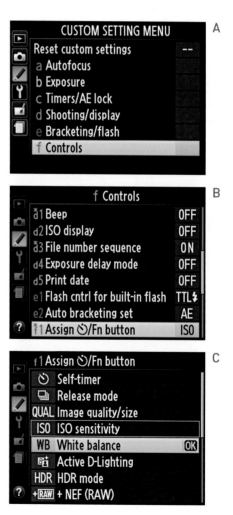

3. While holding the Function button, use the Command dial to select from among the different white balance choices while viewing the effect on the rear LCD.

4. To lock in your change, just release the Function button and then move the Lv switch to exit Live View mode.

USING THE LANDSCAPE PICTURE CONTROL

When shooting landscapes, I always look for great color and contrast. This is one of the reasons that so many landscape shots are taken in the early morning or during sunset. The light is much more vibrant and colorful at these times of day and adds a sense of drama to an image.

You can help boost this effect, especially in the less-than-golden hours of the day, by using the Landscape picture control (**Figure 7.9**). Just as in the Landscape mode found in the automatic scene modes, you can set up your landscape shooting so that you capture images with increased sharpness and a slight boost in blues and greens. This control will add some pop to your landscapes without the need for additional processing in any software.

Manual Callout

Check out page 91 in the reference manual on the companion CD that came with your camera for more information on setting picture controls.

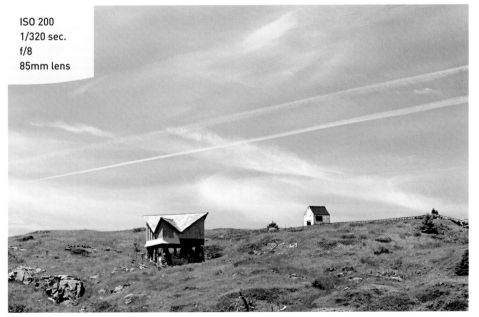

ISO 200
1/320 sec.
f/8
85mm lens

FIGURE 7.9
Using the Landscape picture control can add sharpness and more vivid color to skies and vegetation.

SETTING UP THE LANDSCAPE PICTURE CONTROL

1. Press the **i** button, use the Multi-selector to highlight the Set Picture Control feature (this is normally set to SD), and press OK (**A**).

2. Now use the Multi-selector to scroll down to the LS option and press OK to lock in your change (**B**).

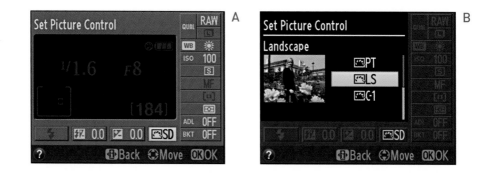

The camera will now apply the Landscape picture control to all of your photos. This style will be locked in to the camera even after turning it off and back on again, so make sure to change it back to SD when you are done with your landscape shoot.

TAMING OVEREXPOSURE WITH EXPOSURE COMPENSATION

Balancing exposure in scenes that have a wide contrast in tonal ranges can be extremely challenging. The one thing you should never do is overexpose your photos (skies are especially vulnerable) to the point of blowing out your highlights (unless, of course, that is the look you are going for). It's one thing to have white clouds, but it's a completely different, and bad, thing to have no detail at all in those clouds. This usually happens when the camera is trying to gain exposure in the darker areas of the image (**Figure 7.10**). The one way to tell if you have blown out your highlights is to turn on the Highlight Alert, or "blinkies," feature on your camera (see the "How I Shoot" section in Chapter 4). When you take a shot where the highlights are exposed beyond the point of having any detail, that area will blink in your LCD display. It is up to you to determine if that particular area is important enough to regain detail by altering your exposure. If the answer is yes, then the easiest way to go about it is to use some exposure compensation.

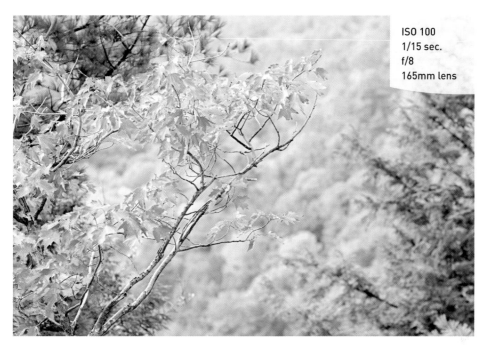

ISO 100
1/15 sec.
f/8
165mm lens

FIGURE 7.10
The darker colors in the background caused the meter to overexpose slightly, which washes out color and loses detail in the highlights. All the highlights on the leaves were blinking on the LCD display.

With this feature, you can force your camera to choose an exposure that ranges, in 1/3-stop increments, from five stops over to five stops under the metered exposure (**Figure 7.11**).

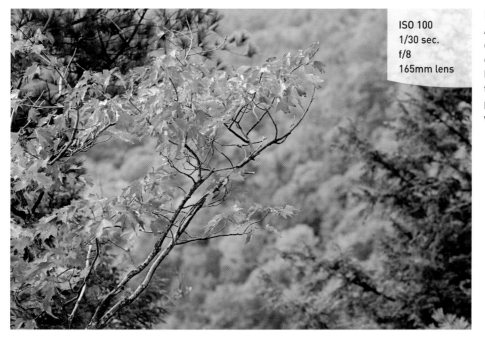

ISO 100
1/30 sec.
f/8
165mm lens

FIGURE 7.11
A compensation of one stop of under-exposure brought back the detail in the highlights and produced a more vibrant photo.

When you hear someone refer to a subject as being *high key*, it usually means that the entire image is composed of a very bright subject with very few shadow areas—think snow or beach. It makes sense, then, that a *low-key* subject has very few highlight areas and a predominance of shadow areas. Think of a cityscape at night as an example of a low-key photo.

USING EXPOSURE COMPENSATION TO REGAIN DETAIL IN HIGHLIGHTS

1. Activate the camera meter by lightly pressing the shutter release button.

2. Using your index finger, press and hold the Exposure Compensation button to change the over-/underexposure setting by rotating the Command dial.

3. Rotate the Command dial to the right one click and take another picture (each click of the Command dial is a 1/3-stop change).

4. If the blinkies are gone, you are good to go. If not, keep subtracting from your exposure by 1/3 of a stop until you have a good exposure in the highlights.

I generally keep my camera set to –1/3 stop for most of my landscape work unless I am working with a location that is very dark or low key.

You can also change the Exposure Compensation setting by using the **i** button on the rear of the camera.

ADJUSTING EXPOSURE COMPENSATION USING THE I BUTTON

1. Press the **i** button to activate the cursor in the information display.

2. Use the Multi-selector to move the cursor to the Exposure Compensation position and press OK.

3. Now press in a downward direction on the Multi-selector to lower the compensation by 1/3 of a stop. Each press downward will continue to reduce the exposure in 1/3-stop increments for up to five stops (although I rarely need to go past one stop).

It should be noted that any exposure compensation will remain in place even after turning the camera off and then on again. Don't forget to reset it once you have successfully captured your image. Also, exposure compensation only works in the

Program, Shutter Priority, and Aperture Priority modes. Changing between these three modes will hold the compensation you set while switching from one to the other. When you change the mode dial to one of the automatic scene modes or to Manual, the compensation will set itself to zero.

SHOOTING BEAUTIFUL BLACK AND WHITE LANDSCAPES

There is almost nothing as timeless as a beautiful black and white landscape photo. For many, it is the purest form of photography. The genre conjures up thoughts of Ansel Adams out in Yosemite Valley, capturing stunning monoliths with his 8x10 view camera. Well, just because you are shooting with a digital camera doesn't mean you can't create your own stunning photos using the power of the Monochrome picture control. (See the "Classic Black and White Portraits" section of Chapter 6 for instructions on setting up this feature.) Not only can you shoot in black and white, you can also customize the camera to apply built-in filters to lighten or darken different elements within your scene, as well as add contrast and definition.

The four filter colors are red, yellow, green, and orange. The most typically used filters in black and white photography are red and yellow. This is because the color of these filters will darken opposite colors and lighten similar colors. So if you want to darken a blue sky, you would use a yellow filter because blue is the opposite of yellow. To darken green foliage, you would use a red filter. Check out the series of shots in **Figure 7.12** with different filters applied.

You can see that there is no real difference in contrast between the color and the black and white image with no filter. The red filter has the effect of darkening the skies slightly and giving a darker look to the grass and trees, while lightening the rusted metal in the foreground. Using the yellow filter makes the rusted metal darker as well as the grass and sky. For this particular shot, I much prefer the look of the yellow filter.

Other options in the Monochrome picture control enable you to adjust the sharpness and contrast, and even add some color toning to the final image. This information is also in the "Classic Black and White Portraits" section of Chapter 6. I like to have Sharpness set to 5 and Contrast set to +1 for my landscape images. This gives an overall look to the black and white image that is reminiscent of the classic black and white films. Experiment with the various settings to find the combination that is most pleasing to you.

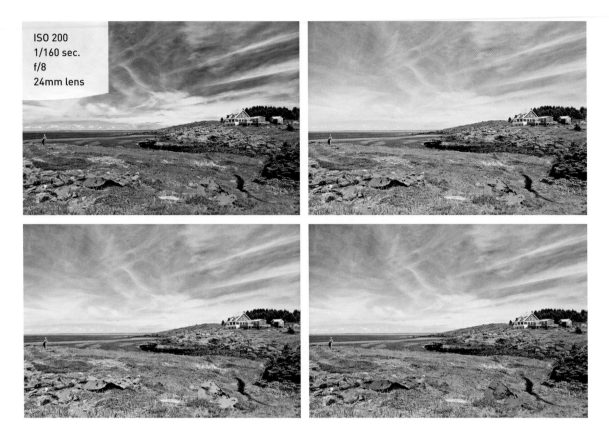

ISO 200
1/160 sec.
f/8
24mm lens

FIGURE 7.12

Adding color filter settings to the Monochrome picture control allows you to lighten or darken elements in your scene. The top right image has no filter applied to it. The bottom left has a red filter, and the bottom right has a yellow filter.

THE GOLDEN LIGHT

If you ask any professional landscape photographer what their favorite time of day to shoot is, chances are they will tell you it's the hours surrounding daybreak and sunset (**Figures 7.13** and **7.14**). The reason for this is that the light is coming from a very low angle to the landscape, which creates shadows and gives depth and character. There is also a quality to the light that seems cleaner and more colorful than the light you get when shooting at midday. One thing that can dramatically improve any morning or evening shot is the presence of clouds. The sun will fill the underside of the clouds with a palette of colors and add drama to your skies.

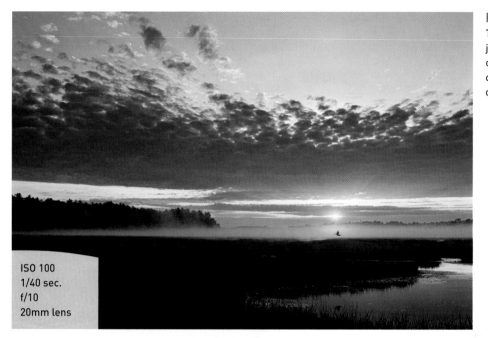

ISO 100
1/40 sec.
f/10
20mm lens

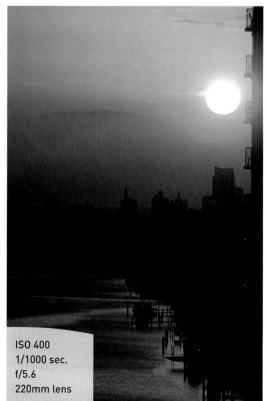

FIGURE 7.14
Late afternoon sun is usually warmer and adds drama and warmth to the clouds.

ISO 400
1/1000 sec.
f/5.6
220mm lens

These two terms are used to describe the overall colorcast of an image. Reds and yellows are said to be *warm*, which is usually the look that you get from the late afternoon sun. Blue is usually the predominant color when talking about a *cool* cast.

WHERE TO FOCUS

Large landscape scenes are great fun to photograph, but they can present a problem: Where exactly do you focus when you want everything to be sharp? Since our goal is to create a great landscape photo, we will need to concentrate on how to best create an image that is tack sharp, with a depth of field that renders great focus throughout the scene.

I have already stressed the importance of a good tripod when shooting landscapes. The tripod lets you concentrate on the aperture portion of the exposure without worrying how long your shutter will be open. This is because the tripod provides the stability to handle any shutter speed you might need when shooting at small apertures. I find that for most of my landscape work I set my camera to Aperture Priority mode and the ISO to 100-200 (for a clean, noise-free image).

However, shooting with the smallest aperture on your lens doesn't necessarily mean that you will get the proper sharpness throughout your image. The real key is knowing where in the scene to focus your lens to maximize the depth of field for your chosen aperture. To do this, you must utilize something called the "hyper focal distance" of your lens.

Hyper focal distance, also referred to as HFD, is the point of focus that will give you the greatest acceptable sharpness from a point near your camera all the way out to infinity. If you combine good HFD practice in combination with a small aperture, you will get images that are sharp to infinity.

There are a couple of ways to do this, and the one that is probably the easiest, as you might guess, is the one that is most widely used by working pros. When you have your shot all set up and composed, focus on an object that is about one-third of the distance into your frame (**Figure 7.15**). It is usually pretty close to the proper distance and will render favorable results. When you have the focus set, take a photograph and then zoom in on the preview on your LCD to check the sharpness of your image.

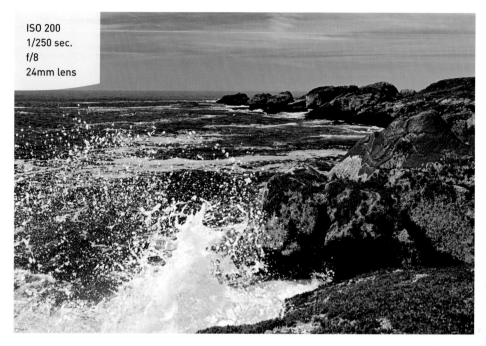

ISO 200
1/250 sec.
f/8
24mm lens

TACK SHARP

Here's one of those terms that photographers like to throw around. *Tack sharp* refers not only to the focus of an image but also to the overall sharpness of the image. This usually means that there is excellent depth of field in terms of sharp focus for all elements in the image. It also means that there is no sign of camera shake, which can give soft edges to subjects that should look nice and crisp. To get your images tack sharp, use a small depth of field, don't forget your tripod, use the self-timer to activate the shutter if no cable release is handy, and practice achieving good hyper focal distance (HFD) when picking your point of focus.

One thing to remember is that as your lens gets wider in focal length, your HFD will be closer to the camera position. This is because the wider the lens, the greater depth of field you can achieve. This is yet another reason why a good wide angle lens is indispensable to the landscape shooter.

EASIER FOCUSING

There's no denying that the automatic focus features on the D5100 are great, but sometimes it just pays to turn them off and go manual. This is especially true if you are shooting on a tripod: Once you have your shot composed in the viewfinder and you are ready to focus, chances are that the area you want to focus on is not going to be in the area of one of the focus points. Often this is the case when you have a foreground element that is fairly low in the frame. You could use a single focus point set low in your viewfinder and then pan the camera down until it rests on your subject. But then you would have to press the shutter button halfway to focus the camera and then try to recompose and lock down the tripod. It's no easy task.

But you can have the best of both worlds by having the camera focus for you, then switching to manual focus to comfortably recompose your shot (**Figure 7.16**).

GETTING FOCUSED WHILE USING A TRIPOD

1. Set up your shot and find the area that you want to focus on.

2. Pan your tripod head so that your active focus point is on that spot.

3. Press the shutter button halfway to focus the camera.

4. Switch the camera to manual focus by sliding the switch on the lens barrel from A to M.

5. Recompose the composition on the tripod and then take the shot.

The camera will fire without trying to refocus the lens. This works especially well for wide-angle lenses, which can be difficult to focus in manual mode.

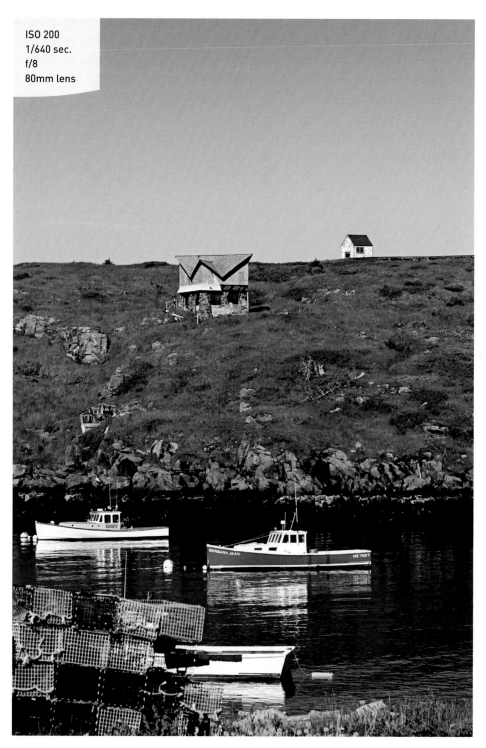

ISO 200
1/640 sec.
f/8
80mm lens

FIGURE 7.16
Using the DOF
(depth of field) one-
third rule, I focused
on the red lobster
boat, then switched
the lens to manual
focus before recom-
posing for the final
shot.

MAKING WATER FLUID

There's little that is quite as satisfying for the landscape shooter as capturing a silky waterfall shot. Creating the smooth-flowing effect is as simple as adjusting your shutter speed to allow the water to be in motion while the shutter is open. The key is to have your camera on a stable platform (such as a tripod) so that you can use a shutter speed that's long enough to work (**Figure 7.17**). To achieve a great effect, use a shutter speed that is at least 1/15 of a second or longer.

SETTING UP FOR A WATERFALL SHOT

1. Attach the camera to your tripod, then compose and focus your shot.
2. Make sure the ISO is set to 200 (or lower).
3. Using Aperture Priority mode, set your aperture to the smallest opening (such as f/22 or f/36).
4. Press the shutter button halfway so the camera takes a meter reading.
5. Check to see if the shutter speed is 1/15 of a second or slower.
6. Take a photo and then check the image on the LCD.

You can also use Shutter Priority mode for this effect by dialing in the desired shutter speed and having the camera set the aperture for you. I prefer to use Aperture Priority to ensure that I have the greatest depth of field possible.

If the water is blinking on the LCD, indicating a loss of detail in the highlights, then use the Exposure Compensation feature (as discussed earlier in this chapter) to bring details back into the waterfall. You will need to have the Highlight Alert feature turned on to check for overexposure (see "How I Shoot" in Chapter 4).

There is a possibility that you will not be able to have a shutter speed that is long enough to capture a smooth, silky effect, especially if you are shooting in bright daylight conditions. To overcome this obstacle, you need a filter for your lens—either a polarizing filter or a neutral density filter. The polarizing filter redirects wavelengths of light to create more vibrant colors, reduce reflections, and darken blue skies, as well as lengthening exposure times by two stops due to the darkness of the filter. It is a handy filter for landscape work (**Figure 7.18**). The neutral density filter is typically just a dark piece of glass that serves to darken the scene by one, two, or three stops. This allows you to use slower shutter speeds during bright conditions. Think of it as sunglasses for your camera lens. You will find more discussion on filters in bonus Chapter 11.

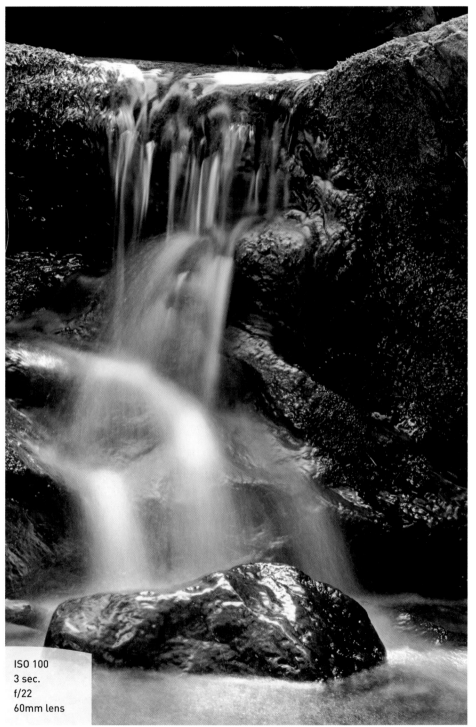

ISO 100
3 sec.
f/22
60mm lens

FIGURE 7.17
I used a tripod
and a long expo-
sure time to give
the waterfall its
silky look.

FIGURE 7.18
I used a neutral density filter to add two stops of exposure, thus allowing for a longer exposure time under the rising sun and transforming the waves into a silky mist. I got the added benefit of darkening the sky.

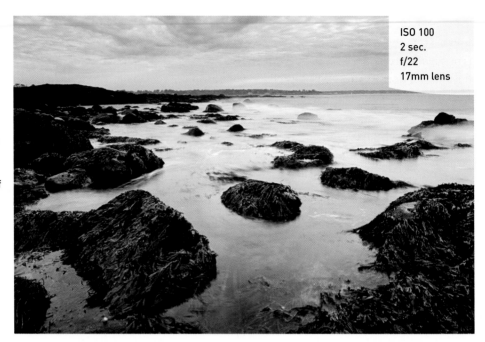

ISO 100
2 sec.
f/22
17mm lens

DIRECTING THE VIEWER: A WORD ABOUT COMPOSITION

As a photographer, it's your job to lead the viewer through your image. You accomplish this by utilizing the principles of composition, which is the arrangement of elements in the scene that draw the viewer's eyes through your image and holds their attention. As the director of this viewing, you need to understand how people see, and then use that information to focus their attention on the most important elements in your image.

There is a general order at which we look at elements in a photograph. The first is brightness. The eye wants to travel to the brightest object within a scene. So if you have a bright sky, it's probably the first place the eye will travel to. The second order of attention is sharpness. Sharp, detailed elements will get more attention than soft, blurry areas. Finally, the eye will move to vivid colors while leaving the dull, flat colors for last. It is important to know these essentials in order to grab—and keep—the viewer's attention and then direct them through the frame.

In **Figure 7.19**, the eye is drawn to the bright wooden cross at the bottom of the frame. From there, it is pulled toward the contrast of the dark crow perched on top. Moving upward to the bright moon, then down to the sharpness and color of the flowers and grass that is anchoring the lower portion of the image. The elements within the image all help to keep the eye moving but never leave the frame.

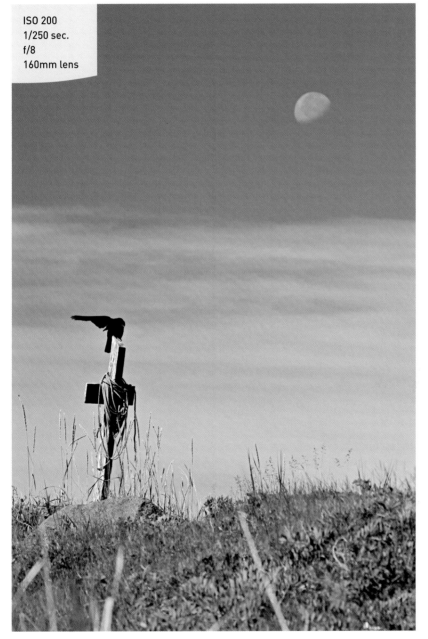

ISO 200
1/250 sec.
f/8
160mm lens

FIGURE 7.19
The composition of the elements pulls the viewer's eyes around the image, leading from one element to the next in a circular pattern.

RULE OF THIRDS

There are, in fact, quite a few philosophies concerning composition. The easiest one to begin with is known as the "rule of thirds." Using this principle, you simply divide your viewfinder into thirds by imagining two horizontal and two vertical lines that divide the frame equally.

The key to using this method of composition is to have your main subject located at or near one of the intersecting points (**Figure 7.20**).

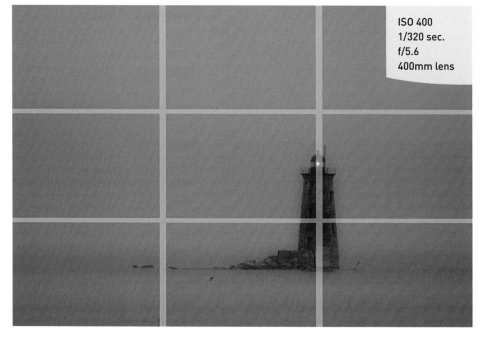

ISO 400
1/320 sec.
f/5.6
400mm lens

By placing your subject near these intersecting lines, you are giving the viewer space to move within the frame. The one thing you don't want to do is place your subject smack dab in the middle of the frame. This is sometimes referred to as "bull's eye" composition, and it requires the right subject matter for it to work. It's not always wrong, but it will usually be less appealing and may not hold the viewer's attention.

Speaking of the middle of the frame: The other general rule of thirds deals with horizon lines. Generally speaking, you should position the horizon one third of the way up or down in the frame. Splitting the frame in half by placing your horizon in the middle of the picture is akin to placing the subject in the middle of the frame; it doesn't lend a sense of importance to either the sky or the ground.

In **Figure 7.21**, I incorporated the rule of thirds by aligning my horizon in the top third of the frame and the shipwreck and rocky shoreline near the bottom third. I have also placed the shipwreck in the foreground near the intersecting lines on the right side of the frame, and a piece of the shipwreck in the bottom-left corner to balance the composition. I achieved this by choosing the right focal length (in this case, it was 200mm) and by moving my camera position until I had all of the key elements in the right place.

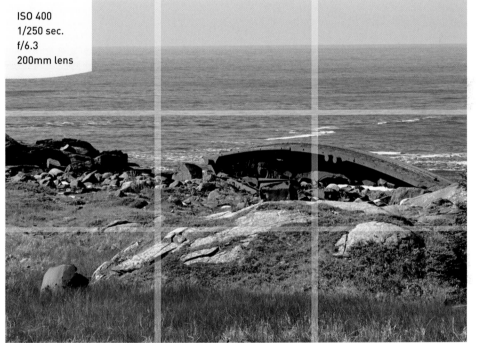

ISO 400
1/250 sec.
f/6.3
200mm lens

FIGURE 7.21
Placing the horizon of this image at the top third of the frame places emphasis on the subjects below it—the sea, the shipwreck, and interesting stones.

The D5100 has a visual tool for assisting you in composing your photo in the form of a grid overlay in Live View (unfortunately, the grid overlay is not available in the viewfinder like it was on the D5000).

USING A GRID OVERLAY IN LIVE VIEW

1. Rotate the Lv switch under the Mode dial to activate Live View.

2. Press the Info button on the top of the camera to cycle through the Live View display options until you see the grid overlay (**A**).

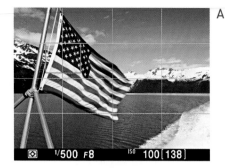

Although the grid in the Live View screen isn't equally divided into thirds, it will give you an approximation for where you should be aligning your subjects in the frame, and it can help you keep your horizon straight.

CREATING DEPTH

Because a photograph is a flat, two-dimensional space, you need to create a sense of depth by using the elements in the scene to create a three-dimensional feel. This is accomplished by including different and distinct spaces for the eye to travel: a foreground, middle ground, and background. By using these three spaces, you draw the viewer in and render depth to your image.

The salt marsh scene, shown in **Figure 7.22**, illustrates this well. The fallen tree strongly defines the foreground area. The misty marsh leading to the forest helps separate the tree from the middle ground, and the sky full of puffy clouds and color creates a perfect backdrop for the scene.

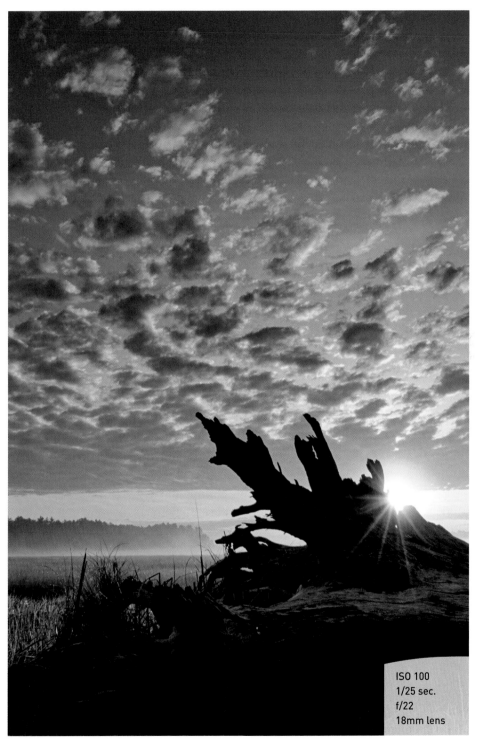

FIGURE 7.22
The fallen tree,
misty marsh hills,
and sky all add to
the feeling of depth
in the image.

ISO 100
1/25 sec.
f/22
18mm lens

ADVANCED TECHNIQUES TO EXPLORE

This section comes with a warning attached. All of the techniques and topics up to this point have been centered on your camera. The following two sections, covering panoramas and high dynamic range (HDR) images, require you to use image-processing software to complete the photograph. They are, however, important enough that you should know how to correctly shoot for success, should you choose to explore these two popular techniques. But wait, what about the in-camera HDR function that is new to the D5100? Don't worry, we'll cover that too, but as you'll soon see, it has its limitations, so I want to show you an alternative HDR method that will give you more data in your captures and more control over the finished product.

SHOOTING PANORAMAS

If you have ever visited the Grand Canyon, you know just how large and wide open it truly is—so much so that it would be difficult to capture its splendor in just one frame. The same can be said for a mountain range, or a cityscape, or any extremely wide vista. There are two methods that you can use to capture the feeling of this type of scene.

THE "FAKE" PANORAMA

The first method is to shoot with your lens set to its widest focal length, and then crop out the top and bottom portion of the frame in your imaging software. Panoramic images are generally two or three times wider than a normal image.

CREATING A FAKE PANORAMA

1. To create the look of the panorama, find your widest lens focal length. The 18mm setting on the 18–55mm AF-S kit lens is a great starting point.

2. Using the guidelines discussed earlier in the chapter, compose and focus your scene, and select the smallest aperture possible.

3. Shoot your image. That's all there is to it, from a photography standpoint.

4. Now, open the image in your favorite image-processing software and crop the extraneous foreground and sky from the image, leaving you with a wide panorama of the scene. A typical panoramic aspect ratio is 3:1, where the longest side is three times longer than the short side.

Figure 7.23 shows an example using a photo taken in Glacier Bay, Alaska.

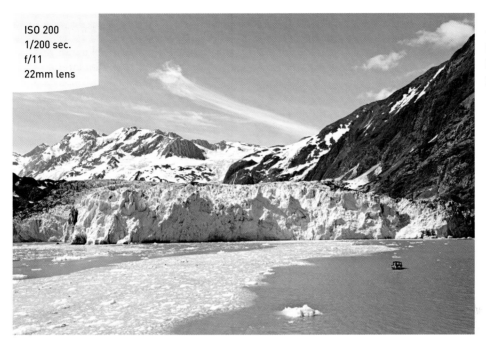

ISO 200
1/200 sec.
f/11
22mm lens

FIGURE 7.23
This is a nice
image, but it could
look good as a
panorama too.

As you can see, the image was shot with a very wide perspective, using a 22mm lens. While it is not a bad photo, it has the potential to have more of an impact with the right crop. Now look at the same image, cropped for panoramic view (**Figure 7.24**). As you can see, it makes a huge difference in the image and gives much higher visual impact by zeroing in on the glacier, drawing your eyes across the length of the horizon, and allowing you to better see the small boat in the foreground.

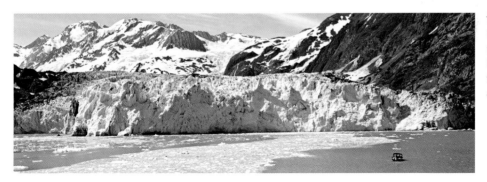

FIGURE 7.24
Cropping gives the
feeling of a sweep-
ing vista and makes
the shot visually
appealing.

THE MULTIPLE-IMAGE PANORAMA

The reason the previous method is sometimes referred to as a "fake" panorama is because it is made with a standard-size frame and then cropped down to a narrow perspective. To shoot a true panorama, you need to use either a special panorama camera that shoots a very wide frame, or the following method, which requires the combining of multiple frames.

The multiple-image pano has gained in popularity in the past few years; this is principally due to advances in image-processing software. Many software options are

FIGURE 7.25
Here you see the makings of a panorama, with ten shots overlapping by about 30 percent from frame to frame.

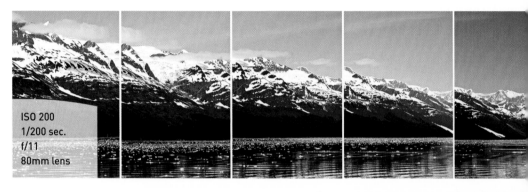

ISO 200
1/200 sec.
f/11
80mm lens

FIGURE 7.26
I used Adobe Photoshop to combine all of the exposures into one large panoramic image.

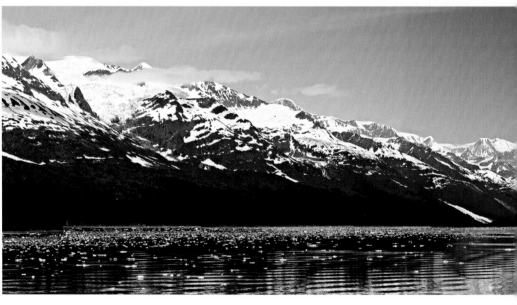

available now that will take multiple images, align them, and then "stitch" them into a single panoramic image. The real key to shooting a multiple-image pano is to overlap your shots by about 30 percent from one frame to the next (**Figures 7.25** and **7.26**). It is possible to handhold the camera while capturing your images, but the best method for capturing great panoramic images is to use a tripod.

Now that you have your series of overlapping images, you can import them into your image-processing software to stitch them together and create a single panoramic image.

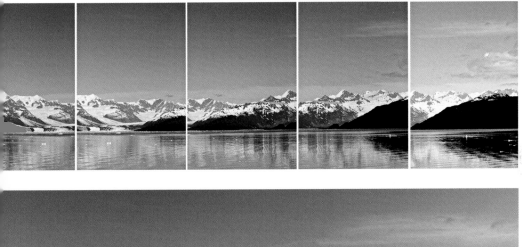

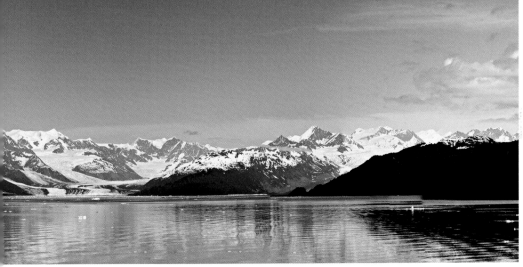

SHOOTING PROPERLY FOR A MULTIPLE-IMAGE PANORAMA

1. Mount your camera on your tripod and make sure it is level.

2. Choose a focal length for your lens that is somewhere between 35mm and 80mm (depending on the distance between you and your subject).

3. In Aperture Priority mode, use a very small aperture for the greatest depth of field. Take a meter reading of a bright part of the scene, and make note of it.

4. Now change your camera to Manual mode (M), and dial in the aperture and shutter speed that you obtained in the previous step.

5. Set your lens to manual focus, and then focus your lens for the area of interest using the HFD method of finding a point one-third of the way into the scene. (If you use the autofocus, you risk getting different points of focus from image to image, which will make the image stitching more difficult for the software.)

6. While carefully panning your camera, shoot your images to cover the entire area of the scene from one end to the other, leaving a 30 percent overlap from one frame to the next.

7. The final step involves using your favorite imaging software to combine all of the photographs into a single panoramic image and then cropping off any excess areas to achieve the desired aspect ratio.

SORTING YOUR SHOTS FOR THE MULTI-IMAGE PANORAMA

If you shoot more than one series of shots for your panoramas, it can sometimes be difficult to know when one series of images ends and the other begins. Here is a quick tip for separating your images.

Set up your camera using the steps listed here. Now, before you take your first good exposure in the series, hold up one finger in front of the camera and take a shot. Now move your hand away and begin taking your overlapping images. When you have taken your last shot, hold two fingers in front of the camera and take another shot.

Now, when you go to review your images, use the series of shots that falls between the frames with one and two fingers in them. Then just repeat the process for your next panorama series.

SHOOTING HIGH DYNAMIC RANGE (HDR) IMAGES

One of the more recent trends in digital photography is the use of high dynamic range (HDR) to capture the full range of tonal values in your final image. Typically, when you photograph a scene that has a wide range of tones from shadows to highlights, you have to make a decision regarding which tonal values you are going to emphasize and then adjust your exposure accordingly. This is because your camera has a limited dynamic range, at least as compared to the human eye. HDR photography allows you to capture multiple exposures for the highlights, shadows, and midtones and then combine them into a single image using software. A number of software applications allow you to combine the images and then perform a process called "tonemapping," whereby the complete range of exposures is represented in a single image. I will not be covering how to use the various software applications, but I will explore the process of shooting a scene to help you render properly captured images for the HDR process. Note that using a tripod is absolutely necessary for this technique, since you need to have perfect alignment of each image when they are combined.

Before we look at how to shoot for HDR photos to be processed in specialized software, let's take a look at the HDR function built into the D5100. The in-camera HDR function on the D5100 takes two exposures—one slightly underexposed and one slightly overexposed—and then blends the two photos together automatically in the camera to create a new photo that contains a wider dynamic range (meaning more detail in the highlights and shadows) than a single exposure does. This is not far off from the Active D-Lighting function that automatically reduces the exposure and then uses software in the camera to increase the brightness in the shadows while preserving more detail in the highlights. Both functions have their place, and you should know how to use them.

That said, the downside of the in-camera HDR function is that it only combines the data from two captures (many photographers shooting HDR images combine three to seven exposures worth of data) and it only works in JPEG mode. You also have limited control over the blending process, and you have to make your decision before you shoot. Of course you can massage the final JPEG image a little to tease out more detail, but if you are going to do that you lose one of the benefits of the in-camera process.

SHOOTING AN IN-CAMERA HDR PHOTO

1. Mount your camera on your tripod and make sure it is level.

2. Press the **i** button and set the image quality to JPEG (Fine) and the ISO to 100.

3. Press the Menu button and use the Multi-selector to navigate to the Shooting menu (**A**).

4. Use the Multi-selector to navigate to HDR (high dynamic range) and press OK to go to the HDR (high dynamic range) screen (**B**).

5. Scroll down to Exposure Differential and press the Multi-selector to the right to see its options (**C**).

6. For testing purposes, set the Exposure differential to Auto and let the camera decide how the exposure value should be for the scene. Generally speaking, the greater the contrast in the scene, the higher the EV value you would choose. Press OK to set the value.

7. Back on the HDR screen, go to Smoothing and press the Multi-selector to the right to see its options (**D**).

8. Set Smoothing to Normal and press OK.

9. Scroll back up to HDR mode, press the Multi-selector to the right, and set it to On (**E**).

A

SHOOTING MENU

Color space	Adobe
Active D-Lighting	OFF
HDR (high dynamic range)	OFF
Long exposure NR	ON
High ISO NR	NORM
ISO sensitivity settings	--
Release mode	S
Multiple exposure	OFF

B

HDR (high dynamic range)

HDR mode	OFF ▶
Exposure differential	2EV
Smoothing	HIGH

C

HDR (high dynamic range)
Exposure differential

Auto	OK
1 EV	
2 EV	
3 EV	

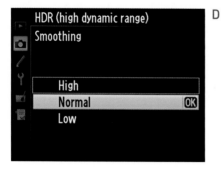

D

HDR (high dynamic range)
Smoothing

High	
Normal	OK
Low	

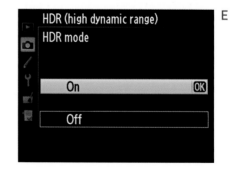

E

HDR (high dynamic range)
HDR mode

On	OK
Off	

10. Press the shutter button halfway to leave the menu.

11. Set your program mode to Aperture Priority so that you can control the depth of field while the camera does everything else.

Note that HDR will be displayed in the viewfinder and on the LCD screen as a reminder you are in HDR mode. Compose your photo and press the shutter button once. You'll hear the shutter fire twice, and then the camera will churn away for a few seconds as it processes the images and blends them together into the final HDR photo. What you should see is a photo with slightly more detail in the highlights and shadows than a typical capture would have (**Figure 7.27**). In my testing, the difference was often rather subtle, but I did see more detail in the HDR version.

Manual Callout

Check out page 76 in the reference manual on the companion CD that came with your camera for more information on the HDR function.

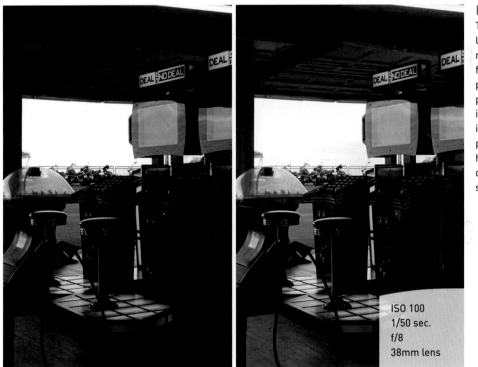

FIGURE 7.27
The photo on the left is a normal, non-HDR capture for comparison purposes. The photo on the right is the result of the in-camera HDR process, which has slightly more detail in the sky and shadows.

ISO 100
1/50 sec.
f/8
38mm lens

By all means, give this feature a good test drive to get a feel for the conditions under which it will deliver the best results. If you are shooting in JPEG already, it is a real nice trick to have in your back pocket (again, much like Active D-Lighting). That said, if you are interested in delving a little further into HDR photography, you can take advantage of the D5100's autoexposure bracketing function to take three different exposures (in RAW mode, even) and combine them in dedicated HDR software. I think you'll be impressed by how much more detail you are able to capture (**Figures 7.28–7.31**).

FIGURE 7.28
(left) Underexposing two stops will render more detail in the highlight areas of the clouds.

FIGURE 7.29
(right) This is the normal exposure as dictated by the camera meter.

FIGURE 7.30
(left) Overexposing by two stops ensures that the darker areas are exposed for detail in the shadows.

FIGURE 7.31
(right) This is the final HDR image that was rendered from the three other exposures you see here.

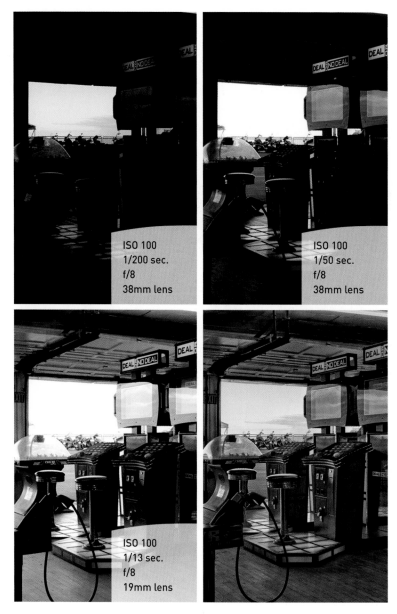

ISO 100
1/200 sec.
f/8
38mm lens

ISO 100
1/50 sec.
f/8
38mm lens

ISO 100
1/13 sec.
f/8
19mm lens

As you can see, the final tonemapped result from this process (I used a program called Oloneo PhotoEngine to create this HDR image) contains a lot more visual data than the in-camera HDR. Did it take more work? Yes, undoubtedly, but I want you to have these tools in your repertoire so that you can choose what fits best with your style and workflow. The other benefit of this technique is that you have total control over the look of the final image, and you can even reprocess the same RAW captures in a myriad of ways depending on your style and taste (**Figure 7.32**).

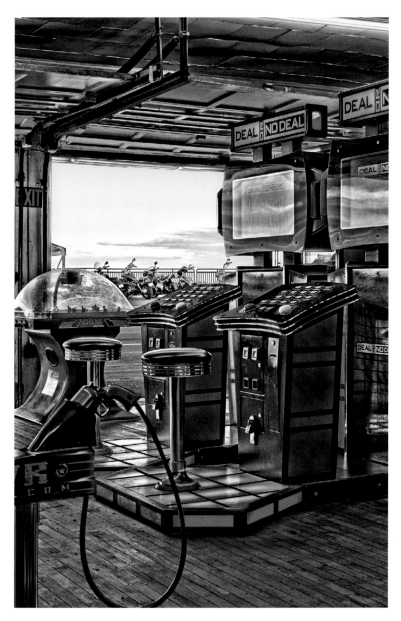

FIGURE 7.32
I reprocessed those same three captures for a slightly grungier look. Whether you love it or hate it, shooting HDR opens new worlds of creativity.

SETTING UP FOR SHOOTING AN HDR IMAGE

1. Set your ISO to 100 to ensure clean, noise-free images.

2. Set your program mode to Aperture Priority. During the shooting process, you will be taking three shots of the same scene, creating an overexposed image, an underexposed image, and a normal exposure. Since the camera is going to be adjusting the exposure, you want it to make changes to the shutter speed, not the aperture, so that your depth of field is consistent.

3. Set your camera file format to RAW. This is extremely important because the RAW format contains a much larger range of exposure values than a JPEG file, and the HDR software needs this information.

4. Change your shooting mode to Continuous. This will allow you to capture your exposures quickly. Even though you will be using a tripod, there is always a chance that something within your scene will be moving (like clouds or leaves). Shooting in the Continuous mode minimizes any subject movement between frames.

5. Adjust the autoexposure bracket (BKT) mode to shoot three exposures in two-stop increments. To do this, you will first need to set the BKT function for AE bracketing by pressing the Menu button.

6. Navigate to the Custom Setting menu and then enter item e: Bracketing/Flash.

7. Locate item e2: Auto Bracketing Set, and press OK. In the next menu screen, select AE Bracketing and then press the OK button.

8. Press the **i** button twice to enter the function setup screen on the rear LCD, use the Multi-selector to highlight BKT, and press OK. Using the Multi-selector, change the option from OFF to AE2.0 and press OK.

9. Focus the camera using the manual focus method discussed earlier in the chapter, compose your shot, secure the tripod, and hold down the shutter button until the camera has fired three consecutive times. The result will be one normal exposure, as well as one underexposed and one overexposed image.

A software program, such as Adobe Photoshop CS5, Oloneo PhotoEngine, Nik HDR Efex Pro, or HDRsoft Photomatix Pro, can now process your exposure-bracketed images into a single HDR file. You can find more information on HDR photography and creating HDR images in the Tutorials section at www.photowalkpro.com.

Remember to turn the BKT function back to OFF when you are done or the camera will continue to shoot bracketed images.

BRACKETING YOUR EXPOSURES

In HDR, *bracketing* is the process of capturing a series of exposures at different stop intervals. You can bracket your exposures even if you aren't going to be using HDR. Sometimes this is helpful when you have a tricky lighting situation and you want to ensure that you have just the right exposure to capture the look you're after. In HDR, you bracket to the plus and minus side of a "normal" exposure, but you can also bracket all of your exposures to the over or under side of normal. It all depends on what you are after. If you aren't sure whether you are getting enough shadow detail, you can bracket a little toward the overexposed side. The same is true for highlights. You can bracket in increments as small as a third of a stop. This means that you can capture several images with very subtle exposure variances and then decide later which one is best. If you want to bracket just to one side of a normal exposure, set your exposure compensation to +1 or –1, whichever way you need, and then use the bracketing feature to automatically bracket your exposures.

Chapter 7 Assignments

We've covered a lot of ground in this chapter, so it's definitely time to put this knowledge to work in order to get familiar with these new camera settings and techniques.

Comparing depth of field: Wide-angle vs. telephoto

Speaking of depth of field, you should also practice using the hyper focal distance of your lens to maximize the depth of field. You can do this by picking a focal length to work with on your lens.

If you have a zoom lens, try using the longest length. Compose your image and find an object to focus on. Set your aperture to f/22 and take a photo.

Now do the same thing with the zoom lens at its widest focal length. Use the same aperture and focus point.

Review the images and compare the depth of field when using wide angle as opposed to a telephoto lens. Try this again with a large aperture as well.

Applying hyper focal distance to your landscapes

Pick a scene that once again has objects that are near the camera position and something that is clearly defined in the background. Try using a wide to medium wide focal length for this (18–35mm). Use a small aperture and focus on the object in the foreground; then recompose and take a shot.

Without moving the camera position, use the object in the background as your point of focus and take another shot.

Finally, find a point that is one-third of the way into the frame from near to far and use that as the focus point.

Compare all of the images to see which method delivered the greatest range of depth of field from near to infinity.

Using Live View and the rule of thirds

Now let's get some practice using the rule of thirds for improving composition. To do this, you need to employ Live View with the grid overlay turned on for a little visual assistance.

Using the Live View grid, practice shooting while placing your main subject in one of the intersecting line locations. Take some comparison shots with the subject at one of the intersecting locations, and then shoot the same subject in the middle of the frame.

Placing your horizons

Finally, find a location with a defined horizon and, using the Live View grid, shoot the horizon along the top third of the frame, in the middle of the frame, and along the bottom third of the frame.

Test drive the in-camera HDR function

Now that you know the feature exists, look for high-contrast scenes (where there are areas of bright highlight with detail and dark shadow with detail) and put that HDR function through its paces. You may not like all the images, but learning to recognize the situations where it comes in handy is worth the practice.

Share your results with the book's Flickr group!

Join the group here: flickr.com/groups/nikond5100fromsnapshotstogreatshots/

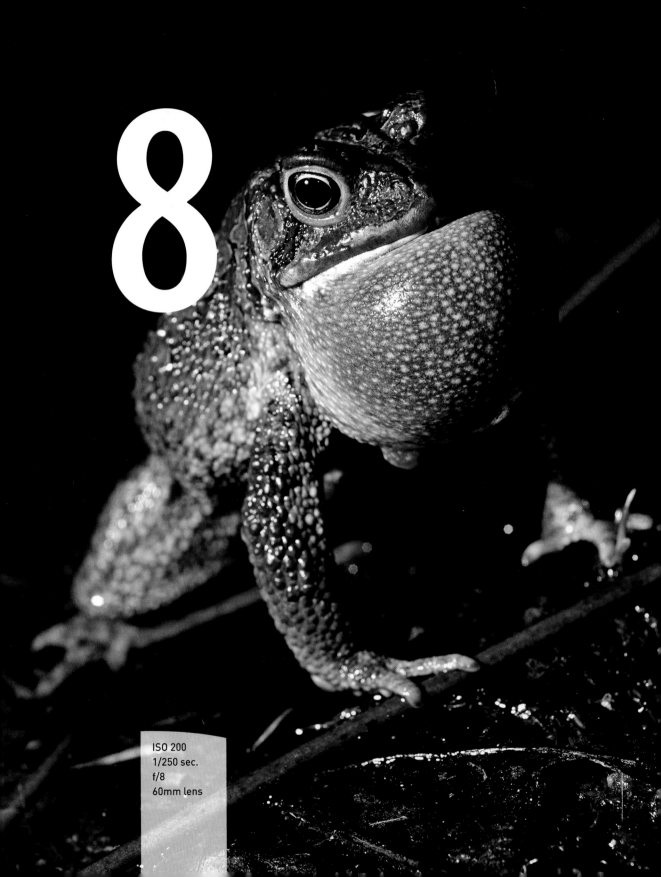

8

ISO 200
1/250 sec.
f/8
60mm lens

Mood Lighting

SHOOTING WHEN THE LIGHTS GET LOW

There is no reason to put your camera away when the sun goes down. Your D5100 has some great features that let you work with available light as well as the built-in flash. In this chapter, we will explore ways to push your camera's technology to the limit in order to capture great photos in difficult lighting situations. We will also explore the use of flash and how best to utilize your built-in flash features to improve your photography. But let's first look at working with low-level available light.

Before dragging out the tripod, I decided to try handholding the camera for this poppy shot in natural light. The flower was near a north-facing window with a white diffusion panel placed between the window and the flower. This created a clean white background and provided the necessary light for the photo.

The tilt of the flower toward the open white space gives compositional balance to the image.

To get a sharp image, I set the shutter speed to 1/250 of a second.

The kit lens at 55mm allowed me to fill the frame nicely.

ISO 4000
1/250 sec.
f/11
55mm lens

There is a bit of noise from the high ISO that is visible in the stem and flower petals.

RAISING THE ISO: THE SIMPLE SOLUTION

Let's begin with the obvious way to keep shooting when the lights get low: raising the ISO (**Figure 8.1**). By now you know how to change the ISO by using the **i** button and the Multi-selector. In typical shooting situations, you should keep the ISO in the 100–800 range. This will keep your pictures nice and clean by keeping the digital noise to a minimum. But as the available light gets low, you might find yourself working in the higher ranges of the ISO scale, which could lead to more noise in your image.

FIGURE 8.1
Some moments just need to be captured in the available light, no matter how little light is available.

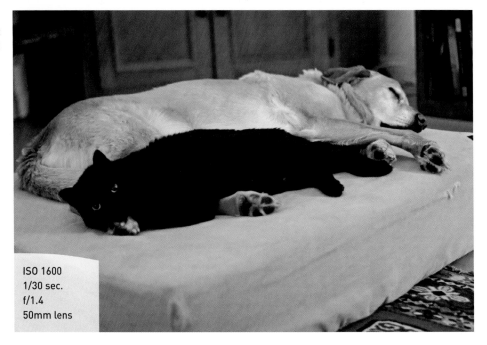

ISO 1600
1/30 sec.
f/1.4
50mm lens

You could use the flash, but that has a limited range (15–20 feet) that might not work for you. Also, you could be in a situation where flash is prohibited, or at least frowned upon, like at a wedding or in a museum. Sometimes the flash just kills the mood of the scene you are viewing, and that feeling is an important part of the subject you are trying to capture.

And what about a tripod in combination with a long shutter speed? That is also an option, and we'll cover it a little further into the chapter. The problem with using a tripod and a slow shutter speed in low-light photography, though, is that it performs best when subjects aren't moving. Besides, try to set up a tripod in a museum and see how quickly you grab the attention of the security guards.

So if the only choice to get the shot is to raise the ISO to 800 or higher, make sure that you turn on the High ISO Noise Reduction feature (**Figure 8.2**). This custom menu function is set to Normal by default, but as you start using higher ISO values you should consider changing it to the High setting. (Chapter 7 explains how to set the noise reduction features.) If you move on to shooting in RAW mode you will have other tools in the RAW processing software for dealing with noise.

To see the effect of High ISO Noise Reduction, you need to zoom in and take a closer look (**Figures 8.3** and **8.4**).

Raising the noise reduction to the High setting slightly increases the processing time for your images, so if you are shooting in the Continuous drive mode you might see a little reduction in the speed of your frames per second.

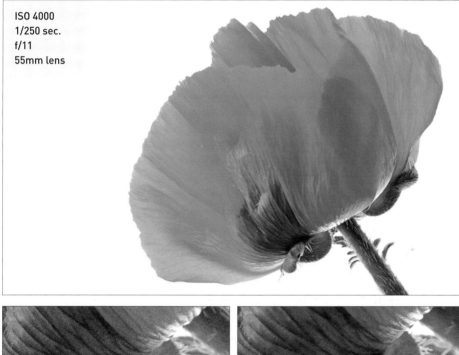

ISO 4000
1/250 sec.
f/11
55mm lens

FIGURE 8.2
Although this looks like a well-lit shot, it was a handheld shot made possible through the use of a very high ISO and the High ISO Noise Reduction feature.

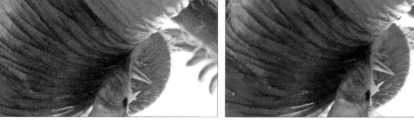

FIGURE 8.3
Here is a close-up of the same flower, so you can get an idea of how things look with High ISO Noise Reduction turned off.

FIGURE 8.4
Here is the same flower photographed with High ISO Noise Reduction turned to High. While it doesn't get rid of all the noise, it certainly reduces the effect and improves the look of your image.

NOISE REDUCTION SAVES SPACE

When shooting at very high ISO settings, running High ISO Noise Reduction at the Normal or High setting can save you space on your memory card. If you are saving your photos as JPEGs, the camera will compress the information in the image to take up less space. When you have excessive noise, you can literally add megabytes to the file size. This is because the camera has to deal with more information: It views the noise in the image as photo information and, therefore, tries not to lose that information during the compression process. That means more noise equals bigger files. So not only will turning on the High ISO Noise Reduction feature improve the look of your image, it will also save you some space so you can take a few more shots.

USING VERY HIGH ISOS

Is ISO 6400 just not enough for you? Well, in that case, you will need to set your camera to one of the expanded ISO settings. These settings open up another stop of ISO, raising the new limit to 25600. The new settings will not appear in your ISO scale as numbers, but as Hi 0.3 for 8063, Hi 0.7 for 10159, Hi 1 for ISO 12800, and Hi2 for ISO 25600.

USING THE HIGHER ISO SETTINGS

1. With the information screen active, press the **i** button to activate the cursor and then use the Multi-selector to place it on the ISO setting (**A**).

2. Press the OK button and then use the Multi-selector to scroll down through the ISO settings until you reach the Hi settings, then select the ISO of choice and press the OK button (**B**).

3. Press the shutter release button to return to active shooting mode.

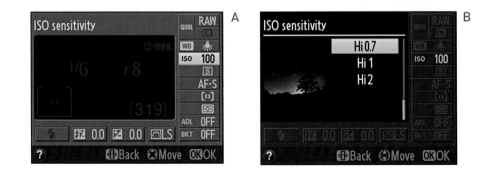

A word of warning about the expanded ISO settings: although it is great to have these high ISO settings available during low-light shooting, they should always be your last resort. Even with High ISO Noise Reduction turned on, the amount of visible noise will be extremely high. If you are going to be shooting frequently in low-light situations, I would urge you to consider investing in a faster lens (with a wide aperture), which, when coupled with ISOs between 3200 and 6400, can allow you to increase your shutter speed fast enough to stop the action under poor lighting conditions (**Figure 8.5**).

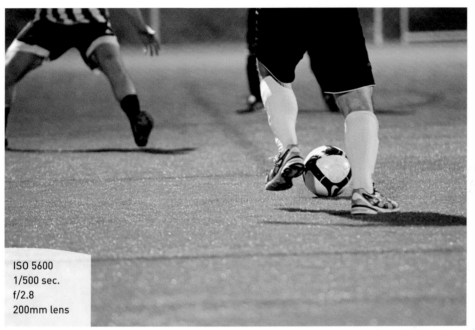

ISO 5600
1/500 sec.
f/2.8
200mm lens

FIGURE 8.5
The only way to get a fast-enough shutter speed during this night game was to raise the ISO to 5600.

Don't forget about the D5100's Night Vision effect (refer to Chapter 3) when there's almost no light at all and you can live with the grainy black and white image (**Figure 8.6**) it produces. Notice the level of noise in the capture makes it almost look like it was snowing at the time.

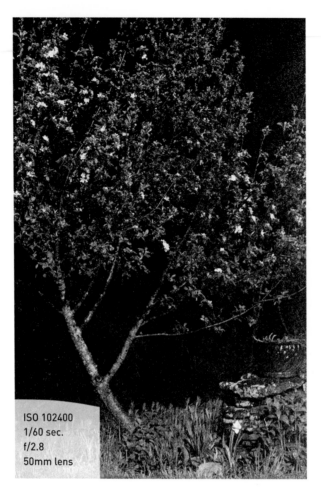

FIGURE 8.6
I used the Night Vision effect in my backyard with only the light from my porch to compose and illuminate this shot of my apple tree.

ISO 102400
1/60 sec.
f/2.8
50mm lens

STABILIZING THE SITUATION

If you purchased your camera with the Vibration Reduction (VR) lens, you already own a great tool to squeeze two stops of exposure out of your camera when shooting without a tripod. Typically, the average person can handhold their camera down to about 1/60 of a second before blurriness results due to hand shake. As the length of the lens is increased (or zoomed), the ability to handhold at slow shutter speeds (1/60 of a second and slower) and still get sharp images is further reduced (**Figure 8.7**).

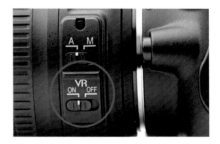

FIGURE 8.7
Turning on the VR switch will allow you to shoot in lower lighting conditions.

The Nikon VR lenses contain small gyro sensors and servo-actuated optical elements, which correct for camera shake and stabilize the image. The VR function is so good that it is possible to improve your handheld photography by two or three stops, meaning that if you are pretty solid at a shutter speed of 1/60 of a second, the VR feature lets you shoot at 1/15, and possibly even 1/8, of a second (**Figures 8.8** and **8.9**). When shooting in low-light situations, make sure you set the VR switch on the side of your lens to the On position.

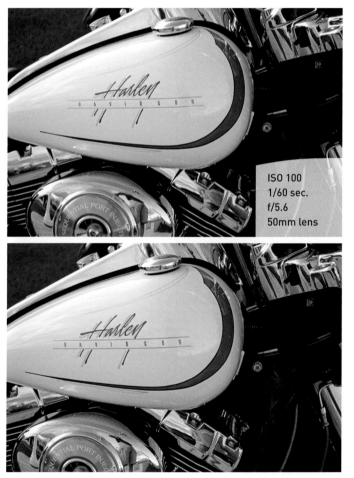

ISO 100
1/60 sec.
f/5.6
50mm lens

FIGURE 8.8
Both of these images were shot at the same camera settings, but the bottom image is with VR and the top is image is without. Note the increased blur in the text of the top photo.

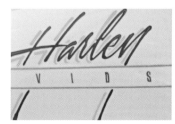 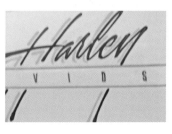

FIGURE 8.9
Here's a closeup of the text. The left is with VR and the right is without.

Whether you are shooting with a tripod or even resting your camera on a wall, you can increase the sharpness of your pictures by taking your hands out of the equation. Whenever you use your finger to depress the shutter release button, you are increasing the chance that there will be a little bit of shake in your image. To eliminate this possibility, try setting your camera up to use the self-timer. The default setting of the Function (Fn) button is the self-timer. To turn on the self-timer, just press the Fn button (directly beneath the flash button). There are four self-timer modes: 2, 5, 10, and 20 seconds. I generally use the 2-second mode to cut down on time between exposures. If you want to use one of the other modes, you will need to change this in the Custom Setting menu under the Timers/AE Lock setting. You can also enable the self-timer via the **i** button and by changing the Release mode.

FOCUSING IN LOW LIGHT

The D5100 has a great focusing system, but occasionally the light levels might be too low for the camera to achieve an accurate focus. There are a few things that you can do to overcome this obstacle.

First, you should know that the camera utilizes contrast in the viewfinder to establish a point of focus. This is why your camera will not be able to focus when you point it at a white wall or a cloudless sky. It simply can't find any contrast in the scene to work with. Knowing this, you might be able to use a single focus point in AF-S mode to find an area of contrast that is of the same distance as your subject. You can then hold that focus by holding down the shutter button halfway and recomposing your image.

Then there are those times when there just isn't anything there for you to focus on. A perfect example of this would be a fireworks display. If you point your lens to the night sky in any automatic focus (AF) mode, it will just keep searching for—and not finding—a focus point. On these occasions, you can simply turn off the autofocus feature and manually focus the lens. Look for the A/M switch on the side of the lens and slide it to the M position. Don't forget to put it back in A mode at the end of your shoot.

Standing in a field one summer morning (way before the dawn) waiting for a lunar eclipse to occur, I passed the time by doing extremely long-exposure captures of my surroundings, such as this dew-covered spiderweb illuminated only by the light of the full moon (**Figure 8.10**). While I could see the web from where I was standing, the camera's autofocus could not. Flipping the switch to manual allowed me to take the shot, then check focus on the LCD.

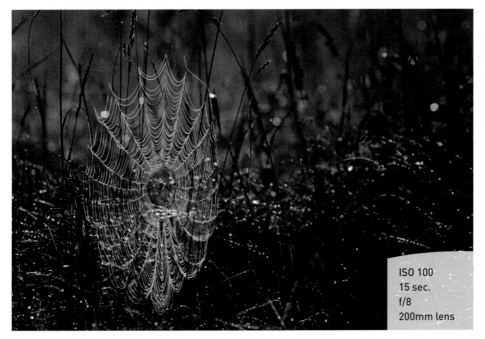

FIGURE 8.10
A very long exposure, manual focus, and a tripod were necessary to catch the moonlight glistening on this spider's web.

AF ASSIST ILLUMINATOR

Another way to ensure good focus is to use the D5100's AF Assist Illuminator. AF Assist uses a small, bright beam of light from the front of the camera to shine some light on the scene, which assists the autofocus system in locating more detail. This feature is automatically activated when using the flash (except in Landscape, Sports, and Flash Off modes for the following reasons: in Landscape mode, the subject is usually too far away; in Sports mode, the subject is probably moving; and in Flash Off mode, you've disabled the flash entirely). Also, the Illuminator will be disabled when shooting in the AF-C or Manual focus mode, as well as when the Illuminator is turned off in the camera menu. The AF Assist should be enabled by default, but you can check the menu just to make sure.

TURNING ON THE AF ASSIST FEATURE

1. Press the Menu button and access the Custom Setting menu.

2. Navigate to the item called a: Autofocus and press the OK button (**A**).

3. Highlight the menu item called a2: Built-in AF-assist Illuminator and press the OK button (**B**).

4. Set the option to On and press the OK button to complete the setup.

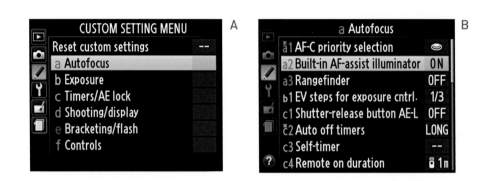

DISABLING THE FLASH

If you are shooting in one of the automatic scene modes, the flash might be set to activate automatically. If you don't wish to operate the flash, you will have to turn it off in the information screen.

DISABLING THE FLASH

1. Press the **i** button to activate the cursor in the information screen and use the Multi-selector to select the Flash Mode item (located in the lower-left portion of the screen) (**C**).

2. Press OK and then use the Multi-controller to find the option to turn off the flash (look for the lightning bolt with the circle and slash) (**D**).

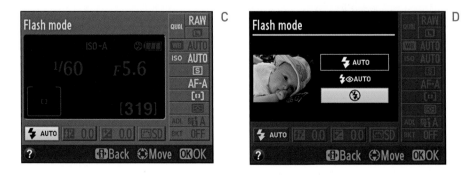

3. Press OK and then make sure the pop-up flash is in the down position before shooting.

To disable the flash in the professional modes, simply keep the flash head in the lowered position. It will not be active unless you raise it.

SHOOTING LONG EXPOSURES

We have covered some of the techniques for shooting in low light, so let's go through the process of capturing a night or low-light scene for maximum image quality. The first thing to consider is that in order to shoot in low light with a low ISO, you will need to use shutter speeds that are longer than you could possibly handhold (longer than 1/15 of a second). This will require the use of a tripod or stable surface for you to place your camera on. For maximum quality, the ISO should be low—somewhere below 400. The long exposure noise reduction should be turned on to minimize the effects of exposing for longer durations (to set this up, see Chapter 7).

I go to Las Vegas at least once a year for Photoshop World, and on my last visit I finally got a room on the strip side of the hotel and couldn't pass up a chance to do a long exposure of the city all lit up (**Figure 8.11**). I didn't have my tripod, but pulling a table right up to the window and using the camera's self-timer worked almost as well. Turning out all the lights in the room eliminated reflections on the glass.

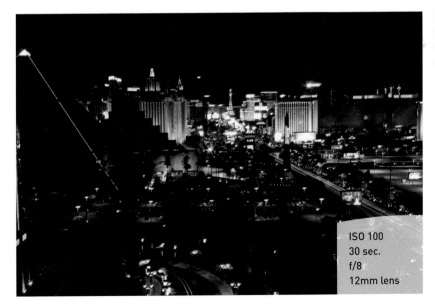

FIGURE 8.11
Las Vegas at night is worth visiting at least once in your life.

ISO 100
30 sec.
f/8
12mm lens

Once you have the noise reduction turned on, set your camera to Aperture Priority (A) mode. That way, you can concentrate on the aperture that you believe is most appropriate and let the camera determine the best shutter speed. If it is too dark for the autofocus to function properly, try focusing manually. Finally, consider using a cable release (see the bonus Chapter 11) to activate the shutter. If you don't have one, check out the sidebar, "Self-time your way to sharper images." Once you shoot the image, you may notice some lag time before it is displayed on the rear LCD. This is due to the noise reduction process, which can take anywhere from a fraction of a second up to 30 seconds, depending on the length of the exposure.

FLASH SYNC

The basic idea behind the term *flash synchronization (flash sync* for short) is that when you take a photograph using the flash, the camera needs to ensure that the shutter is fully open at the time that the flash goes off. This is not an issue if you are using a long shutter speed such as 1/15 of a second but does become more critical for fast shutter speeds. To ensure that the flash and shutter are synchronized so that the flash is going off while the shutter is open, the D5100 implements a top sync speed of 1/200 of a second. This means that when you are using the flash, you will not be able to have your shutter speed be any faster than 1/200. If you did use a faster shutter speed, the shutter would actually start closing before the flash fired, which would cause a black area to appear in the frame where the light from the flash was blocked by the shutter.

USING THE BUILT-IN FLASH

There are going to be times when you have to turn to your camera's built-in flash to get the shot. The pop-up flash on the D5100 is not extremely powerful, but with the camera's advanced metering system it does a pretty good job of lighting up the night...or just filling in the shadows.

If you are working with one of the automatic scene modes, the flash should automatically activate when needed. If, however, you are working in one of the professional modes you will have to turn the flash on for yourself. To do this, just press the pop-up flash button located on the front of the camera (**Figure 8.12**). Once the flash is up, it is ready to go (**Figure 8.13**). It's that simple.

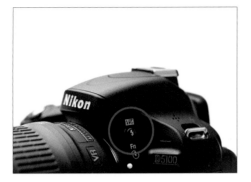

FIGURE 8.12
A quick press of the pop-up flash button will release the built-in flash up to its ready position.

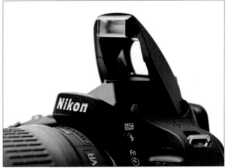

FIGURE 8.13
The pop-up flash in its ready position.

FLASH RANGE

Because the pop-up flash is fairly small, it does not have enough power to illuminate a large space. The effective distance varies depending on the ISO setting. At ISO 200, the range is about 14 feet. This range can be extended to as far as 27 feet when the camera is set to an ISO of 6400. For the best image quality, your ISO setting should not go above 800. Anything higher will begin to introduce excessive noise into your photos. Check out page 53 of the reference manual on the CD that came with the camera for a chart that shows the effective flash range for differing ISO and aperture settings.

SHUTTER SPEEDS

The standard flash synchronization speed for your camera is between 1/60 and 1/200 of a second. When you are working with the built-in flash in the automatic and scene modes, the camera will typically use a shutter speed of 1/60 of a second. The exception to this is when you use the Night Portrait mode, which will fire the flash with a slower shutter speed so that some of the ambient light in the scene has time to record in the image.

The real key to using the flash to get great pictures is to control the shutter speed. The goal is to balance the light from the flash with the existing light so that everything in the picture has an even illumination. Let's take a look at the shutter speeds for the modes in the professional modes.

Program (P): The shutter speed stays at 1/60 of a second. The only adjustment you can make in this mode is overexposure or underexposure using the exposure compensation or flash compensation settings.

 Shutter Priority (S): You can adjust the shutter speed to as fast as 1/200 of a second all the way down to 30 seconds. The lens aperture will adjust accordingly, but typically at long exposures the lens will be set to its largest aperture.

 Aperture Priority (A): This mode will allow you to adjust the aperture but will adjust the shutter speed between 1/200 and 1/60 of a second in the standard flash mode.

METERING MODES

The built-in flash uses a technology called TTL (Through The Lens) metering to determine the appropriate amount of flash power to output for a good exposure. When you depress the shutter button, the camera quickly adjusts focus while gathering information from the entire scene to measure the amount of ambient light. As you press the shutter button down completely, the flash uses that exposure information and fires a predetermined amount of light at your subject during the exposure.

The default setting for the flash meter mode is TTL. The meter can be set to Manual mode. In Manual flash mode, you can determine how much power you want coming out of the flash, ranging from full power all the way down to 1/32 power. Each setting from full power on down will cut the power by half. This is the equivalent of reducing flash exposure by one stop with each power reduction.

SETTING THE FLASH TO THE MANUAL POWER SETTING

1. Press the Menu button and then navigate to the Custom Setting menu.
2. Using the Multi-selector, highlight the item labeled e: Bracketing/Flash and press the OK button (**A**).

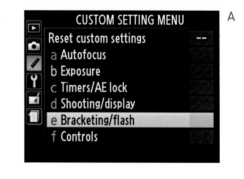

3. Highlight item e1: Flash Cntrl for Built-in Flash and press OK (**B**).

4. Change the setting to Manual (**C**) and then press the OK button to adjust the desired power—Full, ½, ¼, etc.—and then press the OK button (**D**).

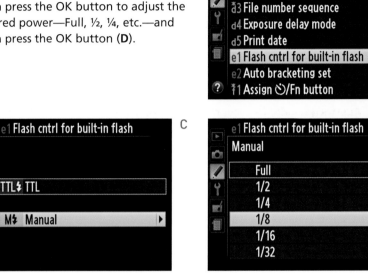

Don't forget to set it back to TTL when you are done because the camera will hold this setting until you change it.

COMPENSATING FOR THE FLASH EXPOSURE

The TTL system will usually do an excellent job of balancing the flash and ambient light for your exposure, but it does have the limitation of not knowing what effect you want in your image. You may want more or less flash in a particular shot. You can achieve this by using the Flash Exposure Compensation feature.

Just as with exposure compensation, flash compensation allows you to dial in a change in the flash output in increments of 1/3 of a stop. You will probably use this most often to tone down the effects of your flash, especially when you are using the flash as a subtle fill light (**Figures 8.14, 8.15**, and **8.16**). The range of compensation goes from +1 stop down to –3 stops.

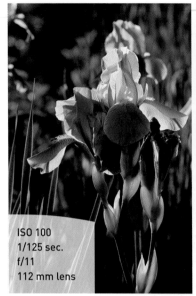

ISO 100
1/125 sec.
f/11
112 mm lens

FIGURE 8.14
I love the look of flowers backlit by the
setting sun. Unfortunately, it leaves
the shadow side very dark when
exposing for the bright highlights.

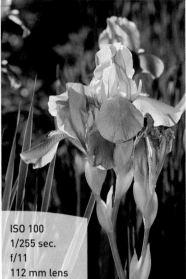

ISO 100
1/255 sec.
f/11
112 mm lens

FIGURE 8.15
Turning on the flash without any compensation completely overpowers the
scene and looks harsh.

ISO 100
1/255 sec.
f/11
112 mm lens

FIGURE 8.16
Reducing the flash exposure compensation by 2 stops fills in the shadow areas
with a much more natural look.

USING THE FLASH EXPOSURE COMPENSATION FEATURE TO CHANGE THE FLASH OUTPUT

1. With the flash in the upright and ready position, press and hold the flash compensation (the same button used to pop the flash) and exposure compensation (just behind the shutter) buttons at the same time.

2. While holding down these two buttons, rotate the Command dial to set the amount of compensation you desire. Turning to the right reduces the flash power 1/3 of a stop with each click of the dial. Turning left increases the flash power.

3. Press the shutter button halfway to return to shooting mode, and then take the picture.

4. Review your image to see if more or less flash compensation is required, and repeat these steps as necessary.

You can also change the flash compensation by using the information screen on the back of the camera.

ADJUSTING THE FLASH COMPENSATION USING THE INFORMATION SCREEN

1. Press the **i** button to activate the cursor in the information screen and use the Multi-selector to set it to the flash compensation item (located along the bottom portion of the screen) (**A**).

2. Press the OK button, use the Multi-selector to select the amount of compensation, and then press the OK button (**B**).

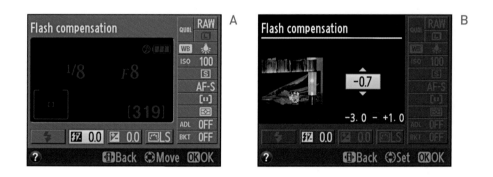

The Flash Exposure Compensation feature does not reset itself when the camera is turned off, so whatever compensation you have set will remain in effect until you change it. Your only clue to knowing that the flash output is changed will be the presence of the Flash Exposure Compensation symbol in the viewfinder. It will disappear when there is zero compensation set.

REDUCING RED-EYE

We've all seen the result of using on-camera flashes when shooting people: the dreaded red-eye! This demonic effect is the result of the light from the flash entering the pupil and then reflecting back as an eerie red glow. The closer the flash is to the lens, the greater the chance that you will get red-eye. This is especially true when it is dark and the subject's pupils are fully dilated. There are two ways to combat this problem. The first is to get the flash away from the lens. That's not really an option, though, if you are using the pop-up flash. Therefore, you will need to turn to the Red-Eye Reduction feature.

This is a simple feature that shines a light from the camera at the subject, causing their pupils to shrink, thus eliminating or reducing the effects of red-eye (**Figure 8.17**).

FIGURE 8.17
Red-eye begone!

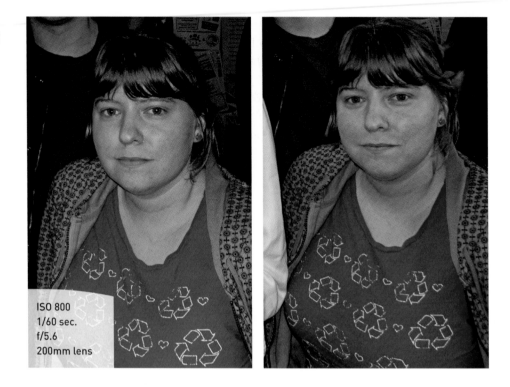

ISO 800
1/60 sec.
f/5.6
200mm lens

TURN ON THE LIGHTS!

When shooting indoors, another way to reduce red-eye, or just shorten the length of time that the reduction lamp needs to be shining into your subject's eyes, is to turn on a lot of lights. The brighter the ambient light levels, the smaller the subject's pupils will be. This will reduce the time necessary for the red-eye reduction lamp to shine. It will also allow you to take more candid pictures because your subjects won't be required to stare at the red-eye lamp while waiting for their pupils to reduce.

The feature is set to Off by default and needs to be turned on by using the information screen or by using a combination of the flash button and the Command dial.

TURNING ON THE RED-EYE REDUCTION FEATURE

1. Press the **i** button to activate the cursor in the information screen and use the Multi-selector to set it to the Flash Mode item (located along the lower-left portion of the screen) (**A**).

2. Press the OK button and then use the Multi-selector to select the Red-Eye Reduction mode, represented by an eye icon (**B**).

3. With red-eye reduction activated, compose your photo and then press the shutter release button to take the picture.

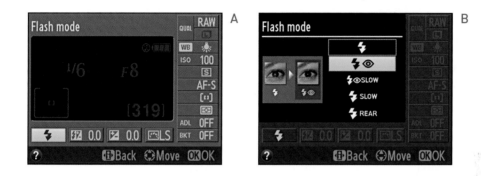

When red-eye reduction is activated, the camera will not fire the instant that you press the shutter release button. Instead, the red-eye reduction lamp will illuminate for a second or two and then fire the flash for the exposure. This is important to remember because people have a tendency to move around, so you will need to instruct them to hold still for a moment while the lamp works its magic.

Truth be told, I rarely shoot with red-eye reduction turned on because of the time it takes before being able to take a picture. If I am after candid shots and have to use the flash, I will take my chances on red-eye and try to fix the problem in my image processing software or even in the camera's retouching menu. The Nikon Picture Project software that comes with your D5100 has a red-eye reduction feature that works really well, although only on JPEG images.

REAR CURTAIN SYNC

There are two flash synchronization modes in the D5100. There's front curtain and rear curtain. You may be asking, "What in the world does synchronization do, and what's with these 'curtains'?" Good question.

When your camera fires, there are two curtains that open and close to make up the shutter. The first, or front, curtain moves out of the way, exposing the camera sensor to the light. At the end of the exposure, the second, or rear, curtain moves in front of the sensor, ending that picture cycle. In flash photography, timing is extremely important because the flash fires in milliseconds and the shutter is usually opening in tenths or hundredths of a second. To make sure these two functions happen in order, the camera usually fires the flash just as the first curtain moves out of the way (see the "Flash Sync" sidebar, earlier in this chapter).

In Rear Curtain Sync mode, the flash will not fire until just before the second shutter curtain ends the exposure. So, why have this mode at all? Well, there might be times when you want to have a longer exposure to balance out the light from the background to go with the subject needing the flash. Imagine taking a photograph of a friend standing in Times Square at night with all the traffic moving about and the bright lights of the streets overhead. If the flash fires at the beginning of the exposure and then the objects around the subject move, those objects will often blur or even obscure the subject a bit. If the camera is set to Rear Curtain Sync, though, all of the movement is recorded using the existing light first, and then the subject is "frozen" by the flash at the end by the exposure.

There is no right or wrong to it. It's just a decision on what type of effect it is that you would like to create. Many times, Rear Curtain Sync is used for artistic purposes or to record movement in the scene without it overlapping the flash-exposed subject (**Figure 8.18**). To make sure that the main subject is always getting the final pop of the flash, I leave my camera set to Rear Camera Sync most of the time.

Figure 8.19 shows an example of what happens with a slow shutter speed, fast action, and rear curtain sync. It was a handheld shot, so there is camera shake with the 3-second exposure, but thanks to the Rear Curtain Sync setting, the result conveys the sense of movement, the low ambient light of the playground at dusk, and a clear shot of the child leaving the slide.

Note that if you do intend to use a long exposure with first curtain synchronization, you need to have your subject remain fairly still so that any movement that occurs after the flash goes off will be minimized in the image.

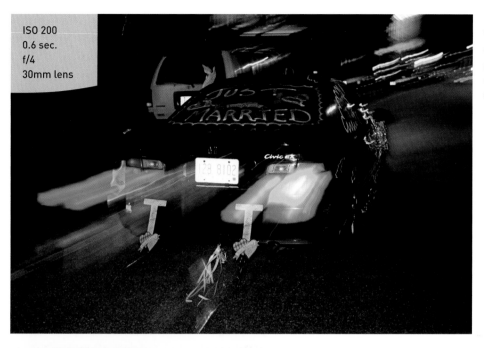

ISO 200
0.6 sec.
f/4
30mm lens

FIGURE 8.18
The effect of Rear
Curtain Sync is
most evident
during long flash
exposures.

FIGURE 8.19
This effect is possible
because the flash fired at
the end of the exposure
using Rear Curtain Sync.

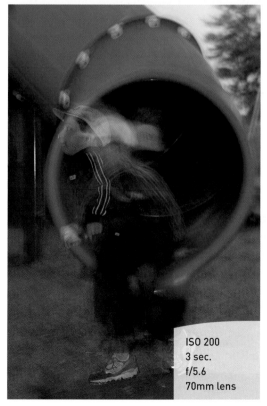

ISO 200
3 sec.
f/5.6
70mm lens

1. Press the **i** button to activate the cursor in the information screen and use the Multi-selector to set it to the Flash Mode item (located along the lower-left portion of the screen) (**A**).

2. Press the OK button and then use the Multi-selector to select the Rear mode (**B**).

3. With Rear Curtain Sync activated, compose your photo, adjust your shutter or aperture depending on the shooting mode you are using, and then press the shutter release button to take the picture.

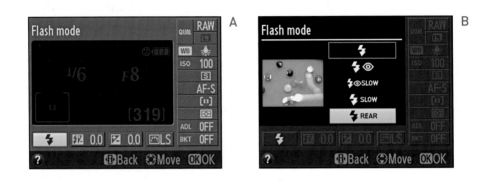

FLASH AND GLASS

If you find yourself in a situation where you want to use your flash to shoot through a window or display case, try placing your lens right against the glass so that the reflection of the flash won't be visible in your image (**Figures 8.20** and **8.21**). This is extremely useful in museums, aquariums, and capturing the fortune-teller at the amusement park.

A FEW WORDS ABOUT EXTERNAL FLASH

We have discussed several ways to get control over the built-in pop-up flash on the D5100. The reality is that, as flashes go, it will only render fairly average results. For people photography, it is probably one of the most unflattering light sources that you could ever use. This isn't because the flash isn't good—it's actually very sophisticated for its size. The problem is that light should come from any direction besides the camera to best flatter a human subject. When the light emanates from directly above the lens, it gives the effect of becoming a photocopier. Imagine putting your face down on a scanner: The result would be a flatly lit, featureless photo.

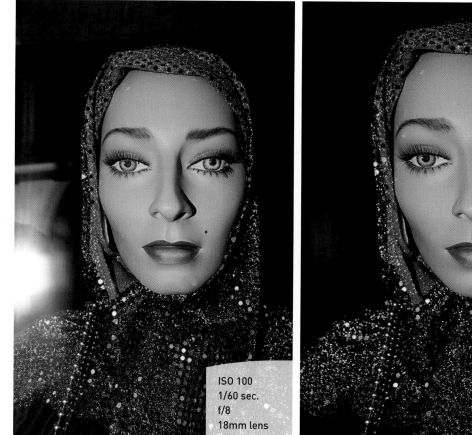

ISO 100
1/60 sec.
f/8
18mm lens

ISO 100
1/60 sec.
f/8
18mm lens

FIGURE 8.20
The bright spot on the left of the frame is a result of the flash reflecting off the display glass.

FIGURE 8.21
To eliminate the reflection, place the lens against the glass or as close to it as possible. This might also require zooming the lens out a little.

To really make your flash photography come alive with possibilities, you should consider buying an external flash such as the Nikon SB-600 AF Speedlight. The SB-600 has a swiveling flash head and more power, and it communicates with the camera and the TTL system to deliver balanced flash exposures. For more information about the Nikon Speedlight system, be sure to check out bonus Chapter 11.

Manual Callout

For more information on the use of external Speedlight flashes on your D5100, check out page 202 of the reference manual on the CD that came with the camera.

Chapter 8 Assignments

Now that we have looked at the possibilities of shooting after dark, it's time to put it all to the test. These assignments cover the full range of shooting possibilities, both with flash and without. Let's get started.

How steady are your hands?

It's important to know just what your limits are in terms of handholding your camera and still getting sharp pictures. This will change depending on the focal length of the lens you are working with. Wider-angle lenses are more forgiving than telephoto lenses, so check this out for your longest and shortest lenses. Using the 18–55mm zoom as an example, set your lens to 55mm and then, with the camera set to ISO 200 and the mode set to Shutter Priority, turn off the VR and start taking pictures with lower and lower shutter speeds. Review each image on the LCD at a zoomed-in magnification to take note of when you start seeing visible camera shake in your images. It will probably be around 1/60 of a second for a 55mm lens.

Now do the same for the wide-angle setting on the lens. My limit is about 1/30 of a second. These shutter speeds are with the Vibration Reduction feature turned off. If you have a VR lens, try it with and without the VR feature enabled to see just how slow you can set your shutter while getting sharp results.

Pushing your ISO to the extreme

Find a place to shoot where the ambient light level is low. This could be at night or indoors in a darkened room. Using the mode of your choice, start increasing the ISO from 100 until you get to Hi 2. Make sure you evaluate the level of noise in your image, especially in the shadow areas. Only you can decide how much noise is acceptable in your pictures. I can tell you from personal experience that I never like to stray above that ISO 800 mark unless I absolutely need to get the shot regardless of the noise.

Getting rid of the noise

Turn on High ISO Noise Reduction and repeat the previous assignment. Find your acceptable limits with the noise reduction turned on. Also pay attention to how much detail is lost in your shadows with this function enabled.

Long exposures in the dark

If you don't have a tripod, find a stable place to set your camera outside and try some long exposures. Set your camera to Aperture Priority mode and then use the self-timer to activate the camera (this will keep you from shaking the camera while pressing the shutter button).

Shoot in an area that has some level of ambient light, be it a streetlight, traffic lights, or even a full moon. The idea is to get some late-night low-light exposures.

Reducing the noise in your long exposures

Now repeat the last assignment but with Long Exposure Noise Reduction set to On. Now look at the difference in the images that were taken before and after the noise reduction was enabled. For best results, perform this assignment and the previous assignment in the same shooting session and using the same subject.

Testing the limits of the pop-up flash

Wait for the lights to get low and then press that pop-up flash button to start using the built-in flash. Try using the different shooting modes to see how they affect your exposures. Use the Flash Exposure Compensation feature to take a series of pictures while adjusting from –3 stops all the way to +1 stops so that you become familiar with how much latitude you will get from this feature.

Getting the red out

Find a friend with some patience and a tolerance for bright lights. Have them sit in a darkened room or outside at night and then take their picture with the flash. Now turn on Red-Eye Reduction to see if you get better results. Don't forget to have them sit still while the red-eye lamp does its thing.

Getting creative with Rear Curtain Sync

Now it's time for a little creative fun. Set your camera up for Rear Curtain Sync and start shooting. Moving targets are best. Experiment with Shutter and Aperture Priority modes to lower the shutter speeds and exaggerate the effect. Try using a low ISO so the camera is forced to use longer shutter speeds. Be creative and have some fun!

Share your results with the book's Flickr group!

Join the group here: flickr.com/groups/nikond5100fromsnapshotstogreatshots/

9

ISO 200
1/180 sec.
f/4.8
86mm lens

Creative Compositions

IMPROVING YOUR PICTURES WITH SOUND COMPOSITIONAL ELEMENTS

Creating a great photograph takes more than just the right settings on your camera. To take your photography to the next level, you need to gain an understanding of how the elements within the frame come together to create a compositionally pleasing image. Composition is the culmination of light, shape, and, to borrow a word from the iconic photographer Jay Maisel, gesture. Composition is a way for you to pull your viewing audience into your image and guide them through the scene. Let's examine a few methods you can use to add interest to your photos by utilizing some common compositional elements.

PORING OVER THE PICTURE

I've always loved the mix of bright sun and light rain. There's just something about the contrast and the energy and the rapid changes in light. Plus you might even spot a rainbow. In this photo I tried to simulate a summer sun shower by using the sprinkler on a summer afternoon. The sun was slanting from the west and provided a nice backlight to the flowers and water droplets.

I love the way the out of focus water droplets add energy to the empty space above the flowers.

A wide-open aperture threw the background out of focus.

Water droplets are frozen in mid-flight by the fast shutter speed.

The bright pinks in the flowers leap off the dark greens of the background.

ISO 400
1/2000 sec.
f/2.8
60mm lens

DEPTH OF FIELD

Long focal lengths and large apertures will allow you to isolate your subject from the chaos that surrounds it. I utilize the Aperture Priority mode for the majority of my shooting. I also like to use a longer focal length lens to shrink the depth of field to a very narrow area (**Figure 9.1**).

The blurred background and foreground force the viewer's eye toward the sharper, in-focus areas, which gives greater emphasis to the subject.

Occasionally a greater depth of field is required to maintain a sharp focus across a greater distance. This might be due to the sheer depth of your subject, where you have objects that are near the camera but sharpness is desired at a greater distance as well (**Figure 9.2**).

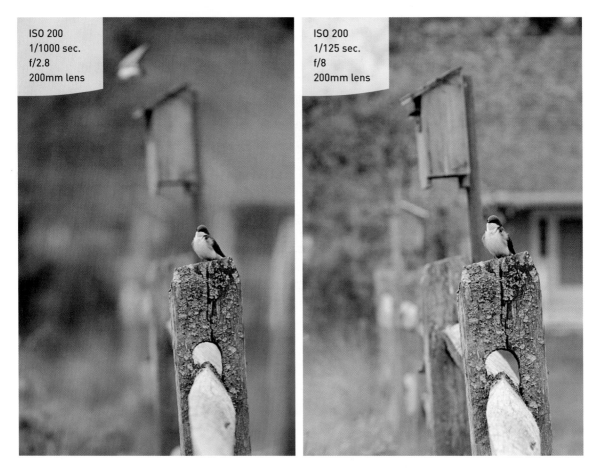

ISO 200
1/1000 sec.
f/2.8
200mm lens

ISO 200
1/125 sec.
f/8
200mm lens

FIGURE 9.1
The combination of a telephoto lens and a large aperture can create a shallow depth of field to isolate the subject.

FIGURE 9.2
Decreasing the size of the aperture extends the depth of field farther.

Or perhaps you are photographing a reflection. We were cleaning out the garage one day and found a baby snake. I placed it on a small mirror and photographed a really unusual scene (**Figure 9.3**). By making the aperture smaller, you will be able to maintain acceptable sharpness in both the near and distant objects. You may not have any snakes or mirrors lying about, but this same technique applies to photographing objects reflected in puddles and windows too.

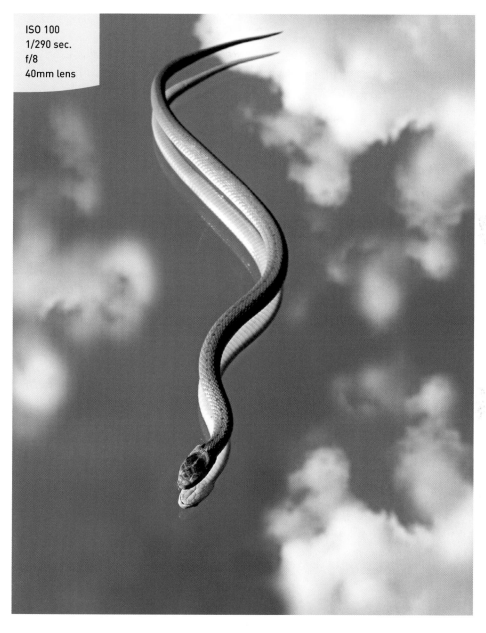

ISO 100
1/290 sec.
f/8
40mm lens

FIGURE 9.3
Getting a distant subject in focus in a reflection, along with the reflective surface, requires a small aperture.

PHOTOGRAPHING REFLECTIONS

A mirror is a two-dimensional surface, so why do I have to focus at a different distance for the image in the mirror? This was one of those questions that drove me crazy when I began to learn about photography. The answer is pretty simple, and it has to do with light. When you focus your lens, you are focusing the light being reflected off a surface onto your camera sensor. So if you wanted to focus on the mirror itself, it would be at one distance, but if you wanted to focus on the subject being reflected, you would have to take into account the distance that the object is from the mirror and then to you. Remember that the light from the subject has to travel all the way to the mirror and then to your lens. This is why a smaller aperture can be required when shooting reflected subjects. Sit in your car and take a few shots of objects in the side view mirrors to see what I mean.

ANGLES

Having strong angular lines in your image can add to the composition, especially when they are juxtaposed to each other (**Figure 9.4**). This can create a tension that is different from the standard horizontal and vertical lines that we are so accustomed to seeing in photos.

FIGURE 9.4
A close-up of a slightly turned solar panel is all angles.

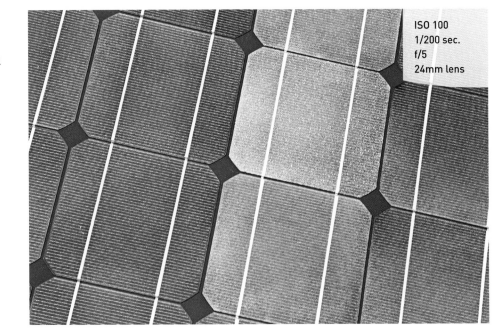

ISO 100
1/200 sec.
f/5
24mm lens

There are times when you can accentuate the angles in your images by tilting the camera, thus adding an unfamiliar angle to the subject, which draws the viewer's attention (**Figure 9.5**).

ISO 200
1/4000 sec.
f/3.5
18mm lens

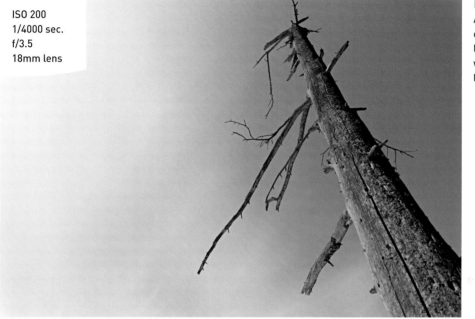

FIGURE 9.5
A tilt of the camera can give a unique look to items that would ordinarily look commonplace.

POINT OF VIEW

Sometimes the easiest way to influence your photographs is to simply change your perspective. Instead of always shooting from a standing position, try moving your camera to a place where you normally would not see your subject. Try getting down on your knees or even lying on the ground. This low angle can completely change how you view your subject and create a new interest in common subjects (**Figure 9.6**).

PATTERNS

Rhythm and balance can be added to your images by finding the patterns in everyday life and concentrating on the elements that rely on geometric influences. Try to find the balance and patterns that often go unnoticed (**Figure 9.7**).

FIGURE 9.6
Put your camera into a position that presents an unfamiliar view of your subject.

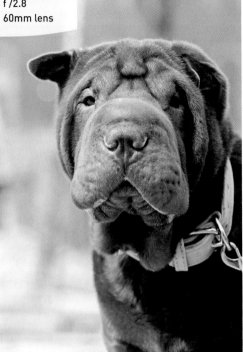

ISO 200
1/1600 sec.
f /2.8
60mm lens

FIGURE 9.7
I found that the pattern of the wall was made more interesting when contrasted with the gentle slope of the road and the row of blue bins.

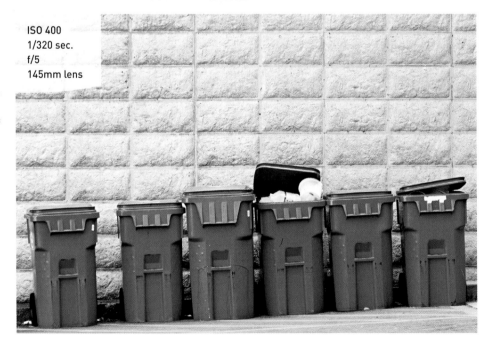

ISO 400
1/320 sec.
f/5
145mm lens

COLOR

Color works well as a tool for composition when you have very saturated colors to work with. Some of the best colors are those within the primary palette. Reds, greens, and blues, along with their complementary colors (cyan, magenta, and yellow), can all be used to create visual tension (**Figure 9.8**). This tension between bright colors will add visual excitement, drama, and complexity to your images when combined with other compositional elements.

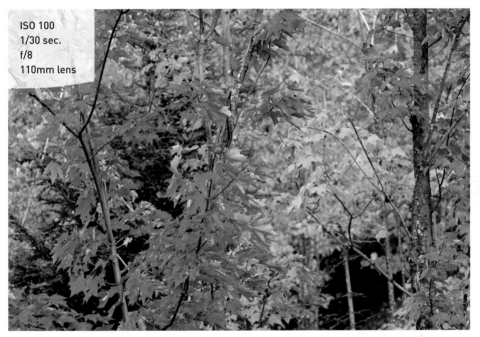

ISO 100
1/30 sec.
f/8
110mm lens

Finding scenes that allow you to combine color, pattern, shape, and point of view are all around you when you start looking for them. One day while out walking, I happened upon a fire truck parked on the curb (**Figure 9.9**).

FIGURE 9.9
Looking at the back
of the truck,
I was struck by the
patterns and colors
as well as the
textures and lines.

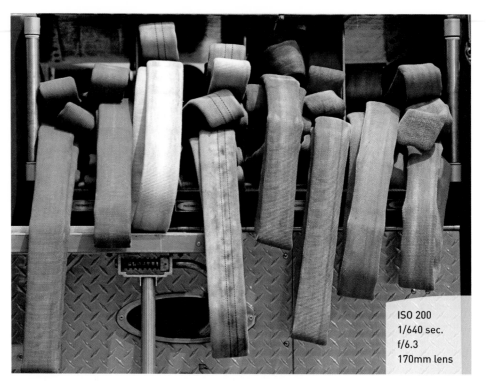

ISO 200
1/640 sec.
f/6.3
170mm lens

CONTRAST

We just saw that you can use color as a strong compositional tool. One of the most effective uses of color is to combine two contrasting colors that make the eye move back and forth across the image (**Figure 9.10**). There is no exact combination that will work best, but consider using dark and light colors, like red and yellow or blue and yellow, to provide the strongest contrasts.

You can also introduce contrast through different geometric shapes that battle (in a good way) for the attention of the viewer. You can combine circles and triangles, ovals and rectangles, curvy and straight, hard and soft, dark and light, and so many more (**Figure 9.11**). You aren't limited to just one contrasting element either. Combining more than one element of contrast will add even more interest. Look for these contrasting combinations whenever you are out shooting, and then use them to shake up your compositions.

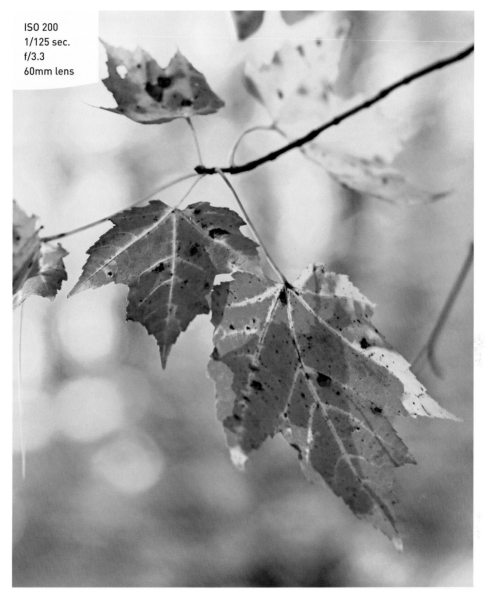

ISO 200
1/125 sec.
f/3.3
60mm lens

FIGURE 9.10
The contrasting colors complement each other and add balance to the scene.

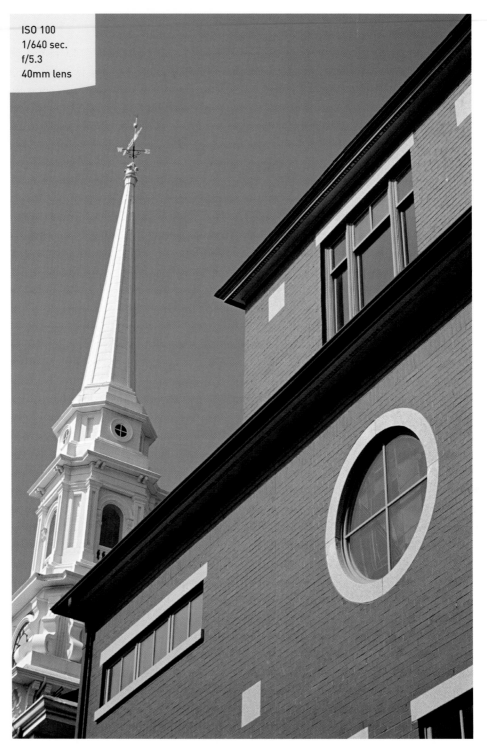

FIGURE 9.11

The horizontal lines of the brick building contrast with the upward-jutting lines of the steeple, but both buildings share a round window, creating another area of visual interest for the eye to discover.

ISO 100
1/640 sec.
f/5.3
40mm lens

LEADING LINES

One way to pull a viewer into your image is to incorporate leading lines. These are elements that come from the edge of the frame and then lead into the image toward the main subject (**Figure 9.12**). This can be the result of vanishing perspective lines, an element such as a river, or some other feature used to move from the outer edge in to the heart of the image.

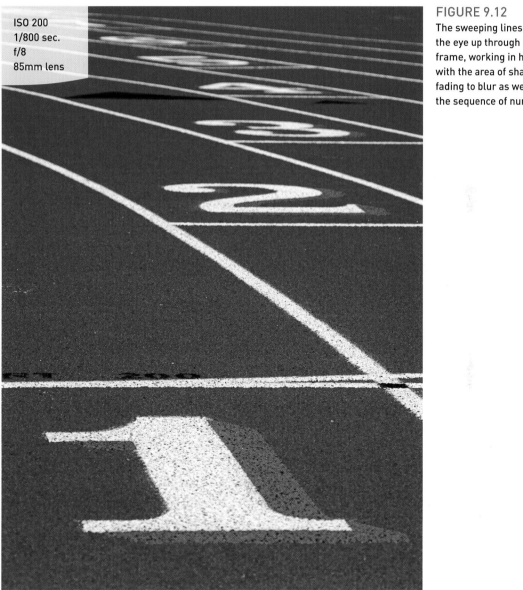

ISO 200
1/800 sec.
f/8
85mm lens

FIGURE 9.12
The sweeping lines all move the eye up through the frame, working in harmony with the area of sharp focus fading to blur as well as with the sequence of numbers.

SPLITTING THE FRAME

Splitting the frame right down the middle is not necessarily your best option. While it may seem more balanced, it can actually be pretty boring. Generally speaking, you should utilize the rule of thirds when deciding how to divide your frame (**Figure 9.13**).

FIGURE 9.13
Not only did I place the tree line at the bottom third of the frame, I also moved the lone tree to the side instead of the middle. This adds more interest to the subject and allows the eyes to move across the image in a more pleasing way.

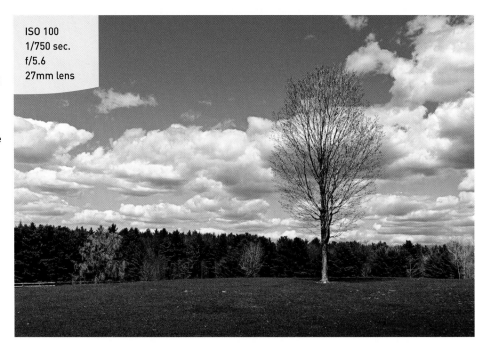

ISO 100
1/750 sec.
f/5.6
27mm lens

With horizons, a low horizon will give a sense of stability to the image. Typically, this is done when the sky is more appealing than the landscape below. When the emphasis is to be placed on the landscape, the horizon line should be moved upward in the frame, leaving the bottom two-thirds to the subject below (**Figure 9.14**).

FRAMES WITHIN FRAMES

The outer edge of your photograph acts as a frame to hold all of the visual elements of the photograph. One way to add emphasis to your subject is through the use of internal frames (**Figure 9.15**). Depending on how the frame is used, it can create the illusion of a third dimension to your image, giving it a feeling of depth.

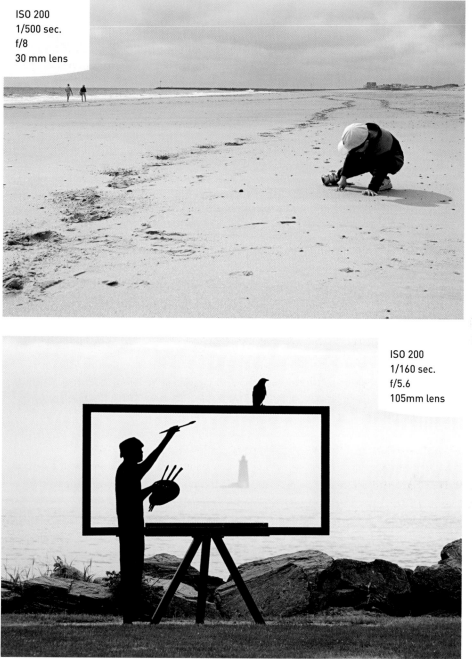

ISO 200
1/500 sec.
f/8
30 mm lens

FIGURE 9.14
The dull gray sky is nothing to look at, so the small boy on the beach is likely the first thing to catch your eye. But then the leading lines of the footprints carry you up the beach to the horizon, which sweeps you to the left to notice the other two figures walking along the shore.

ISO 200
1/160 sec.
f/5.6
105mm lens

FIGURE 9.15
This metal sculpture along the New Hampshire coast provides a perfect frame to watch the sea beyond. It makes a fine perch for a crow too.

Chapter 9 Assignments

Apply the shooting techniques and tools that you have learned in the previous chapters to these assignments, and you'll improve your ability to incorporate good composition into your photos. Make sure you experiment with all the different elements of composition and see how you can combine them to add interest to your images.

Learning to see lines and patterns

Take your camera for a walk around your neighborhood and look for patterns and angles. Don't worry as much about getting great shots as about developing an eye for details.

The ABCs of composition

Here's a great exercise: Shoot the alphabet. This will be a little more difficult, but with practice you will start to see beyond the obvious. Don't just find letters in street signs and the like. Instead, find objects that aren't really letters but that have the shape of the letters.

Finding the square peg and the round hole

Circles, squares, and triangles. Spend a few sessions concentrating on shooting simple geometric shapes.

Using the aperture to focus attention

Depth of field plays an important role in defining your images and establishing depth and dimension. Practice shooting wide open, using your largest aperture for the narrowest depth of field. Then find a scene that would benefit from extended depth of field, using very small apertures to give sharpness throughout the scene.

Leading them into a frame

Look for scenes where you can use elements as leading lines, and then look for framing elements that you can use to isolate your subject and add both depth and dimension to your images.

Share your results with the book's Flickr group!

Join the group here: flickr.com/groups/nikond5100fromsnapshotstogreatshots/

10

ISO 200
1/200 sec.
f/5.6
400mm lens

Advanced Techniques

IMPRESS YOUR FAMILY AND FRIENDS

We've covered a lot of ground in the previous chapters, especially on the general photographic concepts that apply to most, if not all, shooting situations. There are, however, some specific tools and techniques that will give you an added advantage in obtaining a great shot. Additionally, we will look at how to customize certain controls on your camera to reflect your personal shooting preferences and always have them at the ready.

PORING OVER THE PICTURE

I recently started keeping bees, and I find them an endless source of wonder. While pulling frames to check on the colony's progress and health, I took a few photos of each frame, which allowed me to check right up close at a much slower pace back at my desk. There's a lot of activity in the hive, and freezing that action at the macro level is a fun challenge.

Low ISO keeps down noise in the shadows.

I compromised on aperture to keep shutter speed fast and ISO low, which resulted in relatively narrow depth of field.

A fast shutter speed freezes most of the action.

Getting up close provides a look at detail that is normally hard to see.

ISO 100
1/400 sec.
f/4
60mm lens

SPOT METER FOR MORE EXPOSURE CONTROL

Generally speaking, Matrix metering mode provides accurate metering information for the majority of your photography. It does an excellent job of evaluating the scene and then relating the proper exposure information to you. The only problem with this mode is that, like any metering mode on the camera, it doesn't know what it is looking at. There will be specific circumstances where you want to get an accurate reading from just a portion of a scene and discount all of the remaining area in the viewfinder. To give you greater control of the metering operation, you can switch the camera to Spot metering mode. This allows you to take a meter reading from a very small circle in the center of the viewfinder, while ignoring the rest of the viewfinder area.

So when would you need to use this? Think of a person standing in front of a very dark wall. In Matrix metering mode, the camera would see the entire scene and try to adjust the exposure information so that the dark background is exposed to render a lighter wall in your image. This means that the scene would actually be overexposed and your subject would then appear too light. To correct this, you can place the camera in Spot metering mode and take a meter reading right off of—and *only* off of—your subject, ignoring the dark wall altogether (**Figure 10.1**). The Spot metering will read the location where you have your focus point, placing all of the exposure information right on your point of interest.

Other situations that would benefit from Spot metering include:

- Snow or beach environments where the overall brightness level of the scene could fool the meter

- Strongly backlit subjects that are leaving the subject underexposed

- Cases where the overall feel of a photo is too light or too dark

SETTING UP AND SHOOTING IN SPOT METERING MODE

1. Press the **i** button to activate the cursor in the information screen, then move it to the current metering method.

2. Press the OK button and then use the Multi-selector to select the Spot metering option.

3. Press the OK button to lock in your change.

4. Now use the Multi-selector to move the focus point onto your subject and take your photo. The meter reading will come directly from the location of the focus point.

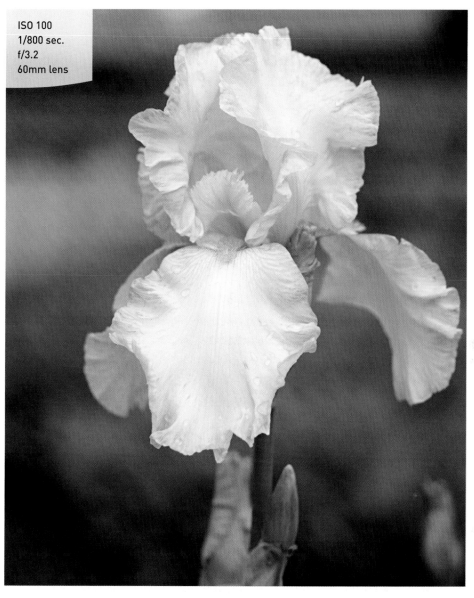

ISO 100
1/800 sec.
f/3.2
60mm lens

FIGURE 10.1
The dark background was making the meter overexpose the light-colored iris. Using the Spot meter on the subject can help you zero in on great exposures.

Note that if you are using the Auto-area focus mode, the camera will use the center focus point as the Spot metering location.

When using Spot metering mode, remember that the meter believes it is looking at a middle gray value, so you might need to incorporate some exposure compensation of your own to the reading that you are getting from your subject. This will come from experience as you use the meter.

METERING FOR SUNRISE OR SUNSET

Capturing a beautiful sunrise or sunset is all about the sky. If there is too much fore-ground in the viewfinder, the camera's meter will deliver an exposure setting that is accurate for the darker foreground areas but leaves the sky looking overexposed, undersaturated, and generally just not very interesting (**Figure 10.2**). To gain more emphasis on the colorful sky, point your camera at the brightest part of it and take your meter reading there. Use the AE Lock to meter for the brightest part of the sky and then recompose. The result will be an exposure setting that underexposes the foreground but provides a darker, more dramatic sky (**Figure 10.3**).

FIGURE 10.2
By metering with all the information in the frame, you get bright skies and more detail in the ground.

FIGURE 10.3
By taking the meter reading from the brightest part of the sky, you will get darker, more colorful sunsets and sunrises.

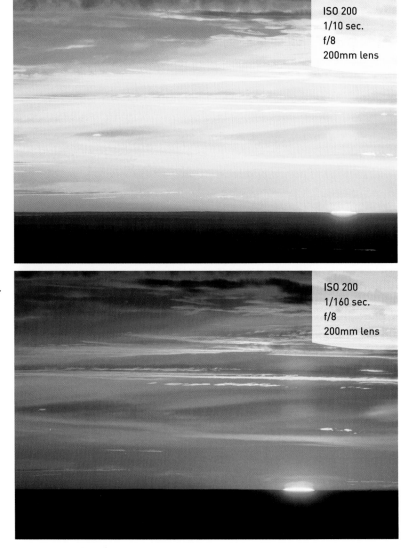

ISO 200
1/10 sec.
f/8
200mm lens

ISO 200
1/160 sec.
f/8
200mm lens

MANUAL MODE

Probably one of the most advanced, and yet most basic, skills to master is shooting in Manual mode. With the power and utility of most of the automatic modes, Manual mode almost never sees the light of day. I have to admit that I don't select it for use very often, but there are times when no other mode will do. A situation that works well with Manual is studio work with external flashes. I know that when I work with studio lights, my exposure will not change, so I use Manual to eliminate any automatic changes that might happen from shooting in Program, Shutter Priority, or Aperture Priority mode.

Since you probably aren't too concerned with studio strobes at this point, I will concentrate on one of the ways in which you will want to use Manual mode for your photography: long nighttime exposures.

BULB PHOTOGRAPHY

If you want to work with long shutter speeds that don't quite fit into one of the selectable shutter speeds, you can select Bulb. This setting is only available in Manual mode, and its sole purpose is to open the shutter at your command and then close it again when you decide. I can think of two common scenarios where this would come in handy: shooting fireworks and shooting lightning.

If you are photographing fireworks, you could certainly use one of the longer shutter speeds available in Shutter Priority mode, since they are available for exposure times of up to 30 seconds. That is fine, but sometimes you don't need 30 seconds' worth of exposure and sometimes you need more.

If you open the shutter and then see a great burst of fireworks, you might decide that that is all you want for that particular frame, so you click the button to end the exposure. Set the camera to 30 seconds and you might get too many bursts, but shorten it to 10 seconds and you might not get the one you want. The same can be said for photographing a lightning storm. Lightning can be very tricky to capture, and using the Bulb setting to open and then close the shutter at will allows for more creativity as well as more opportunity to get the shot.

A safer subject you can practice with from the comfort of your own home is capturing light trails from someone moving a glow stick in a dark room or your backyard at night. Another option for owners of an iPad, iPod Touch, or iPhone is a great app called Holographium (http://holographium.com), which allows you to create holographic text (**Figure 10.4**) captured during long exposures. Check out the gallery of photos on the Holographium Web site to see some of the possibilities.

FIGURE 10.4

I created a holographic long exposure of my name. The ML-L3 wireless remote is very handy for these situations.

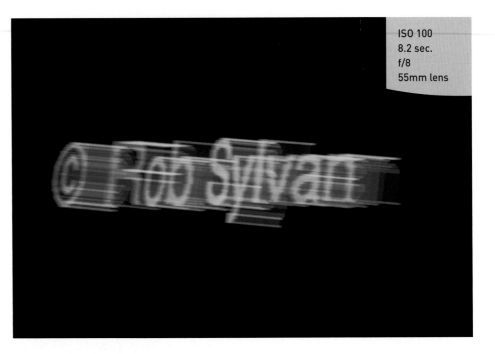

ISO 100
8.2 sec.
f/8
55mm lens

To select the Bulb setting, simply place your camera in Manual mode and then rotate the Command dial to the left until the shutter speed displays Bulb on the rear LCD screen.

When you're using the Bulb setting, the shutter will only stay open for the duration that you are holding down the shutter button. You should also be using a sturdy tripod or shooting surface to eliminate any self-induced vibration while using the Bulb setting.

BULB

If you are new to the world of photography, you might be wondering where in the world the *bulb* shutter function got its name. After all, wouldn't it make more sense to call it the Manual Shutter setting? It probably would, but this is one of those terms that harkens back to the origins of photography. Way back when, the shutter was actually opened through the use of a bulb-shaped device that forced air through a tube, which, in turn, pushed a plunger down, activating the camera shutter. When the bulb was released, it pulled the plunger back, letting the shutter close and ending the exposure.

I want to point out that using your finger on the shutter button for a Bulb exposure will definitely increase the chances of getting some camera shake in your images. To get the most benefit from the Bulb setting, I suggest using a remote cord such as the Nikon MC-DC2 Remote Switch or the ML-L3 wireless remote (see the bonus Chapter 11 for more details). You'll also want to turn on Long Exposure Noise Reduction, as covered in Chapter 7. With the wireless remote, you press once to open the shutter and then press the button on the remote a second time to close it.

SHOOTING LIGHTNING

If you are going to photograph lightning strikes in a thunderstorm, please exercise extreme caution. Standing in the open with a tripod is like standing over a lightning rod. Work from indoors if at all possible.

AVOIDING LENS FLARE

Lens flare is one of the problems you will encounter when shooting in the bright sun. Lens flare will show itself as bright circles on the image (**Figure 10.5**). Often you will see multiple circles in a line leading from a very bright light source such as the sun. The flare is a result of the sun bouncing off the multiple pieces of optical glass in the lens and then being reflected back onto the sensor. You can avoid the problem using one of these methods:

- Try to shoot with the sun coming from over your shoulder, not in front of you or in your scene.

- Use a lens shade to block the unwanted light from striking the lens. You don't have to have the sun in your viewfinder for lens flare to be an issue. All it has to do is strike the front glass of the lens to make it happen.

- If you don't have a lens shade, just try using your hand or some other element to block the light.

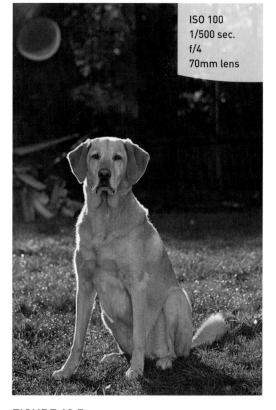

ISO 100
1/500 sec.
f/4
70mm lens

FIGURE 10.5
The bright sun in the upper-left corner has created flare spots that are visible as colored circles radiating across the image.

BRACKETING EXPOSURES

So, what if you are doing everything right in terms of metering and mode selection, yet your images still sometimes come out too light or too dark? There is a technique called "bracketing" that you can use, which will help you find the best exposure value for your scene by taking a normal exposure as well as ones that are over- and under-exposed. Having these differing exposure values will most often present you with one frame that just looks better than the others. I use the Bracketing function all of the time, so I have it assigned to my Function button so that I can access it quickly. You can also change the bracketing by adjusting the setting in your information screen (**Figure 10.6**).

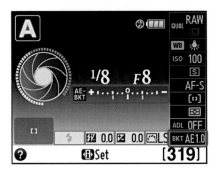

FIGURE 10.6
The Information screen shows you just how much bracketing is being applied on an over/ under scale.

Once you have entered the Auto Bracketing screen, you can decide how much variation you want between bracketed exposures. You can choose from one-third of a stop all the way to two full stops of exposure difference between each bracketed exposure. If I am shooting in the JPEG mode, I will typically bracket in one-stop increments to help zero in on that perfect exposure, and then just delete the ones that didn't make the grade (**Figures 10.7, 10.8,** and **10.9** on the facing page).

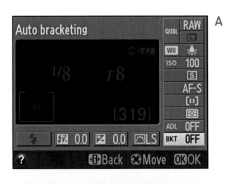

SETTING AUTO EXPOSURE BRACKETING

1. Press the **i** button to activate the cursor in the information screen and move it to the BKT setting (**A**).

2. Press the OK button to enter the Auto Bracketing screen and then use the Multi-selector to set the amount of bracketed exposure you desire (**B**). Press the OK button to lock in your change.

3. Frame your subject in the viewfinder and then take three pictures. The result will be three differently exposed images.

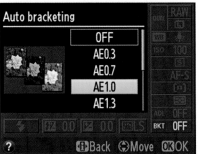

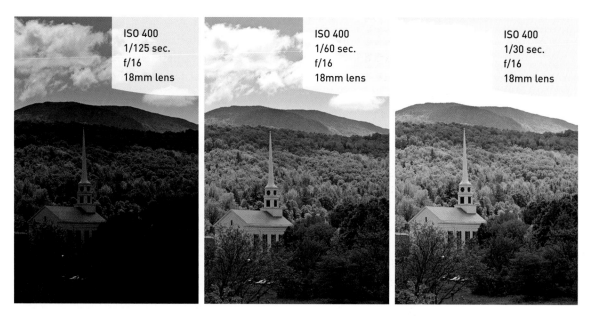

FIGURE 10.7
One stop of exposure below normal.

FIGURE 10.8
The normal exposure as indicated by the camera meter.

FIGURE 10.9
One stop of exposure above normal.

When I am out shooting in the RAW file format, I typically shoot with my camera set to an exposure compensation of −1/3 stop to protect my highlights. If I am dealing with a subject that has a lot of different tonal ranges from bright to dark, I will often bracket by one stop over and under my already compensated exposure. That means I will have exposures of −1 1/3, −1/3, and +2/3. Another thing to remember is that Auto Exposure Bracketing will use the current mode for making the exposure changes. This means that if you are in Aperture Priority mode, the camera will make adjustments to your shutter speed. Likewise, if you are in Shutter Priority, the changes will be made to your aperture value. This is important to remember since it could impact certain aspects of your image, such as depth of field or camera shake. You also need to know that AE Bracketing will remain in effect until you set it back to zero, even if you turn the camera off and then on again.

MACRO PHOTOGRAPHY

Put simply, macro photography is close-up photography. Depending on the lens or lenses that you got with your camera, you may have the perfect tool for macro work. Some lenses are made to shoot in a macro mode, but you don't have to feel left out if you don't have one of those. Check the spec sheet that came with your lens to see what the minimum focusing distance is for your lens.

If you have a zoom, you should work with the lens at its longest focal length. Also, work with a tripod because handholding will make focusing difficult. The easiest way to make sure that your focus is precisely where you want it to be is to use Manual focus mode.

Since I am recommending a tripod for your macro work, I will also recommend using Aperture Priority mode so that you can achieve differing levels of depth of field. Long lenses at close range can make for some very shallow depth of field, so you will need to work with apertures that are probably much smaller than you might normally use. If you are shooting outside, try shading the subject from direct sunlight by using some sort of diffusion material, such as a white sheet or a diffusion panel (see the bonus Chapter 11). By diffusing the light, you will see much greater detail because you will have a lower contrast ratio (softer shadows), and detail is often what macro photography is all about (**Figures 10.10** and **10.11**).

FIGURE 10.10
Color, pattern, lines, and other compositional elements are still useful at the macro level.

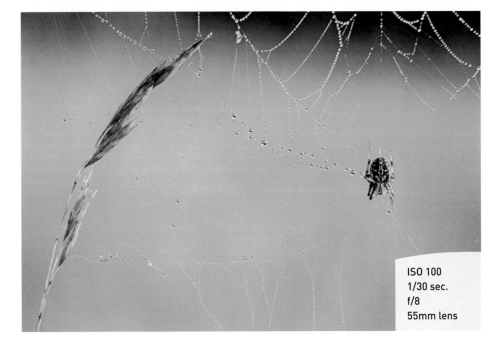

ISO 100
1/30 sec.
f/8
55mm lens

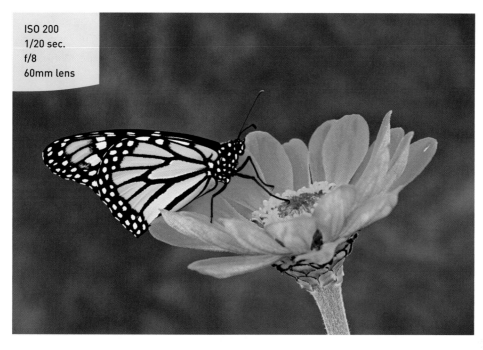

ISO 200
1/20 sec.
f/8
60mm lens

FIGURE 10.11
This monarch had just emerged from its chrysalis. They are pretty tired at this time, so I could get away with a slow shutter speed.

ACTIVE D-LIGHTING

Your camera provides a function that can automatically make your pictures look better: Active D-Lighting. It works this way: The camera evaluates the tones in your image and then underexposes for the highlight areas while lightening any areas that it believes are too dark or lacking in contrast (**Figures 10.12** and **10.13**). The Active D-Lighting is automatically applied to images that are shot in any of the automatic scene modes except for the High Key, Low Key, and Silhouette scene modes.

You can choose from six levels: Off, Low (L), Normal (N), High (H), Extra High (H*), and Auto (A). You will need to evaluate the strength of the effect on your images and change it accordingly. If I am shooting JPEG, I will typically leave it set to Normal so that I have brighter, more detailed shadow areas in my photographs while still maintaining good exposure in my skies. You should know that Active D-Lighting can be adjusted only when using one of the professional modes. Also, you will want to turn it off if you are using flash exposure compensation since it will try to work against you when you alter the flash strength.

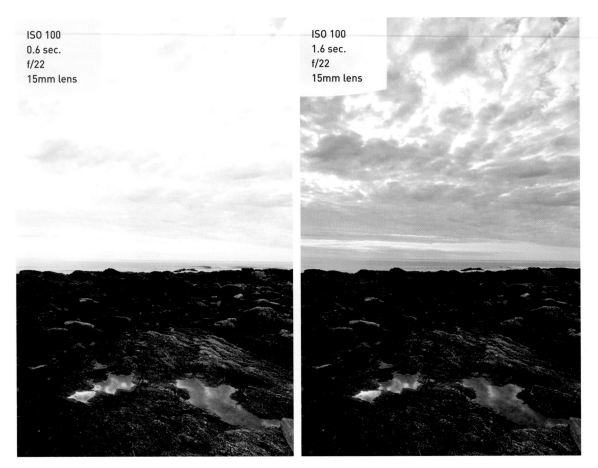

ISO 100
0.6 sec.
f/22
15mm lens

ISO 100
1.6 sec.
f/22
15mm lens

FIGURE 10.12
Without Active D-Lighting, the shadows in the image are dark and contrasty, while the bright sky is almost completely washed out.

FIGURE 10.13
Active D-Lighting on the Extra High setting preserved a lot more detail in the sky even while managing to bring out more detail in the shadows.

Because Active D-Lighting reduces exposure and then uses Nikon's own secret sauce to process the final result in-camera when shooting JPEG, I don't use Active D-Lighting when shooting in RAW mode if I am not going to process the RAW images in Nikon's software (such as ViewNX 2 or Capture NX 2). This is because third-party RAW processing software (such as Adobe Photoshop Lightroom or Apple Aperture) sees only the slightly underexposed image and is unaware of the Active D-Lighting setting. Just keep that in the back of your mind when you decide to make the move up to shooting in RAW mode.

SETTING UP ACTIVE D-LIGHTING

1. Press the **i** button to activate the cursor in the information screen, then navigate to the ADL setting by using the Multi-selector (**A**).

2. Press the OK button and then move the Multi-selector up or down to select the level of Active D-Lighting that you desire (**B**).

3. Press the OK button to lock in your changes and resume shooting.

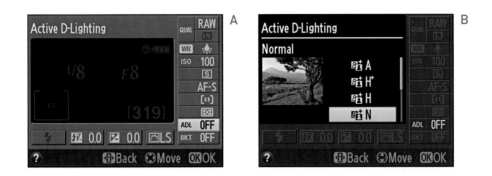

The Active D-Lighting setting can also be changed in the Shooting menu items.

You can also set up your camera to automatically take one shot with Active D-Lighting turned on and another with it turned off, via the Auto Bracketing menu.

BRACKETING WITH ACTIVE D-LIGHTING

1. Press the Menu button and then use the Multi-selector to go to the Custom Setting menu (**A**).

2. Now highlight menu item e: Bracketing/Flash and press OK (**B**).

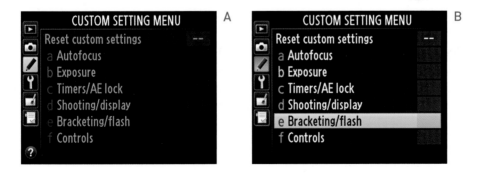

3. Select item e2: Auto Bracketing Set and press OK (**C**).

4. Highlight ADL Bracketing and press OK (**D**).

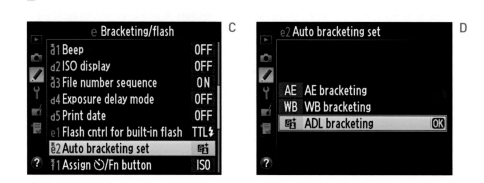

Now you can enable auto bracketing via the **i** button (just like we did earlier for exposure) and see what Active D-Lighting has to offer while comparing shots taken with and without it. Just remember to go back to the Auto Bracketing menu to change it to AE when you want to bracket exposure.

THE MY MENU SETTING

There are a lot of items in the menu that you can change, but some are used and changed more frequently than others. The My Menu function allows you to place up to 20 of your most used menu items in one place so that you can quickly get to them, make your changes, and get on with shooting. About the only menu function that you can't add is Format Card, but pretty much everything else is fair game. You can even add items from the Retouching menu. When you first enter the menu section of the camera, you may not find the My Menu feature because, by default, the camera is set to show you the Recent Settings menu item. Here's how to find and then set up your My Menu setting.

CUSTOMIZING YOUR MY MENU SETTING

1. To activate the My Menu feature, press the Menu button and then use the Multi-selector to locate the Recent Settings menu. Remember that you select among the different menus by moving the cursor to the left using the Multi-selector and then selecting from the different menu icons.

2. Scroll down through the recently viewed menu options until you highlight the option called Choose Tab (**A**).

3. Press OK, then select My Menu and press OK once again (**B**).

4. Now that you are in the My Menu screen, highlight Add Items and press the OK button (**C**).

5. You can now choose items from any of the five different menu sections by highlighting the section (such as Shooting Menu), pressing the Multi-selector to the right or pressing Menu, then highlighting the feature you want to add to My Menu and pressing OK (**D**).

6. Once you are done adding items, you can sort your menu items as you see fit or, if you change your mind, you can delete them. It's all up to you.

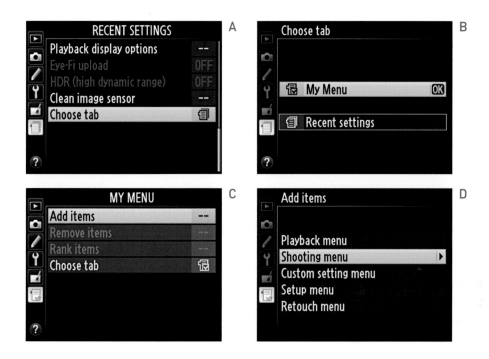

CONCLUSION

As you'll see, the online bonus chapter called "Pimp My Ride" covers a lot of gadgets, filters, and accessories that will make your photography easier and better. It can become an obsession to always have the latest thing out there. But here's the deal. You already have almost everything you need to take great pictures: an awesome camera and the knowledge necessary to use it. Everything else is just icing on the cake. So, although I introduce a few items in the bonus chapter that I do think will make your photographic life easier and even improve your images, don't get caught up in the technology and gadgetry.

Use your knowledge of basic photography to explore everything your camera has to offer. Explore the limits of your camera. Don't be afraid to take bad pictures. Don't be too quick to delete them off your memory card, either. Take some time to really look at them and see where things went wrong. Look at your camera settings and see if perhaps there was a change you could have made to make things better. Be your toughest critic and learn from your mistakes. With practice and reflection, you will soon find your photography getting better and better. Not only that, but your instincts will improve to the point that you will come upon a scene and know exactly how you want to shoot it before your camera even gets out of the bag.

Chapter 10 Assignments

Many of the techniques covered in this chapter are specific to certain shooting situations that may not come about very often. This is even more reason to practice them so that when the situation does present itself you will be ready.

Adding some drama to the end of the day

Most sunset photos don't reflect what the photographer saw because they didn't meter correctly for them. The next time you see a colorful sunset, pull out your camera and take a meter reading from the sky; then take a picture without a meter reading and see what a difference it makes.

Making your exposure spot on

Using the Spot meter mode can give accurate results but only when pointed at something that has a middle tone. Try adding something gray to the scene and taking a reading off it. Now switch back to your regular meter mode and see if the exposure isn't slightly different.

Using the Bulb setting to capture the moment

This is definitely one of those settings that you won't use often, but it's pretty handy when you need it. If you have the opportunity to shoot a fireworks display or a distant storm, try setting the camera to Bulb and then play with some long exposures to capture just the moments that you want.

Bracketing your way to better exposures

Why settle for just one variation of an image when you can bracket to get the best exposure choice? Set your camera up for a 1/3-bracket series and then expand it to a one-stop series. Review the results to see if the normal setting was the best, or perhaps one of the bracketed exposures is even better.

Moving in for a close-up

Macro photography is best practiced on stationary subjects, which is why I like flowers. If you have a zoom lens, check the minimum focusing distance and then try to get right to that spot to squeeze the most from your subject. Try using a diffuse light source as well to minimize shadows.

Share your results with the book's Flickr group!

Join the group here: flickr.com/groups/nikond5100fromsnapshotstogreatshots/

INDEX

Numbers

3D-tracking AF mode, using, 116–117
100 ISO setting, using, 83
200 ISO setting, using, 83
400 ISO setting, using, 83
800 ISO setting, using, 83
1080p resolution, explained, 49

A

A (Aperture Priority) mode, 96
  environmental portraits, 134
  isolating subjects, 111–112
  vs. S (Shutter Priority) mode, 111–112
  using, 89–93, 100, 132–134
accessory terminal, identifying, 51
action. See also movement
  anticipating, 117–119
  camera placement, 124–125
  following, 127
  freezing, 46, 80–81, 109–110
  getting in front of, 124
  panning, 127
  placement of subjects, 123–124
  tips for shooting, 123–125
action shots
  direction of travel, 106
  shutter speeds, 109
  subject speed, 106–107
  subject-to-camera distance, 108
Active D-Lighting feature
  Auto (A) level, 263
  bracketing with, 265–266
  Extra High (H*) level, 263
  High (H) level, 263
  Low (L) level, 263
  Normal (N) level, 263
  Off level, 263
  setting up, 265
  unavailability in scene modes, 75
  using, 263–264
additive color, explained, 16
Adobe RGB color space, 15–17
AE-L (Auto Exposure Lock) feature, using, 137–138, 256
AF Assist Illuminator, using, 215–216
AF (autofocus) modes, 75, 116–117. See also focus modes; M (Manual) focus

AF-A mode, 12, 75
AF-area mode, setting to Dynamic, 116
AF-Assist Illuminator, identifying, 2
AF-C mode, 75
  selecting, 115
  shooting in, 115
AF-F mode, 75
AF-S (Single-servo AF) mode, 11, 25, 75, 138–139
angles, considering in composition, 238–239
aperture
  and f-stops, 92
  function of, 47
  reaching maximum of, 109
  role in exposure triangle, 43
aperture mode, accessing, 79
Aperture Priority (A) mode, 96
  environmental portraits, 134
  isolating subjects, 111–112
  vs. Shutter Priority (S) mode, 112
  using, 89–93, 100, 132–134
audio
  recording, 51
  turning off, 51
Auto (Flash Off) mode
  ISO setting, 59
  using, 59–60
Auto Exposure Bracketing, using, 260–261
Auto Exposure Lock (AE-L) feature, using, 137–138, 256
Auto ISO sensitivity control, 113–114. See also ISO settings
Auto ISO setting
  enabling, 10
  noise associated with, 10
  turning off, 9–11
Auto mode
  problem with, 60
  shooting in, 76
  using, 58–59
Auto Off timer setting, adjusting, 6
AutoExposure/AutoFocus Lock button, identifying, 3
autofocus
  overriding, 17–18
  unavailability in scene modes, 74

autofocus (AF) modes, 75, 116–117. See also focus modes; M (Manual) focus
automatic focus features, turning off, 180
automatic modes, limitations of, 74–75
Autumn Colors scene mode, 70
A/V port, identifying, 51

B

battery
  charging, 5
  keeping backups, 5
Beach/Snow scene mode, 68
BKT mode
  accessing, 260
  using with HDR (high dynamic range), 200
black and white
  filter colors, 175
  landscape scenes, 175–176
black and white portraits
  Filter effects, 142
  Monochrome picture control, 140–143
  taking, 140–142
"blinkies" feature, turning on, 172
Blossom scene mode, 70
bracketing
  with Active D-Lighting feature, 265–266
  exposures, 260–261
  HDR images, 201
buffer, function of, 121
built-in flash. See also fill flash; flash
  Aperture Priority (A) speed, 220
  ISO settings, 219
  metering modes, 220–221
  Program (P) shutter speed, 220
  range of, 219
  setting to manual power setting, 220–221
  Shutter Priority (S) speed, 220
  shutter speeds, 219–220
  TTL (Through The Lens) feature, 220
  using, 218–219
Bulb setting
  selecting, 258
  using, 259, 268
burst mode, using, 119–121